THE
CRUISING
GUIDE
TO THE
VIRGIN ISLANDS

7th Edition

THE
CRUISING
GUIDE

TO THE
VIRGIN
ISLANDS

7th Edition

by Nancy and Simon Scott

A Complete Guide
for Yachtsmen, Divers and
Watersports Enthusiasts

Cruising Guide Publications, Inc. is a special interest publisher of sailing guides to cruising in various areas around the world and other publications of nautical interest. CGP endeavors to provide comprehensive and invaluable materials to both inveterate sailors and less experienced seafarers seeking vital vacationing tips and navigational information relative to the journey to and the enjoyment of their destinations.

The Cruising Guide to the Virgin Islands is intended for use in conjunction with either U.S. National Ocean Survey charts, U.S. Hydrographic Office charts, or British Admiralty charts. Every effort has been made to describe conditions accurately. However, the publisher makes no warranty, express or implied, for any errors or omissions in this publication. Skippers should use this guide only in conjunction with the above charts and/or other navigational aids and not place undue credence in the accuracy of this guide. *The Cruising Guide to the Virgin Islands* is not intended for use for navigational purposes.

Published by
Cruising Guide Publications, Inc.
P.O. Box 1017
Dunedin, Florida 34697-1017
PHONE: (800) 330-9542 • (813) 733-5322 • FAX: (813) 734-8179

BY NANCY AND SIMON SCOTT

Art Director
TOM HENSCHEL

Marketing Director
MAUREEN LARROUX

Photography
JIM SCHEINER
DOUGAL THORNTON

Illustrations and Cartography
ROGER BURNETT

Et Cetera
JANET JOYCE
BARBARA LIEBLING

Special thanks to The Moorings for use of aerial photographs from *Virgin Anchorages*, and George and Luana Marler for use of photographs and diagrams from *The Royal Mail Steamer Rhone*.

Seventh Edition
Printed in the United States of America.

ISBN 0-944428-27-4

TABLE OF CONTENTS

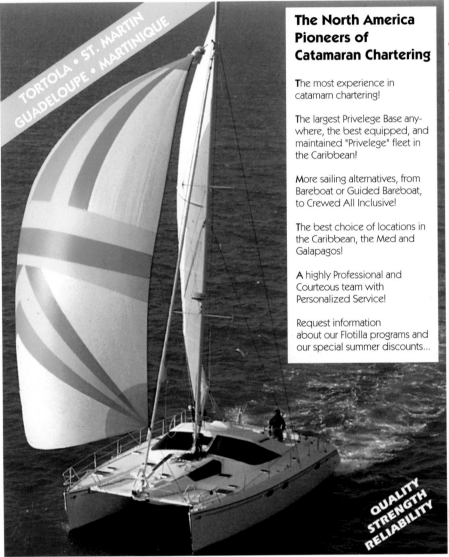

Jim Scheiner

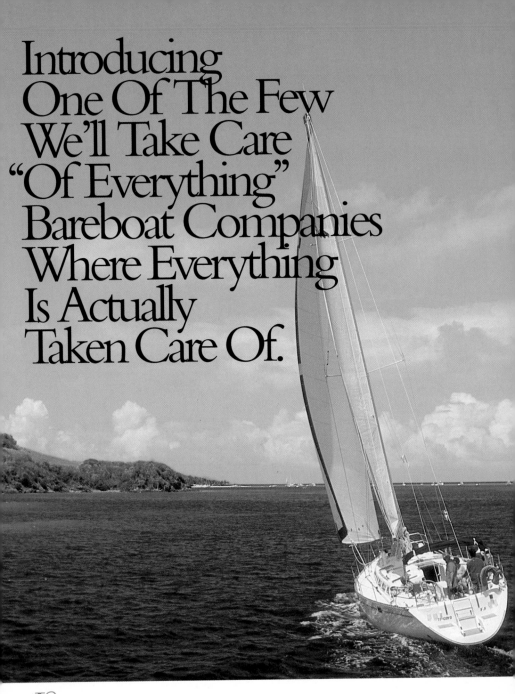

Introducing One Of The Few We'll Take Care "Of Everything" Bareboat Companies Where Everything Is Actually Taken Care Of.

You take a bareboat vacation to enjoy yourself — *not* to sweat the details. That's our job. And nobody does it better than The Moorings.

Keep this in mind before you call your usual bareboat company — and then call us at **1-800-535-7289**.

Life and your vacation are too short to worry about *anything* but having fun.

We'll worry about the rest.

The Moorings®

25 Years Of The Best Sailing Vacations In The World

Caribbean • Mediterranean • South Pacific

The Virgin Islands are a magical Caribbean archipelago that seemed to be created expressly for the pleasures of yachting and watersports.

Whether you are cruising this island paradise aboard your own boat, chartering, or staying ashore, this Guide is designed to help you maximize your visit.

The Guide will assist you in navigation, selection of anchorages, or marinas and resorts, as well as steering you towards exciting attractions, shops and fine dining.

The Guide is intended as an adjunct to, rather than a substitute for, proper navigational charts. We have made all efforts to describe accurately the conditions existing in the anchorages. We would appreciate any input on your part to assist us in making our Guide even more useful for cruising these islands.

Welcome to the Virgin Islands!

Jim Scheiner

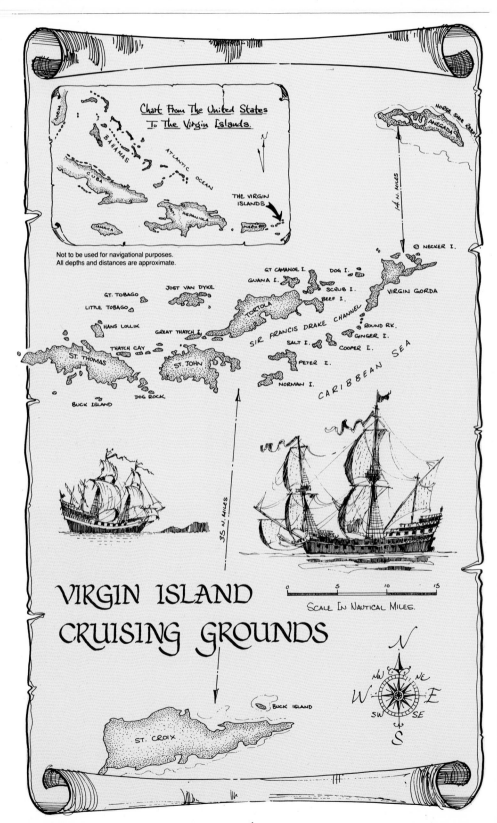

Chart From The United States To The Virgin Islands.

BAHAMAS

ATLANTIC OCEAN

CUBA

HISPANIOLA

JAMAICA

THE VIRGIN ISLANDS

PUERTO RICO

N

Not to be used for navigational purposes.
All depths and distances are approximate.

HORSE SHOE REEF

ANEGADA

14 N. MILES

NECKER I.

GT. CAMANOE I.

DOG I.

GUANA I.

SCRUB I.

VIRGIN GORDA

GT. TOBAGO

JOST VAN DYKE

BEEF I.

LITTLE TOBAGO

TORTOLA

HANS LOLLIK

ROUND RK.

GREAT THATCH I.

SIR FRANCIS DRAKE CHANNEL

GINGER I.

THATCH CAY

SALT I.

COOPER I.

ST. THOMAS

ST. JOHN

PETER I.

CARIBBEAN SEA

NORMAN I.

BUCK ISLAND

DOG ROCK

35 N. MILES

VIRGIN ISLAND
CRUISING GROUNDS

0   5   10   15

SCALE IN NAUTICAL MILES.

BUCK ISLAND

ST. CROIX

N
NW   NE
W   E
SW   SE
S

4

THE VIRGIN ISLANDS

Dougal Thornton

Nothing has influenced the history of the Virgin Islands more profoundly than their geography and physical makeup. Situated at the high point of the curving archipelago that swings from Trinidad to Florida, they survey strategically all of the Americas, and, with their steady trade winds and numerous sheltered harbours, it is not surprising that they rapidly became a centre for sea routes to every point of the compass, providing a welcome pause in the lengthy trade lines between Europe and the riches of South and Central America. Having been described as "the place on the way to everywhere," they have long been desirable for both trading and military advantage, from the days when Spaniards sailed through carrying Aztec loot to Spain until this century when the United States paid $25 million to buy the USVI from Denmark in order to forestall any unfriendly foreign power from parking on her doorstep.

Sailors and sailing have therefore been at the core of Virgin Islands history from the moment the first Ciboney Indians brought their Stone Age canoes from the Americas to drift nomadically through the Antilles, living off the land and the sea.

The Ciboneys were followed from South America a hundred years or so B.C. by the more down-to-earth Arawaks, who settled throughout the Virgin Islands, cultivated the land, made attractive pottery and ornaments (which can still be found) and maintained a strictly hereditary society. The Arawaks believed that their souls were not only in their bodies but also in trees, rocks and other natural phenomena, and constructed idols called "zemis," carving three-cornered stones in the shape of grotesque human beings, birds or natural forms, which they believed could influence crops and weather. They painted their bodies for ceremonies, grew their hair long and flattened the fronts of their childrens' heads to make them more beautiful.

The Arawaks dominated the islands for many years and, even now, we still use

Beneteau. The Choice of Professionals

Charter companies choose Beneteau because our boats are strong, functional and stylish. It's no wonder we're the #1 supplier of charter sailboats in the world.

For over 110 years, Beneteau has built finely-crafted boats that are reliable and fun to sail. This heritage of quality and our spirit of excellence ensures your holidays are everything that you hope for.

You should choose Beneteau for your personal boat for all the same good reasons. Rely on the preferred choice of today's professional. Beneteau.

For more information on the First or Oceanis series sailboats, call, fax or write Beneteau at 8720 Red Oak Boulevard, Suite 102, Charlotte, NC 28217. Fax: (704) 527-0760 Phone: (704) 527-8244.

BENETEAU
THE SEA DEMANDS THE BEST

some of their words: tobacco, barbecue, potato, hurricane and cannibal.

This last referred to the warlike Carib Indians who, about 100 years before Columbus arrived, pillaged their way up from South America like New World Vikings in enormous dug-out canoes. The Caribs were much like the Arawaks and Ciboneys in appearance — medium height, high cheek bones, flat noses and straight, black hair. Unlike the Arawaks they plucked their beards, considering them a deformity. They flattened the fronts and backs of their children's heads to make them beautiful, and scarred and painted their own bodies, presumably toward a similar goal.

The Caribs, quite unlike the Arawaks in temperament, were fierce and aggressive, terrorizing the entire Caribbean with their warlike behaviour. A spartan bunch, they kept on the move, raiding the Arawak settlements, stealing their women and capturing the young boys to be emasculated, fattened and eaten. They thought nothing of piling 100 men into an 80-foot dug-out canoe to traverse 1,000 miles in search of battle and plunder. Their social hierarchy was loose, their leaders chosen according to fighting ability rather than ancestry.

Caribs believed that good spirits were invisible except at night, when they took the form of bats; so each Carib had a bat for his personal deity, to whom he would make offerings of cassava bread and fruit to ensure healthy crops and continued well-being. Like the Arawaks, the Caribs practiced euthanasia to rid themselves of the old and infirm, and blamed most unpleasant occurrences—hurricanes, earthquakes or sickness—on evil spirits.

Columbus discovered the Virgin Islands in 1493 on his second voyage to the New World. He anchored off Salt River Bay in St. Croix for fresh water and then was driven by unfavourable winds to Virgin Gorda. Seeing the numerous islands, he named them "the Virgins" in honour of St. Ursula and the 11,000 virgins who, threatened by the marauding Huns in 4th-century Cologne, sacrificed their lives rather than submit to a fate worse than death. Virgin Gorda got its name (fat virgin) because Columbus, viewing it from seaward, thought that it resembled a reclining woman with a protruding belly.

The Spaniards, whose nation was the most powerful in Europe at this time, had laid claim to the West Indies as they had in their discovery of the Americas. They began to settle in various places throughout the islands to provide stop-over points for their ships carrying spoils from Central and South America to the mother country.

By this time the Caribs had more or less absorbed and digested the Arawaks, either physically or socially, and were thrilled to have new prey to harass, different coloured women to steal and a different flavour of

Simon Scott

7

enemy to fight. The staunchly Catholic Spaniards, right-wing products of the Inquisition's rule, were more than a little horrified at the Caribs' dietary preferences and, by the mid-1500s, had given up any hopes of missionary conversion.

Emperor Charles V ordered that the Indians "should be treated as enemies and given no quarter." Nevertheless, as late as 1620 the Caribs were still raiding mercilessly up and down the Caribbean.

Nor did this fierce tribe confine themselves to settlements. They can truly be described as the first pirates of the Caribbean—the first of many to prey upon the Spanish galleons. They were soon followed in this practice by several European nations who, afraid to challenge Spain directly, gave unofficial backing, in the form of letters of marque, to private enterprise to indulge in smuggling, piracy and the harassment of Spanish settlements.

This combination of privateering and piracy (the distinction between the two wearing very thin at times) was to continue for several hundred years. A vast array of colourful and bizarre characters paused in the Virgin Islands, among them the well-known pirate Henry Morgan and the legendary Sir John Hawkins, who visited the area four times. On his last voyage in 1595 Hawkins sailed with Sir Francis Drake to attack Puerto Rico, the two fleets apparently reconnoitering for a few days in the North Sound of Virgin Gorda to muster their men and prepare for battle.

It was a fateful trip for both of them: Hawkins sickened and died of the fever

8

that was the scourge of the tropics; Drake, himself, after a failed assault on the heavy fortifications of San Juan, soon followed suit.

As the power of Spain waned, other countries began to colonize the West Indies more seriously, although piracy continued for a while, the struggling settlers being happy to trade their agricultural produce and materials for a share of the Spanish gold. The Virgin Islands went through a lengthy period of "musical colonies" with the English, French, Dutch, Spanish and Danish moving from one island to another, shoving previous settlers on to the next, squabbling amongst themselves in Europe and, as a result, warring in the West Indies.

Eventually, however, the treasures from America dried up and the process of colonization gradually steadied. The Danes formally took possession of St. Thomas and, later, St. John; the English ousted the Dutch and gained a firm foothold in Tortola and Virgin Gorda; and the French settled in St. Croix but later sold it to the Danish West India Company.

The Spaniards continued to raid occasionally from their strongholds in Puerto Rico and Hispaniola through the late 1600s and piracy flared up intermittently in the early 1700s.

Considerable cleaning up and law enforcement took place as the casual farming that had begun, merely in order to colonize the islands and break the Spanish monopoly, gave way to serious plantations which, unsubsidized by stolen Spanish gold, needed to trade at a steady profit.

Following the example of the original Spanish settlers, early plantation owners brought slaves from Africa. When the introduction of sugar cane production in the 1640s required a large, cheap and stable labour force, the number of slaves began to increase. For some time the colonies thrived. Sugar and cotton were valuable commodities and the plantations diversified into the production of indigo, spices, rum, maize, pineapples, yams and coconuts. In 1717 the first census taken in Virgin Gorda showed a population of 625, about half of whom were black. By the mid-1700s this population had grown to nearly 2,000 and the proportion of slaves throughout the Virgin Islands had increased dramatically.

Life on the plantations was extremely hard for the slaves and, as their majority on the islands increased, so did the restrictions on them and the severity of the punishments meted out to them for the breaking of these. Conflict over the slave trade was increasing; it had been outlawed in England in 1772 and the impetus for its abolition was growing.

The obstacles to plantation life increased, several hurricanes and droughts ravaged the islands, and the American Revolution and Napoleonic wars created a revival of enemy raids, piracy and fighting within the islands. The slaves suffered as a result and, as news of abolition elsewhere began to filter through to the West Indies, they began to make use of their by now considerable majority to rebel.

The slave rebellions coincided, more or less, with the introduction of the sugar beet in Europe, which dealt a fatal blow to the once great "trade-triangle" based on West Indian cane. By the mid-1800s the slaves were free and the white population had deserted the colonies.

Jim Scheiner

9

For almost 100 years the Virgin Islands dozed peacefully, the freed slaves living quietly off the land and sea, though with some difficulty in years of drought and famine. Government was minimal: In 1893, for example, there were only two white men in the B.V.I.—the Deputy Governor and the doctor.

The islands struggled on with tottering economies. Virgin Gorda was visited briefly by Cornish miners who reopened the old Spanish mine in search of copper. An earthquake leveled all the churches in Tortola and the *H.M.S. Rhone* was wrecked off Salt Island. As late as 1869 the steamship *Telegrafo* was detained in Tortola and charged with piracy. Labour riots and rebellions occasionally protested the hardships. The United States began to show an interest in buying the Danish islands, afraid that they would be sold to a hostile nation such as Germany.

The islands moved into the 20th century without much change. An agricultural station was established in Tortola in 1900 in hopes of boosting the faltering economy, various homestead projects were begun throughout the island with little effect and the parent governments of each colony were forced to accept financial responsibility for the islands, which were fast becoming a liability.

The first world was tightening the purse strings further, and by 1917 the Danes were happy to sell their Virgin Islands to the United States, which was eager to have a military outpost in the Caribbean. St. Thomas had long been a useful coaling station and harbour for steamships and was well positioned to defend the approaches to the Panama Canal.

Over the first half of the 20th century there was gradual social reform and progress towards local government. This process began to speed up as the tourist trade, boosted by the increasing ease of casual travel, began to grow.

Finally the geography and physical advantages of the islands began once more to have a major influence on their fortunes. Situated conveniently close to the United States and blessed with a warm climate and a beautiful, unspoilt environment, the Virgin Islands rapidly became popular with tourists. At last, here was an industry which needed only the natural resources of the islands to sustain their economies.

Now stable, friendly places, the Virgin Islands are once more visited by colourful characters from all over the world. Some just sail through nomadically, like the long-departed Ciboneys; others, like the Arawaks, stay to build homes and businesses.

There is still the occasional pirate, although they are more usually found on land these days, and privateering has yet to be revived—unless one applies this label to the tax department.

With the charter industry becoming the backbone of the islands, particularly in the BVI, sailors continue to make use of one of the finest sailing areas in the world. The quiet coves where Drake, Columbus and Blackbeard used to anchor are once more havens for fleets of sailing vessels and the modern adventurers who come to explore the Virgin Islands.

Jim Scheiner

10

PIRATES
Of The Caribbean

It is just as well that there are no longer any pirates in the Virgin Islands. Imagine yourself reclining in the cockpit of the yacht after a difficult hour trying to make the anchor stay put. The pina colada is nice and cold. The kids' yelling has receded into the distance as they explore the shoreline, collecting sea urchin spines in their feet. Your wife is perfecting her suntan on the foredeck and the other couple, who used to be your oldest friends until you decided to charter a yacht together, are arguing through clenched teeth in the galley. A perfect vacation in the Caribbean.

Then, as the sun begins to sink towards the horizon, a small sloop veers into the cove you thought you had to yourselves. An anchor splashes overboard and, before you have finished spraying your ankles with insect repellent, a horde of noisy, unshaven thugs row across to your boat and, without so much as a by-your-leave, swarm on deck, empty your wallet, your liquor cabinet and your fridge, and steal your camera and your wife.

It wouldn't do much for the charter business.

Although piracy is no longer a popular pastime in the VI, it is really not that long since it was the rage throughout the Caribbean. In the early 1700s, a sympathetic governor in St. Thomas was still fencing goods for pirates like Charles Vane and Edward Teach (the legendary Blackbeard), and as late as 1869 the steamship *Telegrafo* was detained in Tortola and charged with piracy.

Nor is there anything new about sailors dabbling in "the sweet trade." As long as men have transported anything of value across the ocean, there have been others willing to relieve them of it. Even the Bible speaks of "princes of the sea." Julius Caesar had first-hand experience of these—he was kidnapped and held for ransom by them, and his invasion of Britain was partly in order to subdue the Veneti *pirata* and their British crews. For several hundred years the Vikings made annual raids along the coasts of Western Europe, and in the Middle Ages, as trade and travel by

sea expanded, piracy got underway with a vengeance.

"Privateering" also came into vogue at this time. A pirate called Eustace The Monk, who was believed to have black magic powers, did well plundering French ships on behalf of England's King John. Privateering was basically government-sponsored piracy—tacit approval given to raids on the ships of potential enemies. Privately owned vessels manned by civilians were commissioned with "letters of marque" as auxiliaries to the Royal Navy. They were used mainly against merchant shipping and were actively encouraged by monarchs in times of war or hostility. (As the 16th and early 17th centuries saw Europe in a fairly constant state of turmoil, this meant that they were encouraged most of the time.) Since a healthy percentage of the "purchase" went to the Crown, there was an added incentive for Royalty to turn a blind eye to the often extreme actions of the privateers and a deaf ear to the whining and complaining of the Ambassadors from semi-hostile nations.

A prime example of this sanctioning of successful piracy was, of course, the way in which Queen Elizabeth I dealt with Sir Francis Drake. His famous round-the-world voyage actually evolved from a plan to raid the Spanish-American towns along the Pacific coast during an interval when England was theoretically at peace with Spain. However, when he returned with a treasure worth at least $5 million, the Virgin Queen boarded his ship, the *Golden Hind*, ignoring the Spanish demands that "El Draque" be hanged, and knighted him instead. This led Sir Walter Raleigh to make the (still pertinent) comment, "Did you ever know of any

that were pirates for millions? They only that work for small things are pirates."

Having laid claim to all of the Americas and the West Indies, Spain was the most powerful nation in the world at this time. Other nations, though afraid to challenge the monopoly directly, were happy to see pirates siphoning off funds intended for the Spanish Reformation by intercepting the treasure ships loaded with Aztec gold. The increasing number of privateers also provided a handy pool of trained sailors who could be called upon in times of outright conflict.

Numerous ex-pirates played an important role in the eventual defeat of the Spanish Armada. In times of covert hostility they could go back to being privateers (the "legality" made visiting ports for supplies easier), and in the infrequent and uneasy intervals of peace they resorted to plain piracy—their status was largely dependent upon the diplomatic label given to it at the time.

In reality their lives changed very little. If pressganged into the Navy they could expect long voyages, harsh discipline, vile food and a good chance of an early demise—all for a pathetic pittance which would be cut off abruptly in peacetime. As pirates, their conditions at sea were little better but were offset by a freer democratic lifestyle, a similar chance of survival and the possibility of vast financial reward. As Bartholomew Roberts, one of the most successful pirates of the early 18th century, commented, "In an honest service there is thin rations, low wages and hard labor; in this, plenty and satiety, pleasure and ease, liberty and power; and who would not balance creditor on this side, when all the hazard that is run for it, at worst, is only a sour look or two at choking. No, 'a merry life and a short one' shall be my motto."

The defeat of the Armada intensified the harassment of Spanish merchant ships and allowed English, French and Dutch colonies to germinate in the now undefended West Indies.

Some of the first colonists were the itinerant French *boucaniers* who settled on Hispaniola.

They made a meager living barbecuing beef in smokehouses called *boucans* and selling it to passing vessels. Foolishly the Spaniards drove them off the island; in revenge they took to the sea where, instead of hunting wild cattle, they went after Spanish ships instead.

"Buccaneer" became a new and fearful term for "pirate," and their ranks swelled as out of work naval crews drifted to the new world. New colonies struggling desperately to gain a foothold were a willing market for plundered goods. The governors of these new settlements gained a 10% commission for issuing letters of marque to privateers and, as a result, Jamaica's Port Royal became one of the richest towns in the hemisphere because of pirate gold. It also became known as "the wickedest city in the world," but it was largely due to the transient population of fighting sailors that the British were able to keep Jamaica. As late as 1774, historian Edward Long wrote, "It is to the buccaneers that we owe possession of Jamaica to this hour."

So the pirates were a vital part of the colonization of the West Indies. Henry Morgan, for example, dealt terrible blows to Spanish dominance when he attacked Spanish shipping, ransomed Puerto de Principe in Cuba, assaulted Porto Bello and burned Panama City to the ground. Despite a new treaty with Spain, neither Morgan nor the governor who issued the commission was ever punished, possibly because of the shares received by the King and his brother, the Duke of York.

The Spanish meted out their own punishment if they caught pirates or privateers. They made no distinction between the two except that privateers were sent to the gallows with their commissions tied around their necks. Hanging was the usual end for captured pirates, although, if they were unlucky enough to fall into the hands of the Inquisition, they might receive a more drawn-out demise on the rack.

Some of the evil vermin who gravitated to a life of piracy were very capable of perpetrating their own unique atrocities. Most pirates had a weakness for "rumbullion" and in their cups would often torment their prisoners for entertainment. Blackbeard was said to have made one victim eat his own nose and lips; another Englishman named Thomas Cobham sewed 20 Spaniards up in a mainsail and threw the whole squirming package overboard.

"Going on the account" was the term used when a man signed up for a career in piracy; this basically meant "no prey, no pay," but all the crew were shareholders in the "company" and part owners of the ship. The company typically began with a very modest vessel— some of the early buccaneers used dug-out canoes—but after a few killings on the market, they would generally acquire more suitable headquarters.

The ideal pirate vessel was small and fast. Bermudan sloops were felt to be ideal because of their speed (over 11 knots) and maneuverability, and could carry up to 75 men. A bigger company might go for a brigantine, a two-masted vessel that could carry either a square or fore-and-aft rig or a versatile combination of the two.

This was often how pirates made their assaults, sneaking out from the coast in poor light to spring upon a sluggish merchantman. The Virgin Islands made an excellent hunting ground with their myriad coves and passages. Situated right on the treasure route from South America to Europe, the area was visited by many notorious Caribbean pirates such as Edward England, whose kind treatment of prisoners so disgusted his crew that he was deposed; Charles Vane, who Defoe reported, "died in Agonies equal to his Villainies but showed not the least Remorse for the Crimes of his past life"; Calico Jack, well known for his romance with lady pirate Anne Bonny; Bartholomew Roberts, who became one of the greatest pirates of all "for the love of novelty and change alone"; and the formidable Blackbeard, who would go into battle with slow-burning matches alight in his beard and behind his ears to enhance his devilish resemblance.

By the early 18th century, competition for prizes in the Caribbean was strong. A treaty in 1713 allowed the Navy time to begin protecting merchant shipping (for a price that was almost robbery in itself).

As the colonies in the island began to stabilize, law and order made the pirates less welcome as members of the community. Many of them set off for the North American mainland, where the newer colonists, already muttering about Independence, were quite pleased to help the newcomers harass British shipping magnates. Others headed for the Orient, the Red Sea, the Indian Ocean and Madagascar.

Since then piracy has continued to flourish in the Far East, but has been quelled fairly effectively in the West.

Smuggling, however, is another matter—recent years have seen a resurgence in the "sweet trade."

The traditions haven't changed much; seaport bars still abound with tales of sailors sneaking around dark shores in small, fast boats, dodging the authorities, sending coded messages at dead of night and risking life and liberty for high stakes.

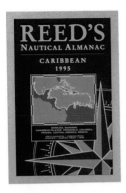

Traveling to and from the Virgins is very straightforward. Most of the larger bareboat companies have travel agents who work closely with them and are in touch with special air fares and hotel accommodations. San Juan, Puerto Rico is the main routing for passengers destined to the BVI, St. Thomas and St. Croix. There are numerous non-stop flights from major U.S. Gateways with ample local connections. St. Thomas and St. Croix have direct service from the U.S. mainland. There are plenty of good hotels throughout the islands and it is advisable to plan a one night stay before checking in at the appropriate marina. This will enable you to "acclimatize" slowly, watching the sun set and sipping a rum punch while the frustrations of the day's travel diminish to insignificance.

The Virgins are an extremely popular tourist destination not only for sailors, but for all sorts of tourists and water sports enthusiasts; consequently, air travel and hotel accommodations should be reserved well in advance.

If you are planning to travel between the islands, there are numerous methods available to you:

INTER-ISLAND AIR TRAVEL

American Eagle .... 776-7450 St. Thomas
.... 494-2449 Tortola

Gorda Aero .... 495-2271 Tortola

LIAT .... 774-2313 St. Thomas,
.... 495-1187 Tortola

WRA Caribbean Air Service 774-9280

The following ferries operate between the U.S. and British Virgin Islands, and between Tortola and Virgin Gorda:

Smith's Ferry	775-7292	St. Thomas
	494-4430	Tortola
The Native Sun	774-8685	St. Thomas
	495-4617	Tortola
Speedy's Fantasy	774-8685	St. Thomas
	495-5240	Tortola

The North Sound Express (494-2746) operates between Beef Island, and North Sound, Virgin Gorda. The Peter Island Ferry (494-2561) runs between the Peter Island dock at Baugher's Bay, Road Town and the Peter Island Yacht Club.

There is ferry service from Underwater Safaris at the Moorings dock to Cooper Island most days. Call them by telephone or radio to confirm times.

Two ferries operate between Jost Van Dyke and Tortola: Reel World at 495-9277 or JVD Ferry Service at 495-2775.

For service between West End and Cruz Bay, call Inter-Island Boat Services at 495-4166 in Tortola or at 776-6597 in the USVI.

From Redhook, St. Thomas to Cruz Bay, St. John, ferries leave at 6:30 a.m. and 7:30 a.m. on weekdays and on the hour from 8 a.m. through noon. From Cruz Bay ,ferries leave from 7 a.m. through 10 p.m. on the hour, and at 11:15 p.m.

Ferries are available between the National Park Dock, St. Thomas, and Charlotte Amalie to Caneel Bay Plantation, St. John. Call 776-6111 for schedules.

Ferries are available directly from Charlotte Amalie to Virgin Gorda—check with the Native Sun, Smith's Ferry and Speedy's Fantasy—as well as between St. Thomas and Jost Van Dyke.

See the directory on page 240 for a complete listing of ferry services.

BOATFAX^{SM}

SHOPPING FOR THE ULTIMATE BOAT ?
LET US FAX YOU THE MARINA.

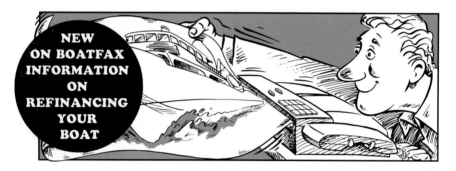

NEW ON BOATFAX INFORMATION ON REFINANCING YOUR BOAT

BOATFAX IS THE SIMPLEST, QUICKEST WAY TO SHOP FOR A BOAT. CALL BOATFAX FROM THE TELEPHONE HANDSET OF YOUR FAX, AND FOLLOWING THE VOICE PROMPTS, INPUT YOUR SELECTION CRITERIA.

BOATFAX FAXES BACK A COMPLETE LISTING OF BOATS WHICH FIT YOUR SPECIFICATIONS. FROM THAT LIST, CHOOSE SPECIFIC BOATS AND CALL BACK TO INSTANTLY RECEIVE DETAILED INFORMATION SUCH AS DESCRIPTIONS, PRICES AND LINE DRAWINGS.

YOUR BOATFAX NUMBER IS 404-399-3077. CALL FROM THE TELE-PHONE HANDSET OF YOUR FAX MACHINE.* BROKERS INTERESTED IN LISTING THEIR BOATS IN BOATFAX CALL 404-399-3078.

FROM NOW ON, BUYING A BOAT IS GOING TO BE SMOOTH SAILING.

BoatFax is a service mark owned by:
CREATIVE SOLUTIONS
G R O U P, I N C

*
**NORMAL TELEPHONE
TOLL CHARGES WILL APPLY**

 **AT&T** | **NCR**
An AT&T Company

— An AT&T/NCR "Solutions Provider"

CUSTOMS AND IMMIGRATION

For visitors entering the U.S. Virgin Islands from the United States, there is no customs or immigration clearance, as you are still in U.S. territory. However, you will have to clear back in on your return from this free port area. U.S. citizens are allowed to bring in $1200 duty-free every 30 days from the USVI.

Those U. S. visitors sailing from British Virgin Island waters and those entering the British Virgin Islands through the airport or West End should be advised that proof of citizenship will be required for all members of your party. A birth certificate, passport or voter registration card is the normal I.D. expected. For all other visitors, a valid passport is required.

BVI customs must be cleared upon entry and little problem will be encountered for bona fide sailors. All items carried for commercial use are subject to local duties at the going tariff.

CURRENCY

The U.S. Dollar is the local currency in both the U.S. and British Virgin Islands. Since you will be spending a lot of time on small islands, it is a good idea to keep traveller's checks in smaller denominations.

Major credit cards are honored at most USVI stores and hotels and the larger BVI establishments, but do not expect to use them at small restaurants during your cruise. Personal checks are not accepted anywhere.

PACKING FOR THE CRUISE

Almost without exception, most sailors coming to the Virgin Islands for a week's sailing bring far too much gear. Try not to carry hard suitcases as they do not stow easily on a boat. If possible, use duffel bags or sea bags that can be folded up when not in use.

If you are travelling from the northern climates during the winter months, try to shed your heavy overcoats and boots prior to boarding the airplane. You will only have to carry them around for the duration of your stay in the islands.

Lay out everything you intend to bring and ask yourself if you really need each item. During the days aboard the boat, you will need only bathing suits and perhaps a cover-up, shorts and a few casual shirts or blouses. If you intend to eat ashore at resorts like Caneel Bay, Little Dix and Peter Island, include a jacket and tie for the men and a light cocktail dress for the ladies. Otherwise, in most island restaurants, casual slacks and shirts are acceptable. You will need some reef shoes for wading in shallow water or coral and several T-shirts.

You may wish to include an inexpensive snorkel for each crew member... using a second hand snorkel can be like borrowing someone else's toothbrush.

PROTECTION FROM THE SUN

Although it may seem difficult to comprehend as you dig your car out of the snow to get to the airport, the tropical sun is *hot*, especially on pale bodies that have been kept undercover throughout a northern winter.

The constant trade breezes keep the temperature pretty much ideal, but be careful not to spend too long out in the sun, as the combined effect of overhead tropical sun and reflection from both sails and water can cause severe sunburns.

Most charter yachts are equipped with bimini tops; however, it is still a good idea to bring along a pair of lightweight or surgical pants and tops if you have access to them. These will enable you to cover up.

If you are fair, then perhaps you should think about a wide-brimmed hat.

Suntan lotions are available throughout the islands. Heed the warnings of dermatologists regarding excessive sun exposure and do not go out into the sun without using an appropriate sun block or coverup. Start with at least SPF-15. If you are careful, you will gradually develop a rich, golden tan without suffering a painful and potentially dangerous sunburn.

WHAT NOT TO BRING

Apart from an abundance of clothing, there are a few items that don't make any sense to lug back and forth:

A) Scuba gear — If you have your own regulator, face mask, etc., fine, but don't bring down weight belts and tanks. They are available for rent from many outlets and dive shops throughout the islands and will save you the hassle of lugging them around.

B) Food items — Once again, unless you have special dietary needs, these items are readily available throughout the islands and the marginal savings on some frozen steaks could be offset if the box thaws or goes astray.

C) Surfboards and windsurfers — These items represent a problem for the major airlines and a nightmare for the smaller commuter airlines. They are available for rent and anyone interested should make prior arrangements with the appropriate charter company or agent.

Remember that you will probably purchase a few items while in the islands and some allowance should be made for such purchases when packing.

The ideal amount of luggage to bring on a sailing holiday should fit in a duffel bag underneath your airline seat. This will save your worrying about checking bags and waiting with baited breath to see if they show up on the other end.

23

CAR RENTAL

Both the British and the U.S. Virgin Islands have developed adequate car rental agencies to cope with the needs of the growing tourist industry.

Prices are slightly higher than on the U.S. mainland, but considering the high cost of freight and the limited life expectancy that vehicles enjoy in the island environment, the differential is not excessive. Most of the major car rental companies have local branches throughout the Virgins and advance reservations can be made through your travel agent.

In addition, many locally owned and operated companies are also represented. If you are chartering during the peak months (December-April), try to reserve well in advance to avoid delays.

TAXI SERVICE

All points of debarkation are more than adequately serviced by taxis. The airports and ferry docks are often lined three deep, with the drivers pushing hard to capture their share of the market.

It is common in the islands to see open safari buses, which can carry up to 20 passengers in natural "air-conditioned" comfort. Taxi fares tend to be expensive throughout the islands and taxis are not metered!

However, there are official taxi rates in both the British and U.S. Virgin Islands, and the prudent traveller should inquire of the rate beforehand so that there are no misunderstandings.

The major charterboat companies will arrange transportation to pick you up upon arrival at the airport, but such service should be arranged at the time of booking the charter.

Most charter companies in and around the Virgin Islands offer the charter party a choice of provisioning programs or options.

The original concept was designed to cope with the lack of supermarkets. But in recent years, both in the U.S. and British Virgin Islands, the selection of goods has increased tremendously. Therefore, your provisioning options are as follows:

A) Allow the charter company to provision for you from a pre-selected plan, to save on sailing time. The main plans are *full provisioning*, which includes 3 meals a day, or the popular *split program*, which eliminates some evening meals so you can eat ashore. If you are considering this, ask the charter company for a sample menu.

B) Provision yourself from one of the local markets or delicatessens. This is a good idea if you have specific dietary needs, but it is time-consuming, and when analyzing costs, taxi fares and sailing time should be considered. However, many of the local markets have a surprisingly sophisticated array of products.

C) Have an independent provisioner prepare your provisions in advance and have them delivered to the boat or swing by and pick them up. Provisioning lists are available in advance, allowing you the luxury of choosing your provisioning from home.

Restocking Along the Way

However you provision your vessel, you will probably wish to augment your supply at some point along the cruise. Major items are normally available only in Road Town, Virgin Gorda Yacht Harbour, Cruz Bay, Charlotte Amalie, Redhook and Christiansted, St. Croix. Many smaller shops have a surprising selection of provisioning items, including those in Nanny Cay, Cane Garden Bay, at the Bitter End Hotel in North Sound, at Harris's Place in Jost Van Dyke, and at Sapphire Beach Marina and Compass Point in St. Thomas.

ICE, WATER & SUPPLIES ARE AVAILABLE FROM THE FOLLOWING AREAS:

Location	Water	Ice	Supplies
Crown Bay Marina, St. Thomas	yes	yes	yes
Yacht Haven Marina, St. Thomas	yes	yes	yes
Sugar Reef Marine, St. Thomas	yes	yes	yes
Compass Point, St. Thomas	yes	yes	yes
Red Hook, St. Thomas	yes	yes	yes
Sapphire Marina, St. Thomas	yes	yes	yes
Cruz Bay, St. John	yes	yes	yes
Sopers Hole Marina, West End	yes	yes	yes
Nanny Cay Marina	yes	yes	yes
Fort Burt Marina, Roadtown	yes	yes	yes
Road Reef Marina	yes	yes	yes
Village Cay Marina, Roadtown	yes	yes	yes
Inner Harbour Marina	yes	yes	yes
The Moorings Marina, Roadtown	yes	yes	yes
Marina Cay, Tortola	yes	yes	yes
Tropic Island Yacht Management, Maya Cove	yes	yes	no
Peter Island Yacht Harbour	yes	yes	no
Seabreeze Marina, Fat Hogs Bay, Tortola	yes	yes	yes
Virgin Gorda Yacht Harbour	yes	yes	yes
Leverick Bay, North Sound, Virgin Gorda	yes	yes	yes
Bitter End, Virgin Gorda	yes	yes	yes
Harris' Place, Jost Van Dyke	yes	yes	yes
St. Croix Marina	yes	yes	yes
Green Cay Marina	yes	yes	yes

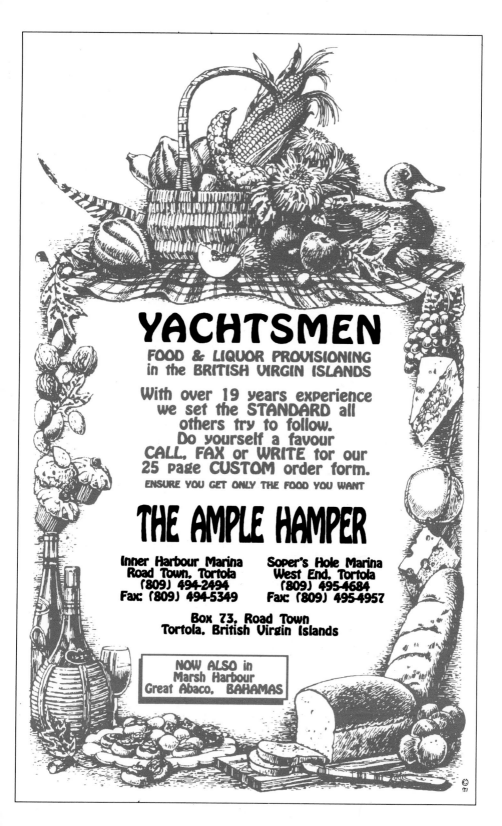

Boatphone Mobility.

Now you don't have to be in port to keep in touch. And your family (or your broker!) can get in touch with you.

CCT BOAT PHONE
Cellular Phone Service offers easy, convenient, private communication <u>throughout</u> the Virgin Islands. Whether you use a phone already installed on most bareboats, rent a phone, or bring your own personal phone, either from the beach, or on the water, you can activate cellular service 24-hours a day by "O" "Snd" on the phone. For further information, or to pre-register (no cost), call us at (809) 494-3825.

Service is now available on most Virgin Island bareboats.

Caribbean Cellular Telephone

BOATPHONE^{SM}

The #1 Cellular Phone Company of the Caribbean.

Mill Mall, P.O. Box 267, Road Town, Tortola, B.V.I.
PHONE (809) 494-3825 • FAX (809) 494-4933

Dial ISLAND FAX (404) 399-3077 • Select Code #1126...For More Information.

28

Jim Scheiner

Camera

The verdant green hillside tumbles down to a deserted golden beach, fringed with majestic coconut palms. Tall ships and sleek yachts glide by on an azure sea. You and your companions spend joyful days sailing, snorkeling and exploring. As the water laps against the side of your yacht, you wonder how you'll ever be able to recapture this carefree feeling after you return to the hustle and bustle of the "real world." How will you convey the unspoiled beauty of the Virgin Islands to your friends back home? Well, while memories and tans fade fast, photos last and last.

It's hard to go wrong with today's cameras; top of the line models now offer auto-everything, simplicity and the basic point and shoot cameras deliver control, sophistication and zoom lens capability previously reserved for high-end machines. Serious shooters will probably want to bring a 35 mm single lens reflex (SLR) with a fullcomplement of lenses. A wide-range zoom lens (35mm to 135mm or longer) will cover most situations. For capturing onboard action, a wider angle lens (24mm) will be good. A long telephoto lens (longer than 210mm) is difficult to use on a moving boat, but can deliver some dramatic shots. Today's automatic "fill flash" is ideal for filling in the deep shadows caused by the tropical sun and for shooting sunset portraits. A polarizing filter can intensify some colors and make the water appear clearer, but it adds a lot of contrast and eats up light. Remember, if you bring every gizmo and accessory you own, you'll spend your entire holiday lugging it around and worrying about its safety. If you're a snap-shooter thinking about upgrading, consider one of the new, water resistant automatic cameras. While not waterproof by any means, they are a little more durable in a marine environment. Even if you're a serious shooter, you might also want to bring a simple camera rather than risk your expensive SLR.

Jim Scheiner

Video

These days, legions of holiday makers are leaving their SLRs and "snap shot" cameras behind and going forth armed with video camcorders. The latest generation of video cameras are small enough to be taken anywhere and deliver an incredible "broadcast quality" picture with point and shoot ease. But they're equally capable of recording endless hours of meaningless, boring video. With a little planning, practice, and discipline, your vacation movies can be quite entertaining.

Here are a few basics: Hold the camera steady (use a tripod or brace yourself), set the zoom at widest angle setting and get close. Don't over do panning and zooming. Film selectively, you don't need record every activity every time it happens. When you do decide to record an activity, shoot it in a logical order--establishing or big view shots to set the scene, medium shots to show the action and close up shots to show details--you should try to tell a story. Keep it short unless something *very* special is happening. Limit each scene to 10 to 20 seconds of meaningful video. Try in-camera editing, where you shoot your scenes in the order and length that you want to view them. Don't forget live "voice over" narration to explain what and where, but don't over do it. And while you don't want to have the date superimposed over *all* your

video, it's not a bad idea to do it for the first shot of each day, sort of like the entry line in a diary. Remember, keep it short, interesting and steady, and think before you push the record button.

Bring plenty of batteries and tape they're not readily available on the islands. A wide angle adapter lens for use in the narrow confines on the boat helps capture all the action. Video cameras are especially sensitive to water/spray damage, including condensation formed when coming from a cold, air conditioned room to warm, humid air. A good case is essential. Charging batteries on board can be complicated so find out in advance how much 110 AC power there is. If there's only 12 volt, then invest in a 12 volt charger, but double check the polarity before plugging it it.

Film

Bring the type of film (print or slide) you normally use. There is plenty of light in the tropics, so make sure you bring some fine-grained, slower speed film (ISO 100 and lower) for crisp and clear shots. Four hundred speed film is great for sunsets and twilight scenes. ISO 200 is great, an all around compromise. For slide film photographers, Fujichrome's new Velvia (ISO 50) is very color saturated and makes the images come alive. Kodak's new "Underwater" film has confused a few people. Basically, it's a slide film with increased sensitivity to red in order to compensate for the predominantly blue light at depths below 20 feet. We've found it to be useful for wide-angle shots in shallow water. For bright colorful shots of divers or marine life, the best technique is to get close, use a strobe and "normal" film. Film processing (both E6 slide and print) is available on the island. As always, keep your film out of the sun and avoid having it repeatedly X-rayed at airport security stations. If you transport your film in a ziplock or mesh bag, it's easy to have it hand checked.

Protecting Your Equipment
Even though you've come all this way for the sun, sea and sand, it doesn't mean that your cameras should partake as well. Salt water and sand kills cameras! While an outright dunking in the sea is certainly catastrophic, it's the cumulative damage caused by spray and carelessness that needs to be prevented. Today's state-of-the-art electronic still and video marvels are especially sensitive to salt water damage. Specialized cameras, protective cases, and preventative measures all help, but a little bit of common sense and awareness go a long way.

Salt water is *very* corrosive and it does most of its damage invisibly, destroying the hidden inner-workings of your camera. Even if you quickly wipe off the occasional splash, the few drops of saltwater that seeped inside your camera will continue to absorb moisture out of the air, damaging your camera long after it appears to be dry..

On board the boat, keep your camera protected from waves and spray. A gallon size, heavy-duty ziplock or even a small (5 gallon) garbage bag will work wonders. Keeping your camera hidden under a light-weight *waterproof* jacket until you're ready to shoot also is a possibility. But if it's really blowing, simply leave your camera below decks, out of harm's way. A UV, or skylight filter, will help protect your lens from salt spray. Don't forget that the salt water "contamination" you collect on your hands and face just from being on a yacht is passed to your camera every time you pick it up. Freshwater face washes and "camera only" towels and paper towels help to minimize this. I always have a dry, clean paper towel in my pocket. Never change film or lenses

when there is any chance of spray or splashes.

Getting your camera ashore is another matter. Dinghies are a lot wetter than you think. On a professional shoot, I place my camera bag inside a heavy duty garbage bag (tied closed) and then place that in a canvas bag. Sometimes I use a waterproof, hard "pelican" case, but they're heavy and bulky and difficult to work out of. Be wary of placing an unprotected camera bag on the floor of the dinghy, there's likely to be a lot of water sloshing around. If you want to take pictures from the dinghy *and* keep your camera dry, slow the dinghy down (stop it if necessary) and avoid shooting while motoring into the wind. A lot of cameras get soaked climbing out of the dinghy to go ashore. Seal everything back up before you splash your way through the surf. If you're at all unsure of your balance, pass your camera bag to someone already ashore and hold it high against big waves.

Ashore, the biggest problem is sand. Even waterproof cameras are not sand-proof; sand gets into the o-ring seals and destroys them. Practice the same care on the beach as you did on you yacht and you'll do fine. A "camera only" ziplock and beach bag will prevent others from inadvertently throwing wet, sandy towels and clothes on top of your camera. After a swim, dry (and rinse) you hands, face and hair before shooting. As discussed below, disposable cameras are perfect for dinghy and beach trips.

Underwater Photography Equipment
The easiest and cheapest way to get started in underwater photography is to purchase a couple of waterproof, disposable "snorkel" cameras (i.e., the Kodak Weekender or Fuji Waterproof). Not only are they waterproof, but they're also dinghy- and beach-proof. Take one everywhere and enjoy worry-free vacation photography. While we don't sanction "one time use" cameras, in this situation it's far better to trash a $10 to $20 disposable camera than your $600.Nikon.

The Weekender is rated to about a dozen feet and ideal for swimming and snorkeling. But if scuba diving is in your plans, you'll need to move up a notch. Ikelite, a manufacturer of professional underwater camera housings and strobes, also makes the Aquashot housing (around $80) for use with Fuji or Kodak disposable cameras-with-flash. The advantage over the snorkeling cameras described above is twofold. First, the cameras have a built-in flash which will bring out the brilliant colors of the fish and corals. Without flash, everything deeper than 20 to 30 feet underwater is blah blue. Second, the Aquashot housing is rated to 125 feet, as deep as you are likely to go. This combination of housing and disposable camera-with-flash is a great trouble-free way to get started in underwater photography with minimal risk or investment. The pictures rival those taken by expensive underwater cameras.

An Underwater Photography Primer

Regardless of what kind of camera you use to take underwater pictures, there is one maxim that holds true--*get close.* The less water you shoot through, the clearer, brighter and more color-saturated your pictures will be. There are exceptions of course, but most good underwater photographs are shot within four feet of the subject, which is quite close within conversational distance. If you can reach out and touch your subject, you're too close, much further away and you're too far. The perfect distance is a handshake distance--reach out and shake hands with your buddy and fire away. If your subject (a fish, say) isn't interested in shaking hands, then just imagine a double arm length. However you measure it, it's pretty close, but that's what it takes to get *good* underwater photos.

With most cameras, at three to four feet from your subject the dimensions of the area photographed will be roughly two by three feet. Angelfish, parrotfish and coral and sponge formations are appropriate subjects. Tiny fish and huge vistas requires specialized lenses. Remember, that while pictures of coral and fish are fun and challenging to take, make sure that you take plenty of your companions. Try to avoid shooting down on your subject. If at all possible, aim across or even up slightly, this helps separate your subject form the background and even adds a little drama to the image.

Most published underwater photographs boast brilliant colors. However, due to the natural absorption of sunlight by water, your pictures will suffer form the underwater "blues," unless you use a flash to bring out the reds and yellows. Smaller cameras with built-in flashes do a fine job of balancing the flash with the available light. Even the most powerful underwater strobe won't reach past five or six feet. Try to avoid stirring up the bottom, the resultant strobe lit "back scatter" will look as if you were diving in a blizzard.

The coral reef and its inhabitants are very fragile, so please, no standing on or grabbing delicate coral structures or removing anything from the sea. Take only pictures, leave only bubbles.

Jim and Odile Scheiner are the owners of Rainbow Visions Photography in Tortola, specializing in underwater photography and video.

Jim Scheiner

THOUSANDS of Cruising World

subscribers who were polled

RATED THE SERVICE

provided by bareboat charter companies.

HERE ARE THE RESULTS.

COMPANY INFORMATION					READER RATINGS		
Company	**Years In Business**	**Base Location**	**#Boats** (this base)	**Age** (years)	**The Base**	**The Boat**	**The Service**
Sunsail	20	Soper's Hole West End, Tortola	65	New-4	Good to Excellent	Good to Excellent	Excellent
		Bitter End Yacht Club, Virgin Gorda	6	1-2	New Base - No Reader Comment Received		
Freedom Yacht Charters	3	Roadtown, Tortola Marina Cay	11	New-1.5	Good	Excellent	Good
Sun Yacht Charters	16	NEW: Hannah Bay, Tortola PREVIOUS: Roadtown, Tortola	17	New-3	Good	Good to Excellent	Good to Excellent
The Moorings	25	Roadtown, Tortola	150	New-6	Good to Excellent	Good	Good
Caribbean Yacht Charters (CYC)	26	Compass Point, Jersey Bay, St. Thomas	40	New-4	Good	Good	Good to Excellent
Tortola Marine Management	15	Roadtown Marina, Tortola	28	New-6	Good	Good	Good to Excellent

Top 6 Charter Companies in the Virgin Islands. Information above condensed from Cruising World's 1994 Reader Chartering Poll.

Offering bareboat, crewed and flotilla

charters for over 20 years.

For Marina Services and

Hotel Accommodations at our

Sunsail Base in Soper's Hole, Tortola,

please call: **(809) 495-4740**

For all other inquiries on

Chartering Worldwide,

please call: **1-800-327-2276**

33

Charts

Pilotage through unknown waters is one of the major concerns of the cruising yachtsman. However, in the Virgins, where there is very little tide rise and fall and only minimal current to worry about, pilotage is extremely simple.

Since the weather is so warm, we don't experience any fog and you can always see the island for which you are heading.

Reefs and shoals are not a major problem as they are well marked and, provided time is taken to study the pertinent charts on a daily basis, your cruise around the island will be most enjoyable.

The islands themselves are high and volcanic, rising steeply from the crystal clear water. In many cases, it is possible to position your bow almost on the beach, providing you have a stern anchor set.

Since the island chain is close together, you will have no difficulty in distinguishing them. Using the contour marks on the charts you will usually be able to pinpoint your location without the use of navigation tools.

Equipment

Every cruising yacht should be equipped with the basic tools of navigation—parallel rules, triangles, dividers, plotters, etc. However, it should be noted that in order to navigate throughout the islands, the only equipment needed is a compass, chart, pencil and leadline or fathometer. Those wishing to brush up on navigational skills will find ample opportunity, although celestial observations are often difficult because of the proximity of the islands.

It is possible to navigate throughout the U.S. and British Virgin Islands with one chart, NOAA 25641, which covers St. Thomas to Virgin Gorda. Many of the charter companies have duplicated this chart in one form or another, which they hand out to each charter group. If you're chartering, be sure to ask the charter company in advance what charts they'll provide and whether the charts are yours to keep. Then look carefully at the areas you intend to cruise and obtain any additional chart coverage you may want.

Charts are sometimes difficult to obtain in the Virgin Islands, so taking your own charts is the best way to be sure that you have coverage you're comfortable with. Your own charts will also serve as nice mementos of your trip. A complete set of Virgin Islands charts will range from $48 to $140, depending upon the charts you select.

The following charts cover the Virgin Islands and are available from larger chart agents in the U.S., Canada and Europe:

U.S. National Ocean Survey (NOAA)
25645 - Christiansted Harbour, St. Croix
25647 - St. Thomas, Pillsbury Sound and St. John
25649 - St. Thomas Harbour
25640 - Puerto Rico and the V.I.
25641 - Virgin Gorda to St. Thomas and St. Croix
25644 - Frederiksted Road and Pier

U. S. Defense Mapping Agency
25609 - Tortola to Anegada
25610 - Approaches to Gorda Sound

25611 - Road Harbour and approaches

British Admiralty
130 - Anguilla to Puerto Rico
485 - St. Croix
2008 - N.E. Virgin Gorda to Anegada
2016 - Virgin Gorda - North Sound
2019 - Tortola to Virgin Gorda
2452 - Tortola to Culebra including St. Thomas

Imray - Iolaire
A23 - The Virgin Islands - St. Croix
A231 - St. Thomas to Virgin Gorda
A232 - Tortola to Anegada

Reef Reading

There is no dark secret attached to the ability to read the reef. It is merely the ability to distinguish water colour. Experience is, of course, the best teacher; however, with a few practical hints, even the novice will be able to feel his way to an anchorage within a few days.

It is important to have the sun overhead in order to distinguish reef areas. That is why most charter companies insist that the boats be at anchor by 1600 hours. Do not attempt to negotiate a reef-fringed entrance with the sun in your eyes, and always have someone on the bow keeping an eye on the water in front of the boat.

Deep water of 50 feet and over will be "inky" blue. This can be lighter if the bottom is white sand.

A light green or turquoise would indicate a depth of 15–25 feet. If the bottom has rocks or coral, these will change the colour to a brownish shade.

Water of 10 feet and under will show as a very pale shade of green if there is a sandy bottom, or a light brown if rocks and coral are present.

Right of Way and Night Sailing

A general rule of thumb is to stay out of everyone's way. There are times, however, when this is impossible and, in such instances, power boats should give way to boats under sail. This being the case, it is important in close quarters to hold your course so that the other skipper can take appropriate action to avoid you, without having to double-guess your actions.

If you are crossing ferry traffic, it is prudent to keep a weather eye on approaching vessels and make every effort to stay well clear.

Many schooners trading between the islands are underway at night, and very few use running lights.

Don't sail at night!

Cruising Etiquette

During your cruise through the Virgins, please remember that there are a limited number of places on the smaller islands capable of dealing with garbage.

Check first before carrying it ashore — *don't throw it over the side*, even if it means keeping it a couple of days in a plastic bag. Always carry any refuse back to your boat, rather than leaving it on the beach.

Many of the beaches throughout the Virgins are private property and the cruising yachtsman must exercise care to respect any notice indicating such restrictions.

THE BUOYAGE SYSTEM
OF THE BRITISH VIRGIN ISLANDS

In an international effort to standard-ize buoyage systems, the International Association of Lighthouse Authorities (IALA) has agreed that, in order to meet conflicting requirements, there will be two systems in use throughout the world. These are to be called systems A and B, respectively. The rules for the two sys-tems were so similar that the "IALA" Executive Committee felt able to com-bine the two sets of rules into one, known as the "IALA Maritime Buoyage Sys-tem."

This single set of rules allows light-house authorities the choice of using red to port or red to starboard on a regional basis, the two regions being known as region A and region B.

The latter system, system B, is used in North and South America and through-out the waters of the Caribbean. In sys-tem B the colour red is used to mark the starboard side of the channel when ap-proaching from seaward.

In this respect, it should be noted that the respective buoyage systems for both U.S. and British Virgins are the same.

RED RIGHT RETURNING!
The lateral 'system B' as seen entering from seaward.

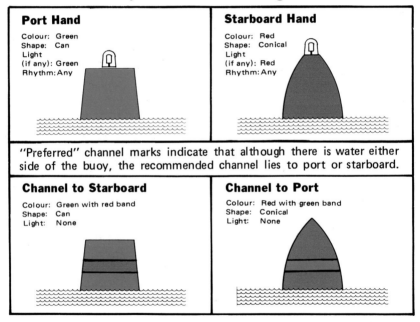

Port Hand

Colour: Green
Shape: Can
Light
(if any): Green
Rhythm: Any

Starboard Hand

Colour: Red
Shape: Conical
Light
(if any): Red
Rhythm: Any

"Preferred" channel marks indicate that although there is water either side of the buoy, the recommended channel lies to port or starboard.

Channel to Starboard

Colour: Green with red band
Shape: Can
Light: None

Channel to Port

Colour: Red with green band
Shape: Conical
Light: None

VIRGIN WEATHER

Located in the northeast trade wind belt, the Virgin Islands are blessed with almost perfect weather the year round. The seas from the north are broken by the island chain, providing the seafarer with ideal weather conditions.

Weather Forecasts

Unlike that of most other parts of the world, the weather in the Virgin Islands is extremely stable. Forecasts are broadcast daily on most of the local stations:

St. Thomas: WIVI-FM 99.5 MHZ (forecasts at 7:30 and 8:30 a.m., 3:30 and 4:30 p.m., daily and hourly updates); WVWI 1000 KHZ-AM; WAH (Virgin Islands radio) broadcasts the weather on VHF 16, switching to VHF 28 and 85 at 6 a.m., 2 and 10 p.m.

St. Croix: WSTX 970 KHZ-AM.

Tortola: ZBVI 780 KHZ-AM; ZROD-FM 103.7 (hourly, 9 a.m.-6 p.m.).

St. Croix: WSTX 970 KHZ-AM.

Puerto Rico: WOJO 1030 KHZ-AM, all day at 6 minutes past the hour. Excellent weather report and reception. English-speaking.

Tides

The tidal range throughout the Virgin Islands is about 12 inches, depending upon the time of year. You will probably be unaware of any fluctuation. However, you cannot rely upon the rising tide to float you off the odd sandbar. Currents in certain areas can reach 1–2 knots, namely through Pillsbury Sound between St. Thomas and St. John, the Durloe Cays in St. John, and in the narrows between St. John and Tortola.

Ground Swells

During the winter months of November through April, any significant weather in the North Atlantic will produce heavy swells along the entire north coast of the Virgins several days later. These ground seas have little effect on vessels under sail, but can turn a normally tranquil anchorage into pounding surf. Most anchorages exposed to the north are prone to this phenomenon—choose your anchorage accordingly.

Winds

Owing to the northeast trade winds, the wind direction throughout the Virgins is dominated by the movements of the Bermuda High. During the winter months of November to January, the prevailing wind is from the northeast at 15-20 knots. The fabled Christmas Winds can produce 25-30 knots for several days at a time. By February, the winds start to move around to the east, and by June, they are blowing out of the southeast at 10-15 knots.

During September to October, the trade winds are weakest, and the weather can be less settled. Although these months are considered hurricane season, Hurricane Hugo was the first to hit in 50-odd years. By November, the high pressure system around Bermuda starts to stabilize and 15-20 knot breezes become the norm.

Rain

While late summer to fall is considered rainy season, rain squalls can come at any time of year. Be aware of approaching squalls by watching the sky and clouds to windward. If a dark squall is approaching, it probably has considerable wind velocity on the squall line, and the prudent skipper should shorten sail beforehand.

It also will give the crew a chance to arm themselves with soap and enjoy a good fresh-water shower.

Winter Storms and Hurricanes

It is a well-known fact that the Virgin Islands have fewer storms than does the Long Island Sound in New York. When the islands do experience a tropical storm or depression, it is usually in the early development of the storm centre, and the storms do not reach full intensity until they are north of the area. Should a storm approach the islands, remember that they travel very slowly; consequently, with the communication systems used today, sailors can be assured of at least 48 hours' warning.

And Now For The Good News

No Surcharge On Credit Card Calls

DIAL 111

Caribbean
PHONECARDS

To use your credit card to call from the British Virgin Islands simply dial 111 from any phone — public or private — and quote your card number and the number you wish to call. You'll be connected in seconds.

No complicated access codes, no fuss and **no credit card surcharge**. You pay only normal operator rates.

Or, by purchasing a prepaid Caribbean Phonecard and inserting it into our specially marked Cardphones, you can dial your call direct. Dial 1 + AREA CODE + NUMBER for North America, and the Caribbean, 011 + COUNTRY CODE + NUMBER for Europe and the rest of the world. Nothing could be easier than calling home from the BVI.

CABLE & WIRELESS
BRITISH VIRGIN ISLANDS

Telephone Service

The U.S. Virgin Islands (area code 809) are on the same system as the United States. Calls can be made at pay phones, as on the mainland, either collect or with a telephone credit card.

The British Virgin Islands, serviced by Cable and Wireless, also share the area code 809 and offer direct dialing, several USA Direct Dial telephones throughout the islands, coin and card telephones, and fax, telex and telegram services.

The customer care office is located on Wickham's Cay near the banks, or by calling (809) 494-3200. When calling a number within the BVI from the BVI, only the last five digits should be dialed.

VHF

Almost every boat sailing the Virgins will be equipped with a VHF radio. Apart from single side band for offshore communications, VHF is used for all local traffic.

The channels vary from boat to boat, but the most commonly used frequencies are listed below.

Channel 16: Standby and international distress frequency
Channel 12: Portside operations (Charter company to yacht)
Channel 6: Ship-to-ship, safety
Channel 27: Radio Tortola
Channel 28: W.A.H. Virgin Islands Radio
Channel 68: Ship-to-ship communications
Channel 22A: Coast Guard
Channel 3: Weather

Channel 16 is used as a calling frequency, but the operator must switch to a second channel once contact has been established in order to keep 16 open.

How Can I Be Reached In An Emergency?

If you are expecting urgent business calls or if you should be needed for a medical emergency, it would be wise to leave the phone number of both Virgin Island Radio and Tortola Radio, and the marina from where you are sailing. The party will not be able to contact you directly unless you happen to be monitoring the radio, but they can leave a message and the list of yachts for which they are holding traffic would be read during traffic hours.

Virgin Island Radio broadcasts traffic every hour on the hour, 24 hours per day. They will place collect calls, credit card calls, third party calls, and take Master Card and Visa. Their telephone number is (809) 776-8282.

Tortola Radio (British Virgin Islands) broadcasts traffic at 7 and 11 a.m., and 3 and 6 p.m. daily. Telephone (809) 494-3425 (or 43425 if calling locally).

Can I Call Home From the Boat?

It is possible for VHF calls made from your vessel via Virgin Island Radio or Tortola Radio to be patched into the phone system.

As stated above, calls may be made through Virgin Island Radio with payment by several methods. Also, Tortola Radio will place collect calls for you. If you are a bareboat charterer, make arrangements with the marina prior to leaving. If you are aboard a crewed charter yacht, the skipper will assist you with radio calls.

Private yachts must make arrangements to open an account with either Tortola Radio or Virgin Island Radio if not using one of the above methods of payment.

Cellular Telephones

For Virgin Island yachtsmen who need to keep in touch, cellular telephone service is now available. Cellular phones can be used for everything from checking in with the office, the family, or for local applications like ordering more provisions and making dinner reservations. Installed on many bareboat charter fleets as well as crewed yachts, this offers the yachtsman

the choice of using a telephone for more privacy, or the radio.

You can rent cellular phones in the Virgins or bring your own from home. There is service by two cellular phone companies, Boatphone in the BVI and Vitel Cellular in the USVI. Information is available from your charter company regarding the availability and operation of cellular phones. All that is required is a major credit card.

How About Dinner Reservations?

Where telephone service is nonexistent, many restaurants stand by the VHF on Channel 16 or 68, which is reserved for ship-to-ship operation.

It is frowned upon by the local licensing authority to use the VHF Channel 12 for reservations if the restaurant can be reached via Tortola Radio on a phone patch.

Radio Procedure

Before attempting to make a VHF radio call, think it through. Understand the procedure and the limitations of the equipment you are using.

The call should begin with two repetitions of the station or vessel being called, followed by the name of your yacht, followed by the word "over." It is important to terminate with the "over" as the other party will then key his mike and reply.

Example: "...Moorings, Moorings, this is the vessel *Bodacious* ZJL 172, over..."

If you get no response, repeat the call. If there is still no response, try again in 5 minutes. When contact is to be terminated, the party will sign off: "...This is *Bodacious*, ZJL 172 clear with Moorings..."

Distress Calls

In case of a real emergency, you should come up on Channel 16, "...Mayday, Mayday, Mayday. This is the vessel *Bodacious*, over..."

Repeat three times until contact is made. Then give your location and the nature of your problem. It is important to state only the pertinent information and not to cloud the situation with emotion.

• Stay calm; *don't panic.*

• Don't allow anyone to use the radio unless they are familiar with the procedure and the problem.

The U.S. Coast Guard in San Juan monitors 24 hours per day.

Virgin Island Radio in St. Thomas monitors 24 hours per day.

Tortola Radio monitors from 0700 to 1900, but in a Mayday situation an operator will respond.

Since the Virgin Islands are divided between the U.S. and Britain, you will be crossing international boundaries during your cruise. Therefore, it is necessary to clear customs when entering and leaving each respective territory. Failure to observe this formality could result in substantial fines or even loss of your vessel. Should you pick up your charter boat in the USVI and wish to cruise the waters of the BVI, it would be necessary to "clear" the vessel with U.S. Customs and Immigration. Then proceed to the nearest British port of entry for clearance "inbound." You are required to clear the vessel out again before departing for U.S. territory. Often, if your stay is short and of a known duration, you will be permitted to clear in and out at the same time.

At the time of clearance, it is necessary to have in your possession the ship's papers and passports or identification for all crew members, in addition to your clearance from the last port. All crew members must be present for clearance. It is also recommended that you wear proper attire when making your clearance.

BVI Cruising Permits

For all charter yachts cruising in BVI waters, there is a daily tax payable at the time of clearance. This does not apply to private vessels cruising the area. In the future, day charter boats, dive boats and sport fishing boats will be required to obtain cruising permits.

The rates are as follows:

A. Charter boats based outside of the BVI:
    $4/person per day all year.
B. Charter boats recorded in the BVI:
    Dec. 1–Apr. 30: $2/person per day;
    May 1-Nov. 30: $0.75/person per day.

Fishing Permits in the BVI

It is illegal for a non-resident to remove *any* marine organism from the waters of the British Virgin Islands without first obtaining a recreational fishing permit.

Locations of Customs

St. Thomas: Wharfside at the ferry dock.
St. John: Waterfront at Cruz Bay.
St. Croix: Gallows Bay at Christiansted.
Tortola: Roadtown at the Government Dock. West End ferry dock.
Virgin Gorda: Airport or Yacht Harbour.
Jost Van Dyke: Great Harbour.

Office Hours

U.S. Customs are open from 8 a.m. to noon and 1-5 p.m. Monday through Sunday, but vessels clearing in on Sunday will incur overtime charges. Vessels arriving after hours must raise their quarantine flag, remain on board and clear the next morning. Customs and immigration are located next to each other for ease in clearing.

British Customs are open: Monday through Friday, 8:30-3:30 for normal business, with extended hours to 6 p.m. (with overtime fees); Saturday, 9-12:30, with extended hours until 6 p.m.; Sunday carries overtime charges all day. Customs officers can be found clearing in the ferries on Sundays for yacht clearance. Outside these hours, raise your quarantine flag and clear at the first available opportunity. Do not leave your vessel except to go straight to customs and immigration.

Schedule of Charges

Clearance into and from U.S. waters is free during normal working hours except for a token charge for the forms involved.

Typical charges for a 10 ton yacht clearing into the BVI are as follows:

Harbour Dues $2.00
Ship's Dues $3.00
Forms .... $ .40
Overtime fees .... additional $4.00

Please note that there is a 10-cent stamp duty payable throughout the BVI on all travelers checks.

BVI Immigration

One of the following types of identification is required by U.S. and Canadian citizens entering the BVI:

A. Passport
B. Birth Certificate
C. Voter's Registration Card

All other countries must have a current passport. If you have questions regarding the need for visas contact your nearest British Embassy or telephone the BVI Immigration department at 809-494-3701.

- All crew members are to present themselves for clearance.

- Yachts dropping passengers off must first clear both customs and immigration.

- All private yachts will be given no more than 30 days' entry. Extensions will incur a fee.

- Late fees, in addition to customs charges, are as much as $8 per vessel and higher on Sundays and public holidays.

WATER SAFETY

The waters of the Virgin Islands are essentially a benign area. When people think of tropical waters, man-eating sharks, barracuda and giant moray eels come to mind. The truth of the matter is that more injuries are sustained by cuts from coral or by stepping on sea urchin spines, than by encounters with underwater predators.

Sharks

There are many large sharks around the waters of the Virgins, but they remain largely in deep water. It is highly unlikely that you will ever see a shark during your cruise.

Barracuda

You will, without doubt, see numerous barracuda of various sizes while snorkeling the reefs. They are curious fish and are likely to stay almost motionless in the water watching your movements. They will not bother you, and it is best to show them the same courtesy.

Moray Eels

These creatures are shy by nature and make their homes in rocks and crevices in the reef. They will protect themselves from perceived danger, so do not reach into caves or crevices unless you can see inside.

Coral

Exercise extreme caution around all coral as cuts and scratches can become infected quickly. Familiarize yourself with the various types of coral and remember to stay well clear of the fire coral.

Wear good foot protection when wading on shallow reefs.

Sea Urchins

These black, spiny creatures are found in abundance throughout the islands. They can be seen on sandy bottoms and on reefs and rocks. If you stand on one or inadvertently place your hand on one, it is likely that one or more of the spines will pierce your skin and break off. Do not try to dig the spines out. (See Medical Information on page 215.)

Don'ts

If you observe the following basic rules on water safety, you will add to your enjoyment of the cruise:

1. Don't swim at night.
2. Don't swim alone.
3. Don't swim in heavy surf.
4. Don't dump refuse in the water—it is illegal and attracts sharks.
5. Don't wear jewelry when swimming or diving.
6. Don't reach into crevices or caves.
7. Don't spear a fish and leave it bleeding in the water or in a bag at your waist.
8. Take *no* marine life without a permit!

moor seacure limited

THE OTHER ALTERNATIVE

Tired of straining the old back? Tired of waking up all night worrying about your anchor dragging, thinking that THIS is supposed to be a vacation! WELL, now there is an alternative… Located throughout the British Virgin Islands at most popular anchorages there are professionally maintained moorings available for overnight use. The small fee for the mooring use is well worth the good night's sleep it affords.

Here are a few tips on picking and leaving a mooring…

1. As in anchoring, approach the mooring area slowly with your dinghy pulled in on a short line.
2. Have a crew member ready with a boat hook at the bow to direct you and to pick up the mooring pennant.
3. Approach the mooring buoy slowly from the direction that keeps the bow of your boat into the wind.
4. You may find that at idle speed by shifting alternately from forward to neutral you can coast to the buoy, then shift into reverse for a second to stop the boat as the crew member lifts the pennant on board and attaches it to the bow cleat.
5. Please do not be embarrassed if you miss picking up the pennant the first time. It happens to all of us at sometime. Just circle around and make another approach.
6. To leave the mooring with your dinghy once again on a short line simply let go the pennant and set off for your next destination. Take care not to run over the mooring buoy and pennant as you leave.

These helpful hints are brought to you by Moor-Seacure Ltd.–the premier mooring company in the BVI.
And remember, "If it doesn't say MOOR-SEACURE, it probably ISN'T!"

Moor-Seacure moorings are available at these and other fine locations…

• LAST RESORT AT TRELLIS BAY
• COOPER ISLAND • MARINA CAY • ANEGADA REEF HOTEL
• RHYMERS AT CANE GARDEN BAY • SOPERS HOLE MARINA AT WEST END
• VIXEN POINT • DRAKES ANCHORAGE • BIRAS CREEK IN NORTH SOUND
• ABE'S BY THE SEA AND HARRIS' AT JOST VAN-DYKE IN LITTLE HARBOUR

DON'T BE A DRAG

P.O. Box 139, Road Town, Tortola, B.V.I. • 809-494-4488

Jim Scheiner

Many sailors visiting the Virgin Islands have all sorts of sailing experience, both inshore and offshore; however, it is interesting to note that many have little experience anchoring.

Since you will be subjected to the constant trade breezes on a heavy displacement-type vessel, follow these suggestions for safe, hassle-free anchoring:

1. Pick your anchorage and arrive there early enough in the afternoon to assure both good light and a choice of spots. Bear in mind that during the peak season, December to April, some of the more popular spots become crowded.

2. Before doing anything else, work out a system of communication between the person on the helm and the crew member dropping the anchor. Remember that your engine will be running and therefore you will be unable to communicate verbally. Hand signals are needed and should be worked out beforehand.

3. Furl the sails and generally make the boat shipshape before entering the anchorage. Also shorten the dinghy painter to prevent its being sucked into the prop.

4. Pick your spot. Make sure you will have enough room to fall back on the anchor without lying too close to the yacht anchored behind, once you have laid out 5-to-1 scope.

5. Motor up to the desired spot slowly, ensuring that you are head to the wind. Stop the boat exactly where you wish the anchor to lay. Take note of the depth.

6. Once the vessel has lost all forward way, lower the anchor to the bottom.

7. Let the wind slowly push the vessel back. Don't try to reverse. Pay out adequate scope as the vessel moves aft. Don't worry about being broadside to the wind.

8. When the desired amount of scope has been paid out, snub the rope and allow the wind to straighten out the vessel.

9. Put the engine into reverse and increase throttle to 1500 rpm. This should set the anchor and the anchor rope should start to tighten. If you notice it "skipping," pay out more scope. Once you are satisfied that the anchor is set, take the engine out of gear. The vessel should spring forward.

10. Put on your snorkel gear and visually check your work. This is the best way to ensure a good night's sleep. If the anchor is lying on its side or caught in coral, or if the rope is caught around a coral head, reset it. Better now than later.

11. Check your position relative to other vessels and/or landmarks. Is there

enough room between you and the boats around you? If swinging room is tight or if you are expecting squalls during the night, you might think about laying out a second anchor at 45 degrees to the first. This can be accomplished best with the dinghy.

If the hook doesn't set the first time, don't feel embarrassed! There is not a skipper afloat who hasn't encountered this problem. It is due not to your technique, but to the nature of the seabed. Discuss the situation with your crew, pick it up and try again.

PUBLIC HOLIDAYS

Although the observance of public holidays will make little difference to you when sailing, it is prudent to plan your cruise so that you are not needing shore based facilities during the following holidays:

MONTH	U.S. VIRGIN ISLANDS	BRITISH VIRGIN ISLANDS
January	New Year's Day Three Kings' Day (Observed) Martin Luther King's Birthday	New Year's Day
February	Presidents' Day	
March	Transfer Day	Commonwealth Day
April	Holy Thursday Good Friday Easter Monday Children's Carnival Parade Adults' Carnival Parade	Good Friday Easter Monday
May	Memorial Day	Whit Monday
June	Organic Act Day	Sovereigns Birthday
July	Emancipation Day (West Indies) Independence Day Supplication Day	Territory Day
August		Festival Monday Festival Tuesday Festival Wednesday
September	Labor Day	
October	Columbus Day Local Thanksgiving Day	St. Ursula's Day
November	Liberty Day Thanksgiving Day	Birthday of Heir to the Throne
December	Christmas Day Christmas Second Day	Boxing Day

Should any holiday fall upon a Sunday, the Monday following shall be a legal holiday.

TROPICAL FISH POISONING

Ciguatera, also known as tropical fish poisoning, is a disease which can affect people who have eaten certain varieties of tropical fish.

The results of such poisoning can be very serious and, although seldom resulting in death, can cause severe discomfort. Victims of ciguatera poisoning are often ill for weeks and some symptoms may persist for months.

Ciguatera occurs only in tropical waters

and in the Atlantic area, predominantly in the waters of south Florida and the islands of the Caribbean.

One problem with fish poisoning is that it is impossible to differentiate between toxic and nontoxic fish. The fish itself is not affected by the toxins and therefore appears quite normal and edible. The toxins cannot be tasted and washing, cooking or freezing will not render them harmless.

Many tales exist throughout the Caribbean on how to tell toxic from nontoxic fish, including cooking silver coins with the fish and if the coin turns black, it is toxic. Another is that flies will not land on a piece of toxic fish. While such homespun ideas are interesting bits of Caribbean folklore, they do not work and should not be relied upon.

Symptoms of Ciguatera

In most cases, the symptoms will appear within three to ten hours after eating the toxic fish. The first signs are nausea, vomiting, diarrhea and stomach cramps.

Later, the patient may also start to suffer from a wide variety of neurological ailments, including pains in the joints and muscles, weakness in the arms and legs, and/or a tingling sensation in the feet and hands. A tingling sensation around the lips, nose and tongue is also common.

At the onset of any of the above symptoms, the patient should ask him- or herself, "Have I eaten any fish today?" If the answer is "yes," seek medical attention.

Types of Fish Carrying Ciguatera

The fish most likely to carry the toxins are the larger predatory fish associated with coral reefs. These include barracudas, grouper, snapper, jacks and parrot fish. It should be noted that only certain species in each family are associated with the toxins. Therefore, it is a good idea to check with a local fisherman before eating your catch.

The fish that are considered safe are offshore fish such as tuna, wahoo, swordfish, marlin, and dolphin. Others include sailfish, Spanish mackerel, small king mackerel and yellowtail snapper.

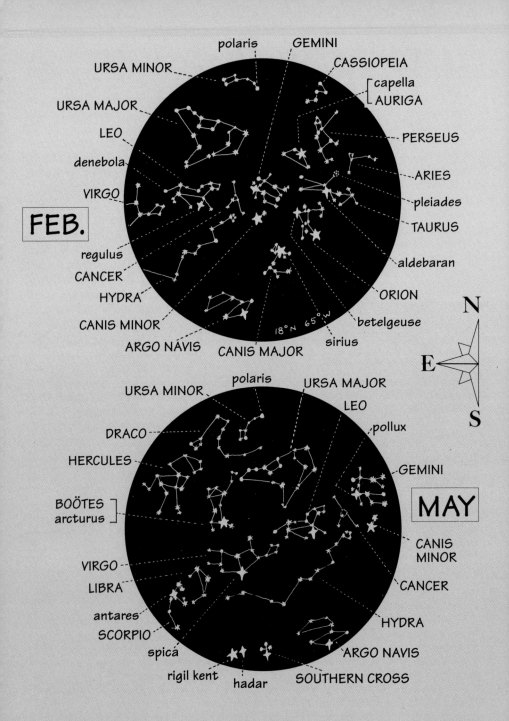

These star charts apply to the following times:

FEBRUARY		MAY	
January 1	2400	April 1	2400
January 15	2300	April 15	2300
February 1	2200	May 1	2200
February 15	2100	May 15	2100
March 1	2000	June 1	2000
March 15	1900	June 15	1900

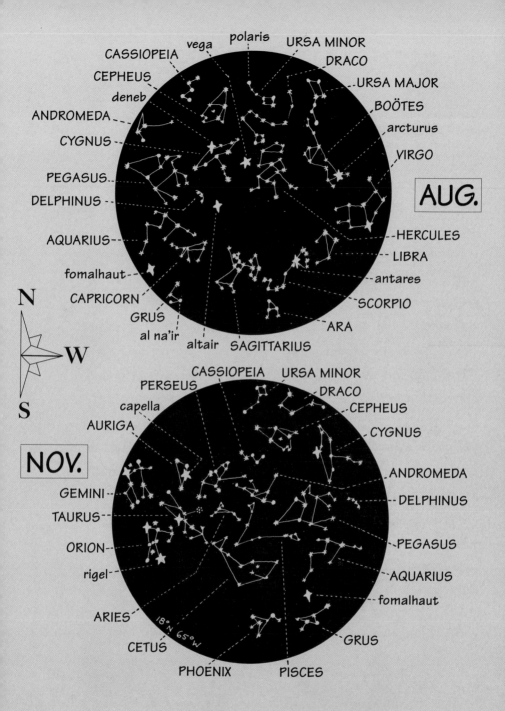

N W S

These star charts apply to the following times:

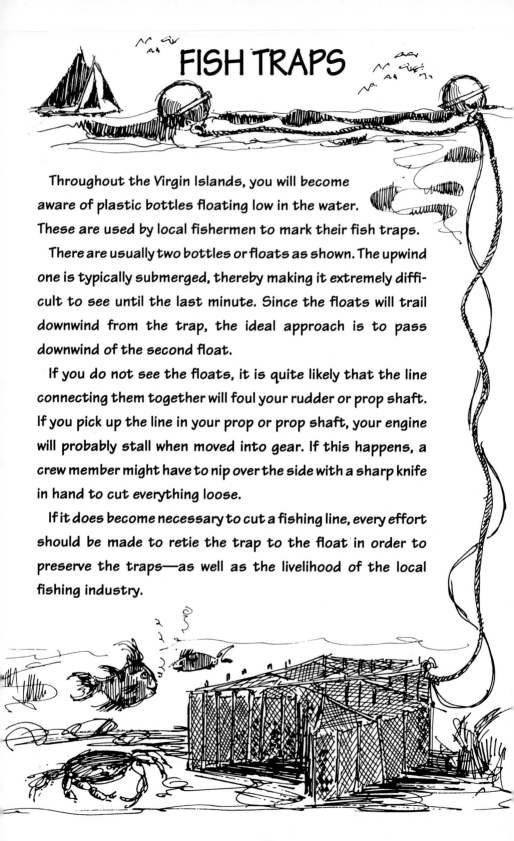

FISH TRAPS

Throughout the Virgin Islands, you will become aware of plastic bottles floating low in the water. These are used by local fishermen to mark their fish traps.

There are usually two bottles or floats as shown. The upwind one is typically submerged, thereby making it extremely difficult to see until the last minute. Since the floats will trail downwind from the trap, the ideal approach is to pass downwind of the second float.

If you do not see the floats, it is quite likely that the line connecting them together will foul your rudder or prop shaft. If you pick up the line in your prop or prop shaft, your engine will probably stall when moved into gear. If this happens, a crew member might have to nip over the side with a sharp knife in hand to cut everything loose.

If it does become necessary to cut a fishing line, every effort should be made to retie the trap to the float in order to preserve the traps—as well as the livelihood of the local fishing industry.

UNDERWATER SAFARIS ....

... A COMPLETE CARIBBEAN DIVING FACILITY

GUIDED DIVE TOURS   INSTRUCTION
EQUIPMENT RENTAL   SALES & SERVICE
HOTEL DIVE PACKAGES   SAIL/DIVE PACKAGES

TWO LOCATIONS
THE MOORINGS — COOPER ISLAND
Airfills at Moorings, Cooper & Marina Cay

Join Us For A Diving Safari ~

- THREE custom built DIVE BOATS, two trips daily...
  MV RENDEZVOUS II — 30 ft. MV MAKO — 42 ft.
  RENDEZVOUS III — 30 ft.
  All fully equipped for diving with everything you need on board.

- Approved PADI TRAINING FACILITY. Professional Instruction
  from RESORT COURSE to INSTRUCTOR.

- RENDEZVOUS TOURS ARE OUR TRADEMARK. We will meet your
  boat at various anchorages throughout the islands, take the
  experienced diver diving, train the beginner or deliver (our tank) air
  fills.

- PLANNING A DIVE IN THE BVI?
  Call direct to book the details with the people you'll be diving with!

800-537-7032

CALL COLLECT TORTOLA RADIO OR VI RADIO

809-494-3965   809-494-3235 BVI   809-494-5322 FAX
P.O. BOX 139, ROAD TOWN, TORTOLA
BRITISH VIRGIN ISLANDS

PROTECTING THE CORAL REEFS

Coral reefs, turquoise lagoons and white sand beaches—these are the delights of cruising in the Caribbean. Unfortunately, much of the life underwater is as delicate as it is beautiful, and the boating community will want to do its part in keeping it special.

Basically, this is an environment where, as the result of higher temperatures and increased salinity, calcium carbonate, a crystalline compound found in chalk, limestone and marble, settles out of solution, creating a friendly environment for many forms of marine life. Some, like corals, use the calcium compound for their own basal and skeletal structures; others, like mollusks, use it for shells; others are simply impregnated or coated with a white precipitate.

Where prolific, corals, aided by the one-celled algae embedded in their tissues, form extensive, fringing reefs off the rocky shores, patches of reef in shallow areas a bit offshore, and, in some places, well-formed outer or barrier reefs.

In all settings the reefs are the home to a rich and varied community of marine life. While they are choice sites for snorkeling and scuba diving, they are a direct menace to navigation.

When sailing or motoring near reefs, be on the lookout for dark brown areas, seen most readily when the sun is high overhead. Unfortunately, shadows cast by passing clouds are hard to distinguish from patches of coral.

Inevitably you will want to anchor near choice reef sites to set forth on a snorkeling or diving venture. This is where you must be especially careful to avoid both smashing the corals and damaging your boat. Look for mooring buoys, which are provided in some areas.

An offshore reef with a lagoon behind is usually approached from the shoreward or lagoon side, as the corals commonly form a crest with high wave action on the seaward exposure. Also, there is no protection or

anchoring in the steep drop-off beyond the reef. Note carefully the currents around the area you are going to explore to be sure you can safely return to your base of operation.

Once overboard and enjoying the reef, always bear in mind that almost everything living in coral communities is very delicate. Touching the sea fans or corals is frowned upon, and collecting anything other than fish is generally taboo. If you turn over a rock or piece of dead coral while exploring the rich life in hidden places, always put it back as you found it. And, by the way, don't feed the fish—food meant for humans is not their best diet, and you would be altering their natural behavior.

A good motto is "Take only pictures; leave only bubbles." Good pictures will last, whereas all that is so beautiful on the reefs will dry out and fade on shore.

Ardent conservationists often regret the widespread fishing that is permitted in the islands: Unfortunately, in the sanctuaries declared off-limits to fishing, the recovery of stocks is not always impressive. Incidentally, fish taken from around the reefs in the Virgin Islands often carry *ciguatera*—a toxin harmless to fish, but quite disastrous if ingested by humans.

The crystal clear waters of the shallows overlie banks of bone-white sand. Unlike the sand of coasts to the north, which consist of ground-up bedrock, these sands are made up of pulverized remnants of corals, shells and the diversity of life with calcium carbonate skeletal structures. Sometimes the lagoon floor supports dense growths of turtle grass. Initially the sea grasses are green, but the blades soon become coated with diverse microscopic growths, interlaced with the white carbonate precipitate.

Take only pictures—
Leave only bubbles.

Along with the white sand of the shallows, you can usually count on finding beautiful, white beaches in the Virgins. Don't be dismayed, however, if you chance upon a beach which, though every bit as clean as the pure white sand, appears gray or black, due to the ground-up volcanic rock mixed with the pulverized carbonate.

Less appreciated than the reefs and beaches are the mangrove stands along the shore. Their role in stablilizing the shoreline, enriching the coastal waters and serving as a nursery for shoreline life closely parallels the role of the salt marshes of temperate regions. The combination of the reefs, lagoons, grassbeds and mangroves is the optimum coastal environment of the tropics, offering high productivity, good shoreline protection, and a continuous source of fascination to the observer.

Due to the growing numbers of boaters and other visitors seeking the delights of these tropical coasts, however, the coastal regions are feeling the stress. The presence alone of the yachtsmen creates this stress, even when they anchor carefully, dispose of all refuse onboard, and take the utmost care in their treatment of the reefs and shore.

Even more disturbing to environmentalists is the deterioration of the environment from causes over which recreational boaters have no control. Freshwater runoff from poor land-use practices (*e.g.*, unlimited land clearing for agriculture and careless construction practices) is a double threat, particularly to corals that are sensitive to lowered salinity and the accompanying smoth-

Jim Scheiner

ering silt. Finally, outfalls of untreated and partially treated domestic sewage tend to increase algal growths that smother corals.

Perhaps the most annoying stresses come from offshore. Until recently, passing ships often discarded great quantities of plastic trash into the water. The accumulation on some shores has been atrocious. Hopefully the problem will ease, however, since the passing of a total ban on discarding plastics overboard; compliance has been quite good. Unfortunately, we have not yet completely eliminated the pump-out of crude oil wastes from tankers, which results in slicks that can wash ashore, even when the shipping routes are some distance away.

As guardians of the earth and its creatures, probably our greatest concern is the possibility that global warming and the consequent rise it will cause in the sea level could kill off the world's reefs.

Current predictions of a sea-level rise are on the order of 30 centimeters by the year 2050—about 6 millimeters per year. Some calculations of calcification rates reassure us that healthy reefs can grow to match rising sea levels, but recent histories of bleaching indicate that corals may lose their embedded algae with the rise in temperature and, if they don't die, may suffer from minimal upward growth as a result.

For visitors to the islands of the Caribbean, this brief overview may explain the makeup of the coral reefs and why there can be no anchoring amongst them.

Man is the reef's greatest enemy. It is essential that the reef viewer, whether diver or snorkeler, adhere to these recommendations if the lush beauty of the coral reefs and the life forms they support are to be preserved for the generations that follow.

NELSON MARSHALL, *Professor Emeritus of Oceanography and Marine Affairs at the University of Rhode Island, the author of "Understanding the Caribbean."*

British Virgin Islands

Visitors come to the Virgin Islands to savor the magnificence of the area's natural resources—the steady, gentle trade winds, glorious sunshine, crystalline waters, the splendor of the coral reefs and abundant sea life. This is a fragile area, however, which must be protected if it is to be enjoyed for many years to come.

The anchors of the charter boats have taken their toll in broken coral, destroying the incredible beauty below the sea that once housed many different forms of sea life. In an effort to defend the reefs against the carelessness of yachtsmen, the National Parks Trust has taken a firm stand and has installed mooring buoys developed by Dr. John Halas of the Key Largo National Marine Sanctuary. This mooring system is being used worldwide to protect reefs and prevent damage from anchors. It calls for a stainless steel pin cemented into the bedrock and a polypropylene line attached to a surface buoy. The system is very strong and extremely effective in eliminating damage when used properly.

Marine Park Regulations:

• Do not damage, alter or remove any terrestrial marine plant, animal or historic artifact.

• All fishing—including spearfishing— is strictly prohibited. Lobstering and collecting live shells are also illegal.

• Use correct garbage disposal points; do not litter the area. Water balloons are prohibited.

• Water skiing and jet skiing are prohibited in all park areas.

• No anchoring in the restricted area in and around the wreck of the *Rhone*. When the mooring system is full, vessels should utilize the Salt Island Settlement anchorage and arrive by tender, using the dinghy mooring system provided.

Mooring Usage Regulations

• Vessels must legally have met BVI Customs and Immigration requirements, and have in their possession valid clearance forms and cruising permits.

• The buoys of the reef protection system are colour-coded:

Red: Non-diving, day use only.

Yellow: Commercial dive vessels only.

White: Non-commercial vessels for dive use only on first-come, first-served basis (90-minute time limit).

Blue: Dinghys only.

• **Large Yellow**: Commercial vessels, or vessels over 55' in length.

• Vessels must attach to the buoy pennant, making sure to avoid chafing of the pennant against the vessel. If the configuration provided is not compatible with your vessel, an extension line must be attached to the pennant eye.

• All buoys are used at user's risk. While the moorings are the property of the BVI Government and are managed by the BVI National Parks Trust, neither bears the responsibility for any loss or injury resulting from the use of the system.

The British Virgin Islands National Parks Trust Maintains Moorings On The Following Islands

• Norman
• Pelican
• The Indians
• Peter Island
• Dead Chest
• Salt
• Cooper

• Ginger
• Guana
• West Dog
• Great Dog
• George Dog
• Cockroach
• Virgin Gorda

Charterers may purchase permits through their charter companies, and visiting private yachts may purchase permits through customs. The fees are nominal and go directly to the Parks Trust for the installation and maintenance of the buoys.

United States Virgin Islands

For years the National Park areas have been a favoured cruising area for many yachtsmen. As a result of increased numbers of pleasure boaters enjoying the park, the damage to the underwater reefs and corals has dramatically escalated. Anchors and, even worse, the sweep of the anchor chains have swept the undersea life away leaving only broken pieces of what were once beautiful living corals. The National Parks Service, with the support of the community, has installed moorings and established protected zones around the more susceptible grass and reef areas.

National Parks Regulations

- Do not damage or take any dead or live marine creatures such as sea fans, coral and shells.
- Anchors must not cause damage to underwater features of the Park.
- All sea turtles are endangered or threatened species. Do not harass or harm them.
- Do not disturb or remove shipwrecks or their contents.
- Tyingto shore vegetation is prohibited.
- Feeding of any wildlife in the park, either on land or in the water, is prohibited.
- Fishing is permitted except in Jumbie and Trunk Bays, with hand-held rod and line.
- Possession or use of any type of spearfishing equipment within park boundaries is prohibited.
- Florida spiny lobsters may be taken by hand or by hand-held snare. *Do not* take female lobsters with eggs. *Limit*: Two per day. *Legal size limit*: 3 ½ inches carapace and a 9-inch overall body length. Do not take rock lobster or the lobster species variously called slipper lobster, buccaneer or locust lobster.

- Overnight stays in park waters are limited to 14 nights per year.
- Maintain quiet aboard boats from 10 p.m. to 6 a.m.
- Water skiing and jet skiing are prohibited in the park.
- National Park rangers may board any vessel in park waters at any time in order to conduct official business.

Trash may be placed in receptacles located at Cruz Bay, Francis Bay, Annaberg, and Little Lameshur.

Mooring Usage Regulations:

- Moorings located within the park boundaries may not be used by vessels greater than 65 feet in length.
- Moorings are maintained by Parks Service personnel. The National Parks Service accepts no liability for damage, loss or injury resulting from the use of defective moorings.
- Help keep moorings safe by reporting and defects or damage to Park personnel.
- National Parks Service moorings are not intended for use in heavy weather conditions when it is recommended that boats anchor in a protected bay.
- No anchoring in Reef Bay, or Little or Great Lameshur Bay, or Salt Pond Bay. Moorings are available in these locations.

The U.S. Virgin Islands National Park Service Maintains Moorings At The Following Locations:

- Lind Point
- Jumbie Bay
- Hawksnext
- Maho Bay
- Francis Bay
- Whistling Cay
- Leinster

- Salt Pond
- Reef Bay
- Greater Lameshur
- Little Lameshur
- Rams Head

DIVING THE VIRGIN ISLANDS

The Virgin Islands are one of the best sailing and cruising areas in the world. They are also recognised as one of the top dive destinations.

The wreck of the *R.M.S. Rhone* has become synonymous with the BVI in dive circles, regarded by many as the best wreck dive of the Western Hemisphere.

Superb reefs for both snorkeling and diving are found in and around most of the anchorages. The U.S. Virgin Islands have a series of underwater parks: Trunk Bay, St. John, Buck Island, St. Croix, Coki Beach, St. Thomas. In the British Virgin Islands, the island of Anegada has over 300 documented shipwrecks.

Servicing the needs of the visiting yachtsmen, many professional dive shops and dive tour operators have set up businesses, providing complete services from equipment rental and air tank refills, to tours and instruction.

For the non-diver, a resort course will enable you to explore the underwater world with the aid of an instructor. Full certification courses are available from the individual dive shop operators conveniently located throughout the islands.

The rules and regulations of the marine parks of both the U.S. and British Virgins are similar. See the story on page 53 for details of these regulations.

Medical Emergencies

In the event of diving-related medical emergencies, contact the U.S. Coast Guard on VHF 16 or telephone (809) 722-2943 or (809) 729-6770 for immediate assistance. There is a recompression chamber in St. Thomas at the Hospital Chamber (telephone 809-776-2886).

Your charter company also can be of great assistance, and should be contacted if you run into a problem.

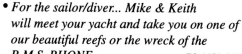

DIVING IN THE BRITISH VIRGIN ISLANDS

The dive operators of the Virgin Islands, through a cooperative effort, have pooled information to give you these brief but picturesque descriptions of 20 of their favourite locations:

Painted Walls — Long canyons, a cave, a sponge-encrusted tunnel, barracudas, rock beauties, angelfish and a variety of pelagic fish make the Painted Walls an exciting and picturesque dive with 28- to 50-foot depths.

The *Rhone* — Just about everyone in diving has heard of the classical wreck, the *RMS Rhone*. Even those who have not visited the B.V.I. have seen the *Rhone* in Columbia Pictures' treasure diving epic, *The Deep*. An ocean steamer 310 feet in length, this magnificent vessel sank off Salt Island during an extremely violent hurricane in 1867. After 117 years of silent slumber in 20–80 feet of water, this great ship remains remarkably intact with much of her decking, rigging, steam engine and propeller still visible. Gilded with colourful sponges and flourishing corals, the *Rhone* is perhaps the most impressive shipwreck in the entire Caribbean.

Rhone Reef — Two coral-encrusted caves are located in less than 25 feet of water at Rhone Reef, Salt Island. A variety of hard and soft corals, fish, turtles and the occasional shark can be found here. Due to its proximity to the *Rhone,* it is a protected area.

Great Harbour — Directly across the channel from Road Town Harbour lies a large, protected bay on the north side of Peter Island. At the centre of this bay is a shallow coral reef less than 20 yards offshore, beginning in 8 feet of water. Loaded with colourful sponges and a marvelous array of small marine life, the reef slopes gently to approximately 18 feet, then drops vertically to a depth of 40 feet.

Indians — The Indians are four large rock formations that rise from the ocean floor to a height of about 90 feet. Deepest depth is 50 feet on the westward side. The Indians have just about everything for the snorkeler as well as the scuba diver: brain, finger, star and elkhorn corals are abundant, as are gorgonians and sea fans.

Caves — The caves at Norman Island can provide many hours of fun for snorkelers. There is a large variety of subjects for the underwater photographer such as schools of dwarf herring or fry. These fish provide food for the many pelicans in the area. The reef in front of the shallow caves slopes downward to a depth of 40 feet.

Angelfish Reef — One of the best sightseeing dives is a sloping reef located off the western point of Norman Island. Depths here range from 10–90 feet. The high point of your dive will be a visit to the

bottom of the channel where a large colony of angelfish resides. There is plenty of fish action at this particular site because of the swiftly flowing currents in the nearby channel and the close proximity to the open sea.

Cooper Island — The southeastern shore of Cooper Island, called Markoe Point, is a sheer rock wall that plunges some 70 feet to the ocean floor. Nurse sharks are frequently encountered lying on sandy floors at the base of small canyons formed by the rugged walls of the island.

Scrub Island — The south side of Scrub Island is a splendid reef with depths of up to 60 feet.

Little Camanoe — The northeastern tip of Little Camanoe offers a 30-foot reef dive. The coral overhangs in this area are exceptionally good. *Caution*: ground seas.

Seal Dog Rock — Plenty of pelagic fish. Depth of 80 feet. *Caution*: may have a current. This dive is recommended for experienced divers.

George Dog — The rocky point in the anchorage at George Dog is an easy 25-30 foot dive for beginning divers.

Invisibles — (East of Necker Island) Spectacular soaring peaks from 4-70 feet from surface. Flashing schools of every kind of fish, sleeping nurse sharks and all forms of sea life abound.

Visibles — (Southwest under Water Pinnacle off Cockroach Island) Caves, canyons, resident 8-foot green moray and nurse shark. Depths to 70 feet. Spawning area for many species of jacks, snappers, groupers.

Chimney — (West Bay of Great Dog) Winding canyon goes to a colourful underwater arch. Many coral heads with an unbelievable variety of small sea creatures.

Joe's Cave — (West Dog Island) Cathedral-effect cave with schooling glassy-eyed sweepers. Clouds of silversides overshadow a variety of eels, pelagic fish and other species, with an occasional school of bulky, splashing tarpon.

Van Ryan's Rock — (Off Collison Point, Virgin Gorda) Huge lobsters, turtles, and plenty of fish among brilliant corals and swaying sea fans.

Ginger Island — Mushroom coral heads 15–20 feet high, great visibility. Graduated shelves ending at 70–90 feet in a huge sand patch. Pet the stingrays and play with huge jewfish.

Southside of Great Dog Island — Reef runs east and west, 100 yards of island coral, butterfly fish. Exciting dive locations, each more unusual than the next. Expect to see just about anything!

Anegada Reef — Graveyard of some 300 documented shipwrecks dating from the 1600s to the present. Spanish galleons and English privateers with uncountable treasure.

The Chikuzen — This 245-foot ship was sunk in 1981 and provides a fantastic home for all varieties of fish, including big rays and horse-eye jacks. The depth here is less than 80 feet. Located about 5 miles north of Camanoe Island.

DIVING IN THE U. S. VIRGIN ISLANDS

Cartenser Sr. — (Off St. Thomas, near Buck Island) A spectacular dive on the intact, coral-encrusted hull of a World War I cargo ship in 50-foot depths. Tours easily arranged.

Cow and Calf — Two rocks between Christmas Cove and Jersey Bay, 5 feet below the surface. The lee side of the western rock provides intricate arches, ledges and caves. Many angelfish and beautiful coral.

Christmas Cove — Good beginner's dive on the northwest side of Fish Cay in 40 feet of water. Swim amongst the coral heads. Plenty of fish.

Dog Rock — For advanced divers on the northwestern side of Dog Island in 40-50 foot depths. Rock and coral ledges and caves. *Caution:* This one can be rough.

Coki Beach — A good place to snorkel off the beach. Coral ledges close to the Coral World Underwater Tower.

Little Saint James — A 40-foot dive on the lee side has some deep ledges to explore, sheltering various schools of fish.

Twin Barges — Located off Limetree Beach lie two wrecks sunk approximately in the 1940s. Although visibility is limited outside the wrecks, the clarity improves inside the ships' chambers.

Carvel Rock — Off of the northern side of this rock, near St. John, in depths to 90 feet, big schools of pelagic fish pass through colourful, sponge-encrusted caves.

Thatch Cay — Divers at the Tunnels here explore 8 different arches and tunnels. The average depth is 40 feet.

Scotch Bank — Off St. Croix, this popular dive spot is a favourite for spotting stingrays and manta rays.

Long Reef — A 6-mile-long reef which provides dives at depths from 30–50 feet. A forest of coral, including pillar and elkhorn colonies.

Salt River — This area has 2 distinct walls. The East Wall plunges from depths of 50–100 feet, revealing many caves and caverns. The West Wall peaks at 30 feet and tumbles to 125 feet. The colours of the sponges grasping the crevices and pillars are awesome.

Buck Island — Off St. Croix, this national monument features abundant tropical fish and a jungle of huge staghorn and elkhorn coral. An absolute must for anyone visiting St. Croix.

Frederiksted Pier — (St. Croix) 30-foot-deep pilings offer splendid diving day or night. The pilings provide a home for bright sponges and algae, as well as sea horses, crabs and octopus.

Cane Bay, Davis Bay and Salt River — All have walls of coral from 20 feet to over 1000 feet. Several anchors have been discovered along the wall. One of the most-photographed anchors is nestled in sand at 60 feet on the Northstar Wall.

THE *ROYAL MAIL STEAMER RHONE*

On the morning of October 29, 1867, the *R.M.S. Rhone* was at anchor outside Great Harbour, Peter Island. The *Rhone*, under the command of Captain Robert F. Wooley, had left Southampton on October 2, 1867, and was taking on cargo and stores for the return crossing.

The *R.M.S. Conway*, commanded by Captain Hammock, lay alongside.

The stillness of the tropical day was undisturbed as the sun blazed down from a clear sky upon calm seas. As the morning wore on, the barometer began to fall, hinting the weather might deteriorate. The seas, however, remained untroubled. Although the captains alerted themselves, work was allowed to continue. Captain Wooley hailed Captain Hammock that he did not like the look of the weather and, as the hurricane season was over, it must be a northerly brewing. Wooley felt they should shift to the northern anchorage of Road Harbour, Tortola.

About 11 a.m., the barometer suddenly fell to 27.95 degrees. The sky darkened, and with a mighty roar a fearful hurricane blew from the north/northwest. The howling wind whistled through the shrouds and tore at the rigging. With engines going at full speed, the ships rode the storm.

At noon there came a lull in the storm. The *Conway* weighed anchor and headed toward the northern anchorage of Road Harbour. As she steamed across the Sir Francis Drake Channel, she was hit by the second blast of the hurricane. Her funnel and masts were blown away, and she was driven onto the island of Tortola.

The *Rhone* tried to weigh anchor during the lull, but the shackle of the cable caught in the hawse pipe and parted, dropping the 3,000-pound anchor and some 300 feet of chain. With engines running at full speed, she steamed seaward in order to seek sea room to weather the second onslaught. She had negotiated most of the rocky channel and was rounding the last point when the hurricane, blowing from the south/southeast, struck, forcing her onto the rocks at Salt Island where she heeled over, broke in two, and sank instantly, taking most of her company with her.

— **Courtesy of *R.M.S. Rhone* by George and Luana Marler**

Jim Scheiner

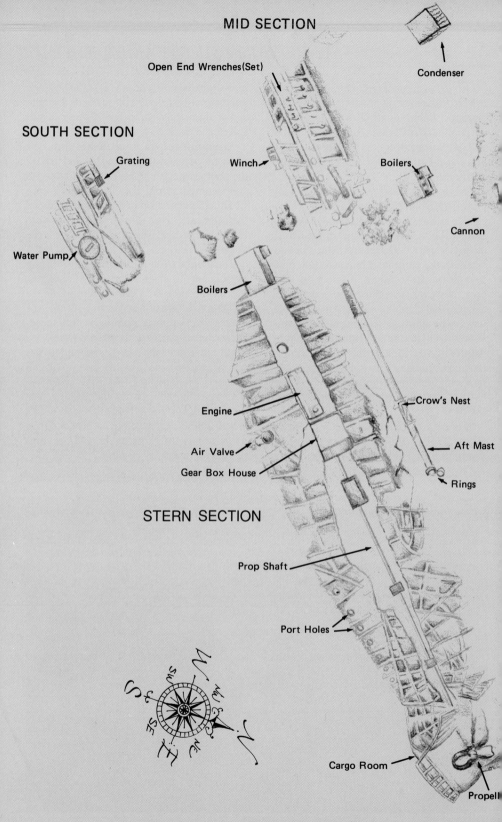

MID SECTION

Open End Wrenches(Set)

Condenser

SOUTH SECTION

Grating

Winch

Boilers

Water Pump

Cannon

Boilers

Crow's Nest

Engine

Aft Mast

Air Valve

Gear Box House

Rings

STERN SECTION

Prop Shaft

Port Holes

Cargo Room

Propell

BLACK ROCK POINT

Hatch

BOW SECTION

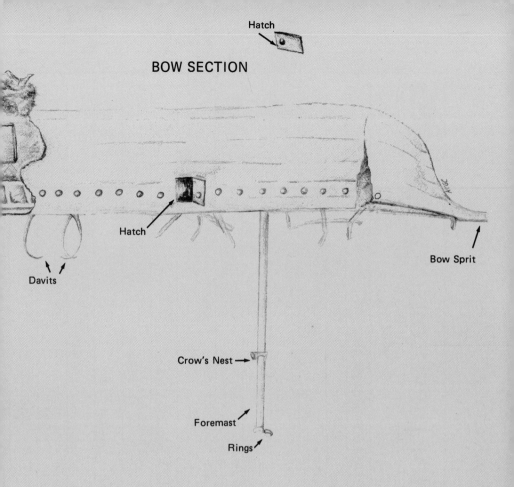

Hatch

Davits

Bow Sprit

Crow's Nest →

Foremast

Rings

R.M.S. RHONE NATIONAL PARK
No Spearfishing, Linefishing, Taking of
Coral or Shells, or Anchoring in the Wreck.
GOVERNMENT OF THE BRITISH VIRGIN ISLANDS

This is a diagram to the Rhone
as it is positioned underwater.

Rudder

LEE BAY
↓

DIVE SHOP DIRECTORY

UNITED STATES VIRGIN ISLANDS

Operator	Location	Address	Telephone	Certification & Resort Instruction	AirFills	Tours†
Anchor Dive Center	St. Croix	Salt River	809-778-1522	Yes	Yes	G, C
Aqua Action	Secret Harbor Hotel	P.O. Box 12138 St. Thomae, USVI 00801	809-775-6285	Yes	Yes	G, C, R
Caribbean Divers	Redhook	USVI 00801	809-775-6384	Yes	Yes	C
Cruz Bay Watersports	Cruz Bay	P.O. Box 252 St. John, USVI 00831	809-776-6234	Yes	Yes	G, C, R
Cruzan Divers, Inc.	St. Croix	12 Strand Street Frederiksted, St. Croix, USVI 00840	809-772-3701 800-247-8186	Yes	Yes	G, C
Joe Vogel Diving Co.	St. Thomae	Villa Olga, St. Thomae, USVI 00801	809-775-7610 800-448-6224 809-774-1376 (Fax)	Yes	Yes	G, C
Chris Sawyer Diving Center	St. Thomas	41-6-1 Estate Frydenhoj, St. Thomas, USVI 00802	809-775-7320	Yes	Yes	G, C
Chris Sawyer Diving Center	Smith Bay	Stouffer Grand Beach Resort Smith Bay, St. Thomae, USVI 00802	809-775-1510, Ext. 7850	Yes	Yes	G, C, R
St. John Water Sports The Dive Shop	St. John	P.O. Box 70 Cruz Bay, St. John, USVI 00830	809-776-6256	Yes	Yes	G, C
St. Thomas Diving Club	St. Thomas	P.O. Box 7337 Bolongo Bay, St. Thomas, USVI 00801	809-776-2381	Yes	Yes	G, C
Underwater Safaris	Yachthaven Frenchman's Reef	P.O. Box 8469 St. Thomas, USVI 00801	809-774-1350	Yes	Yes	G, C
Underwater St. Croix	St. Croix	P.O. Box 26126 Green Cay, St. Croix, USVI 00824	809-778-7350	Yes	Yes	G, C, R

Name	Location	Address	Phone			Tours*
V.I. Divers / The Antoines	St. Croix	Pan Am Pavilion, Christiansted, St. Croix, USVI 00820	809-775-6045, 800-544-5911	Yes	Yes	G, C
Virgin Islands Diving School	St. Thomas	P.O. Box 9707, St. Thomas, USVI 00801	809-774-8687, 809-774-7368 (Fax)	Yes	Yes	G, C
Dive Experience	St. Croix	P.O. Box 4254, Christiansted, St. Croix 00820	809-775-3307	Yes	Yes	G, C

BRITISH VIRGIN ISLANDS

Name	Location	Address	Phone			Tours*
Baskin In The Sun	Prospect Reef, Soper's Hole, Village Cay	P.O. Box 108, Road Town, Tortola	809-494-2858, 809-494-2859, 800-233-7938, 809-494-5853 (Fax)	Yes	Yes	G, C
Blue Water Divers / Mike & Keith Royle	Nanny Cay	P.O. Box 846, Road Town, Tortola, BVI	809-494-2847	Yes	Yes	G, C, R
Dive BVI / Joe Giacinto	V.G. Yacht & Leverick Bay, Peter Island	P.O. Box 1040, Virgin Gorda, BVI	809-848-7078, 809-495-5513, 809-495-5347 (Fax)	Yes	No	G, C, R
Kilbride's Underwater Tours / Bert Kilbride	Virgin Gorda	P.O. Box 46, Virgin Gorda, BVI	800-932-4286, 809-495-9638	Yes	Yes	G, C, R
Rainbow Visions Photography / Jim & Odile Scheiner (Underwater Video)	Prospect Reef Resort	P.O. Box 680, Road Town, Tortola BVI	809-494-2749	No	No	R
Underwater Safaris / Tony & Maureen Green	Road Town, Cooper Island & Marina Cay	P.O. Box 139, Road Town, Tortola BVI	809-494-3235, 809-494-3965	Yes	Yes	G, C, R

*Tours: G = Group; C = Custom; R = Rendezvous)

Sail Caribe

The Most Popular Chartering Destination in the World

Surprisingly, yachting vacations can be had for an all-inclusive price that may be no more than the cost of a normal first class hotel vacation.

Whether you are bareboating, needing a captain for a day, or perhaps the whole crew to pamper and guide you to the fascinating sights of the islands...

You can learn to sail, snorkle, windsurf or scuba dive off your own private charter yacht.

Leave the details to us. As experienced sailors and charterers, we know the boats, the crews, and the islands.

Call Executive Travel Associates Caribbean Yacht Charter Agents
TOLL-FREE 1-800-785-SAIL

Mark Fox

Mark Fox

Mark Fox

GOVERNMENT OF THE BRITISH VIRGIN ISLANDS

CHIEF MINISTER
ADMINISTRATION BUILDING

ROAD TOWN TORTOLA

Dear Yachtsmen:

Welcome to the Yacht Chartering Capital of the World! The British Virgin Islands is homeport of the largest bareboat fleet in the world.

The BVI is an archipelago of some 40 islands, islets, rocks and cays offering a wide variety of water-based activities. Whether you are a first-time charterer or a seasoned sailor, you will find that the British Virgins are ideal for testing your skills.

If you wish to test your angling skills, the BVI is renowned for sportsfishing, deep and shallow water, e.g., bonefishing on Anegada. Or, if your wish is to get even closer to nature, you may explore our undersea world. We have some of the most varied dive sites in the Caribbean and, perhaps, more wrecks than any other Caribbean destination, several completely unexplored.

Our waters are safe and extremely manageable, surrounded by numerous protected anchorages. Our people are warm and as friendly as the balmy tradewinds constantly blowing over the islands.

I have always been a strong advocate of making sure that the BVI remains a competitive "Yachtsman-Friendly Destination." To this end, the Government has enacted legislation to make sure that the destination remains on the cutting edge of the chartering industry, and to broaden the mix of yachts based in the British Virgin Islands. This legislation also streamlines the process of clearing customs and immigration at our ports of entry, ensuring that you have more time to enjoy your vacation.

We are glad to have you and we look forward with anticipation to your next visit, with your friends.

Sincerely,

H. Lavity Stoutt
Chief Minister and Minister of Tourism

THE ANCHORAGES

Dougal Thornton

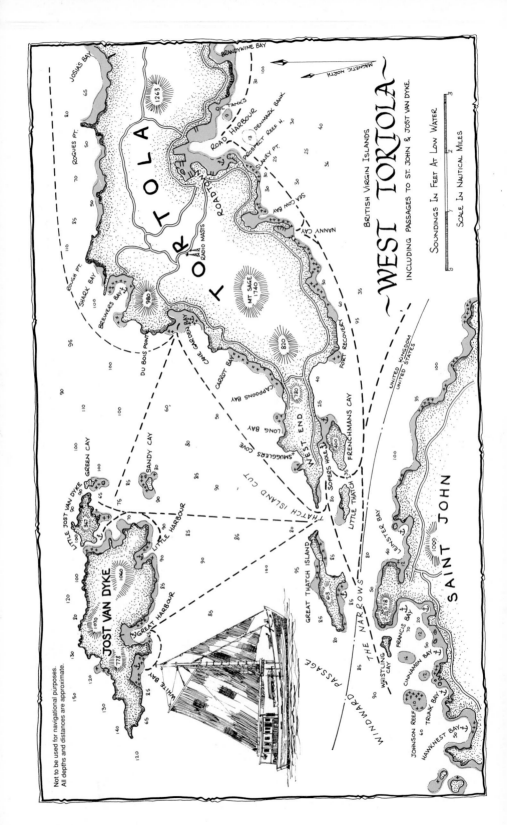

~WEST TORTOLA~

BRITISH VIRGIN ISLANDS

INCLUDING PASSAGES TO ST. JOHN & JOST VAN DYKE.

SOUNDINGS IN FEET AT LOW WATER

SCALE IN NAUTICAL MILES

Not to be used for navigational purposes.
All depths and distances are approximate.

JOSIAS BAY

ROGUES PT.

BRANDYWINE BAY

MAGNETIC NORTH

OIL TANKS

ROAD HARBOUR

DENMARK BANK

PROSPECT REEF H.

SLANEY PT.

SEA COW BAY

NANNY CAY

T O R T O L A

ROAD

RADIO MASTS

MT. SAGE
1740

FORT RECOVERY

UNITED KINGDOM
UNITED STATES

ROUGH PT.

SHARK BAY

BREWER'S BAY

DU BOIS POINT

CANE GARDEN BAY

CARROT BAY

CAPPOONS BAY

LONG BAY

SMUGGLERS COVE

WEST END

SOPERS HOLE

FRENCHMANS CAY

LITTLE THATCH

THATCH ISLAND CUT

SAINT JOHN

GREEN CAY

SANDY CAY

LITTLE JOST VAN DYKE

LITTLE HARBOUR

JOST VAN DYKE

GREAT HARBOUR

WHITE BAY

778

GREAT THATCH ISLAND

THE NARROWS

WINDWARD PASSAGE

WHISTLING CAY

FRANCIS BAY

CINNAMON BAY

TRUNK BAY

JOHNSON REEF

HAWKSNEST BAY

LEINSTER BAY

74

TORTOLA
panorama
British Virgin Islands

SAILING ROUTES of the BRITISH VIRGIN ISLANDS

ANEGADA

MOSQUITO I.

DOG ISLANDS

VIRGIN GORDA

GUANA I.

GREAT CAMANOE I.

LITTLE J.V.D.

JOST VAN DYKE

TORTOLA

BEEF I.

FALLEN JERUSALEM

ROUND ROCK

GREAT THATCH

DRAKE CHANNEL

GINGER I.

SIR FRANCIS

COOPER I.

SALT I.

ST. JOHN

PETER I.

NORMAN I.

SCALE IN NAUTICAL MILES

0   5   10

Not to be used for navigational purposes.
All depths and distances are approximate.

76

JOST VAN DYKE

A large, high island, Jost Van Dyke lies to the north of Tortola and becomes visible to yachtsmen sailing from St. Thomas upon entering Pillsbury Sound. With a population of approximately 200, the island remains relatively unspoilt. The largest settlement is at Great Harbour which is also a port of entry into the BVI.

Named after a Dutch pirate, the island is known as the birthplace of Dr. John Lettsome, born on Little Jost Van Dyke in 1744. Dr. Lettsome later returned to England and founded the London Medical Society and the Royal Humane Society. Known for his good sense of humour, Dr. Lettsome wrote the following:

I, John Lettsome,
Blisters, bleeds and sweats 'em.
If, after that, they please to die,
I, John Lettsome.

White Bay

White Bay is the westernmost harbour on the south side of the island. Aptly named for its beautiful stretch of white sandy beach, White Bay is an excellent anchorage under normal sea conditions. During the winter months, however, ground seas can make it an untenable anchorage, suitable for day stops only.

Navigation

White Bay is a relatively small anchorage with limited swinging room once inside the reef; however, there is room for several boats anchored properly. Although there are three entrances through the reef, it is recommended that you make your approach between the middle of the two reefs, leaving the red buoy to starboard and the green to port.

Anchoring

The channel will carry 10–12 feet. Once inside the reef, anchor to port or starboard in approximately 7–10 feet of water with a sandy bottom. Do not anchor in the channel, and stay well clear of the shoal spot just off the black rocks to starboard of the channel entrance.

Ashore

White Bay Sandcastle is a small, attractive resort that serves luncheon and dinner by reservation. Call on VHF 16. The reef provides excellent snorkeling.

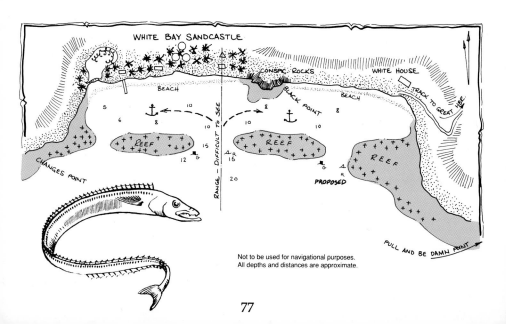

Not to be used for navigational purposes.
All depths and distances are approximate.

77

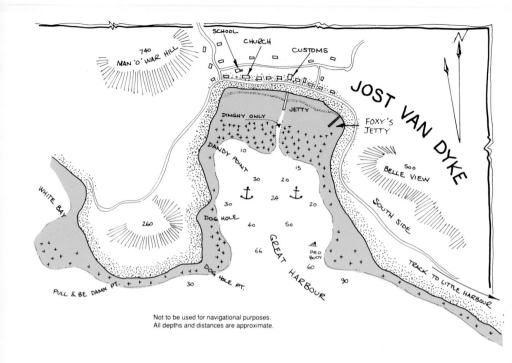

Not to be used for navigational purposes.
All depths and distances are approximate.

Great Harbour

A normally sheltered harbour lying at the foot of 1000-foot-high peaks, Great Harbour is a port of entry into the BVI and is the largest settlement on the island.

Navigation

This is a straightforward entrance and no real hazards exist. Entering the harbour from east or west, it is advisable to give both shorelines a reasonable berth. There is a large reef, extending out 300 yards, ringing the inner shoreline, so anchor before you reach it.

Anchoring

Anchor anywhere outside the reef in 15–30 feet of water. It can be difficult to get your anchor to hold, but once well set you should be okay.

Ashore

Take the dinghy ashore through the break in the reef. Head directly for the dock in order to avoid shallow coral heads. The customs officer for Jost Van Dyke will clear vessels in or out of British waters for both customs and immigration.

Down the beach to the west is Club Paradise Bar. Christine's Bakery and her delectable fresh baked bread can be found following the road next to customs. Ali Baba's is a local West Indian bar/restaurant which also sells crafts, and Happy Laury's offers informal dining with occasional entertainment.

Foxy's Tamarind Bar and Grill is located in the eastern end of Great Harbour, with the dock in front. It has become an institution for cruising boats over the years. Foxy and Tessa hosted the Wooden Boat Regatta for many years. They are open for lunch and dinner daily with Foxy entertaining often, singing his calypso ballads. Don't miss their gift shop!

The Jost Van Dyke ferry operates between West End and Great Harbour.

To rid your boat of unpleasant freight, there is a garbage disposal bin located near customs.

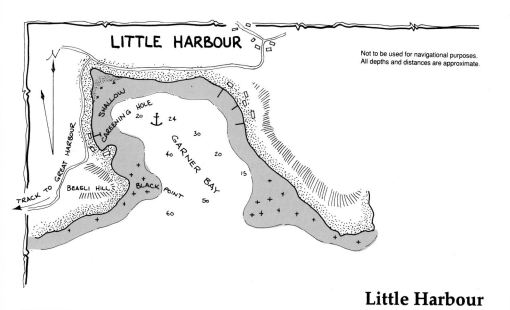

Not to be used for navigational purposes. All depths and distances are approximate.

Little Harbour

Little Harbour, or Garner Bay, as it is sometimes called, lies to the east of Great Harbour. Once used as a careenage for island sloops, the harbour now caters to charter parties, with three restaurants ashore.

Navigation

The entrance to Little Harbour is straightforward and deep. There is a shoal area to port when entering, but the channel is wide and clear.

Anchoring

The traditional anchorage is off the western end of the bay in 12 feet of water, but in recent years boats have been anchoring all over the bay.

The shore is rocky along the east side, but the bottom is clean, hard sand. Ensure that your anchor is well set with sufficient scope, as parts of the harbour are very deep. Or pick up one of the moorings and pay for it ashore at the appropriate restaurant.

Ashore

For those who enjoy hiking, there is a small track that takes you about 1000 feet up the mountain. For those ambitious enough to make the climb, the views are spectacular.

There are three restaurants in the bay. On the eastern side is Abe's By the Sea, and on the other side of the bay are Sidney's Peace & Love and Harris's Place. Harris's can provide for many of your needs, offering ice, groceries, fax and phone facilities, as well as serving breakfast, lunch and dinner.

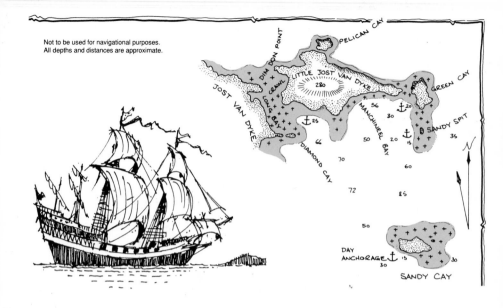

Sandy Cay, Green Cay, Little Jost Van Dyke

The following three anchorages offer spectacular beaches and snorkeling, but should be considered day stops only.

Little Jost Van Dyke

There is a small anchorage on the southeastern end of Little Jost Van Dyke. Entrance from the south presents no hazards. You will find a concrete bulkhead and should anchor off it in 15–25 feet of water. The bottom is sandy and provides excellent holding.

If the wind is out of the south, the anchorage becomes very sloppy and during northerly ground seas the surge is excessive.

There is no passage between Jost Van Dyke and Little Jost Van Dyke, but good snorkeling exists along the south side.

Green Cay

Green Cay offers a superb daytime stop with excellent snorkeling. Anchor due west of the sand bar in 20 feet of water. It is better to stay close to the bar, as the prevailing wind will keep you clear and the water depth increases rapidly once you are off the bar. During the winter months the ground swell man-

ages to work around the island, making the area untenable as an overnight anchorage.

The best snorkeling will be found on the reef that extends south of the cay.

Sandy Cay

To the East of Jost Van Dyke is Sandy Cay. Owned by Laurence Rockefeller, there is a botanical tour on the small path that encircles the island. It also affords some spectacular views of the surrounding islands.

The anchorage is on the southwest side close to shore, in the lee of the island. The holding ground is good, but be careful to avoid the coral heads.

Extreme caution should be exercised during winter ground seas, as the waves make their way around both sides of the island, causing surf to break on the beach, making landing a dinghy difficult, if not disastrous.

To the north of the cay is a ragged breaking reef that provides excellent snorkeling when the seas are flat.

80

Cruise the BVI's
...ON THE DOUBLE!

Tortola Marine Management has doubled its existing fleet of mono-hulls with a new range of sleek, fast CATS from Fountaine-Pajot, Lagoon, Privilege and Gemini. If you want to see more of the BVI in comfort and style call for our new colour brochure and rate guide.

1-800-633-0155
809-49-42751 • Fax 809-49-45166

Dial ISLAND FAX (404) 399-3077 • Select Code #1128

Dougal D. Thornton Associates

TMM

Boats Are Our Business
Our Only Business

At Tortola Yacht Services Center we specialize in providing professional services and quality products for boatowners. These include hull, spar and rigging repairs, electronic sales and service, Awl-grip refinishing, outboard, inboard and diesel engine sales and service, a woodshop, a machine shop, a sail loft and our own Golden Hind Chandlery.

All services are coordinated by knowledgeable, responsible management.

Our yacht brokerage office is the largest in the Caribbean.

Our 70 ton Travelift can handle up to 23' beam.

We care for your boat
We care about you

Tortola Yacht Services Ltd.

P.O. Box 74 ● Tortola, B.V.I● (809) 494-2124 ● Fax (809) 474-4707

...Nestled into a grove of palms it provides two levels for dining, drinking and dancing with a panorama of Cane Garden Bay as a background. On Sundays, Myett's hosts a barbeque buffet with rum punches and reggae music that packs the beach with charter sailors, vacationers and islanders alike, who play volleyball and party past sunset.

Virgin Islands Restaurant Guide & Recipe Book

Myett's

On The Beach,
Cane Garden Bay
Live Music
Fri., Sat., Sun. & Mon.

Lunch 11:00-3:00 Daily
Dinner 6:30-9:30 Daily
Tel/Fax 5-9543

Regarded by many as one of the more beautiful anchorages in the BVI, Cane Garden Bay is picture-postcard material, with a white palm-fringed beach stretching the entire length of the bay. When approaching from the west, you will sail past Smugglers Cove, Belmont, Long Bay and Carrot Bay before reaching Cane Garden Bay. If you have any doubt, line up the south side of Jost Van Dyke directly under the peak of Tobago, and this range will bring you to the entrance.

Navigation

There are two reefs at the entrance to Cane Garden Bay. Entering boats should favour the northern end of the bay. The BVI government has put in place two unlit buoys which simplify the entrance appreciably. Leave the red buoy to starboard when entering.

Once clear of the reef, you'll have plenty of room to anchor.

Anchoring

If there is a slight ground swell, the northern portion of the bay will afford more protection. If the swell is considerable, however, it is recommended that you reschedule your cruise to return a few days later when it has subsided.

When anchoring, keep clear of the buoys designating the swimming area. The bottom affords excellent holdings in 15–25 feet of water.

Owing to the mountains, the wind tends to change directions, so check your swinging room in relation to other vessels.

Ashore

To avoid any unpleasant surprises from a rising tide, pull your dinghy well up on the beach and lay out the dinghy anchor. Stanley's Welcome Bar caters to charter groups with lobster, fish and steak din-

ners, and a steel band several nights per week. The Gazebo, a small bar on the beach across the street from Ole Works, features live music Quito Rymer on Fridadys.

Rhymer's Beach Bar on the beach offers lunch and evening meals, and alternates with Stanley's for steel band music. Mooring buoys, installed and maintained by Moor Seacure, Ltd., are available off of Rhymer's for an overnight stay and should be paid for in the restaurant.

A leisurely walk towards the western end of the beach brings you past Myett's Bar and Restaurant, a delightful stop with good food and entertainment, to De Wedding at the far end of the beach.

Supplies can be purchased from Callwood's Grocery Store, Rhymer's and a few other local shops. Mr. Callwood's rum distillery affords the visiting yachtsman a glimpse back into history. White and gold rum is still produced from the cane grown on the hillsides. It is recommended that Mr. Callwood be asked permission prior to your wandering through the distillery, and the purchase of a bottle or two is expected.

Not to be used for navigational purposes.
All depths and distances are approximate.

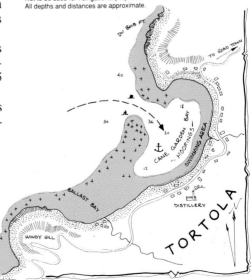

Brewers Bay

This anchorage is off limits to most charter boats. If you are a bareboat charterer, check to be certain that this anchorage is approved by your charter company.

Without question, Brewers Bay on the north side of Tortola is one of the most beautiful anchorages in the Virgin Islands. Fortunately, however, it is seldom used by visiting yachtsmen, owing to its exposure to the northerly ground seas and the extensive coral formations which make access to the anchorage difficult.

During the winter months, it is not advisable to anchor here overnight, and if there is any indication of a ground sea developing, Brewers Bay should not be considered as even a lunch stop.

When entering the anchorage, do so under power. Make sure you have good light in order to read the bottom, and position a crew member on the bow in order to alert you to the presence of coral heads.

There is a reef that fringes the southwest shoreline and another in the centre of the bay. In order to secure a reasonable spot to anchor in, you will have to work yourself up into the southeast corner of the bay, between the reefs, where you can anchor on a sandy bottom in 15–20 feet of water.

Ashore

While the snorkeling is excellent, time should also be taken to explore ashore. For those interested in a short walk, it would be worthwhile walking up the road to the east, toward Mount Healthy, to see the ruins of Tortola's only remaining windmill. Only the base of the original mill has survived the passing years, along with the broken remains of the old distillery buildings.

The visitor should note the stonework of the mill and the surrounding ruins, as it was common to use local rock together with coral and red bricks, which were used as ballast aboard the ships servicing the Caribbean. Owing to the spectacular view, the surrounding hills are now dotted with new homes, some of them quite magnificent.

Not to be used for navigational purposes.
All depths and distances are approximate.

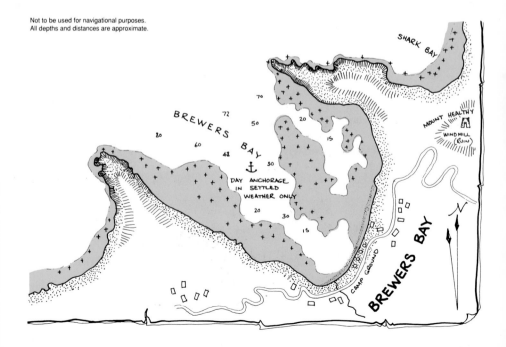

84

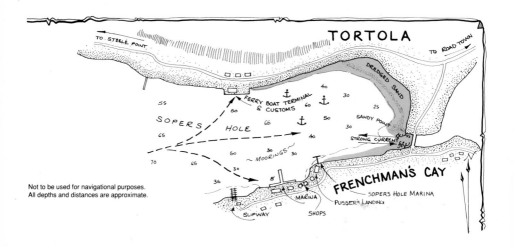

Not to be used for navigational purposes.
All depths and distances are approximate.

Soper's Hole, West End

West End is shown on the charts as Soper's Hole, a protected harbour lying between Frenchman's Cay and Tortola. It is a port of entry for vessels arriving and departing British waters, and a ferry stop between the British and United States Virgin Islands.

Navigation

Whether you enter Soper's Hole between Frenchman's Cay and Little Thatch or Steel Point and Great Thatch, you will be in deep water at all times. A current of up to 3 knots depending on the tidal flow can be expected. If you are sailing in, then you should cut the points of either Frenchman's Cay or Steel Point as close as is possible.

The government dock is located on the northern shore, but yachtsmen are advised not to tie up while clearing customs because of the movement of the ferries. Rather, it is recommended to pick up a mooring and bring the dinghy in.

Along the front of the ferry dock to the northeast corner of the harbour is a shipping lane for tugboats and sand barges—leave this area clear for their operations.

Anchoring

The harbour is so deep in places that yachts will find themselves in 60–70 feet of water. The best place to anchor is in the northeast corner, where the water depth is 20–35 feet on a sandy bottom. There are, however, moorings off of the Sunsail Marina in the southeast section of the bay, which are maintained regularly by Moor Seacure. These moorings may be picked up and paid for at the Sunsail Marina office ashore.

The sandbar is being dredged for a new marina on the east shore, and yachts anchoring on the bar should do so with caution. Moorings are also available in the vicinity of the West End Slipway and are marked accordingly. Be advised not to

85

anchor in the way of the slipway, as they need ample room to operate the railway and maneuver vessels during adverse wind conditions.

West End Slipway has a 200-ton railway for repairs and modifications to just about any vessel. The yard's specialty is rebuilding wooden boats as well as building new wooden boats.

Ashore

The West End customs office is located in the building on the ferry dock. Some supplies are available from the grocery and snack bar across from the customs building and from the Ample Hamper. Taxis to Road Town are available in abundance when the ferries come in.

On the southeast side of the harbour you will find the two-story Pusser's Landing, featuring waterfront dining in two restaurants and bars, an outdoor terrace and the Pusser's Company Store. Downstairs offers a more casual ambience, with

an open air bar, outdoor dining on the terrace and the Company Store, which carries a unique line of Pusser's own sports and travel clothing, watches, luggage and nautical accessories. Upstairs is an elegant, indoor-outdoor dining room, offering a spectacular view of Soper's Hole and the islands beyond. Pusser's is open 7 days a week. Call on VHF 16 for reservations or more information.

Other restaurants close to West End include the hotels on the north shore of Tortola, such as Long Bay Hotel, Sugar Mill Hotel, Smuggler's Cove, The Apple, Sebastian's, Frenchman's Cay, Kelly's Bar and the Jolly Roger (home of the West End Yacht Club Wednesday evening race series).

Soper's Hole now enjoys a cluster of fanciful pastel West Indian buildings known as Soper's Hole Wharf, housing some terrific shops. The Sunsail Marina at Soper's Hole (formerly Soper's Hole Marina) is a full service marina in 25 feet of water. It is home to Sunsail's fleet of 70 bareboat, crewed and flotilla charter yachts as well as the Sunsail Sailing School. The marina offers dockage with water and electricity, fuel and guest suites for overnight accommodations. The marina monitors VHF 16 and is conveniently located next to the Ample Hamper gourmet provisioning shop.

Island Treasures will delight you with their collection of unique, handmade West Indian artifacts and treasures, from fine art to screenprinted fashions.

Sea Lion is a boutique with tropical wear, novelties and gifts. Zenaida carries wonderful textile products in a variety of textures and colors. A short walk away is Walter's Superette, offering a variety of provisions.

A dinghy passage behind the sandbar, between Frenchman's Cay and Tortola, affords good fishing at either end.

With SunYacht Charters, you're always on island time.

Just choose your island and leave the details to us. Because taking life easy is what a sailing vacation is all about. And no one does more than **SYC** to make your charter pure pleasure. We feature the finest bareboat yachts in the world, including our dazzling Sun-Catalina Caribbean Series and the spectacular new Centurion K45 catamarans by Wauquiez.

Call **SYC** today. And relax.

1-800-772-3500
U. S. and Canada

207-236-9611 In Maine • 207-236-3972 Fax
P.O. Box 737, Camden, Maine 04843 U.S.A.

Call us for seasonal specials and group rates.

SunYacht Charters
TORTOLA•ST.MARTIN•ANTIGUA•TAHITI

We Outshine The Rest.

CALL FOR DETAILS OF SYC'S GOLDEN OPPORTUNITY YACHT PURCHASE–MANAGEMENT PROGRAM.

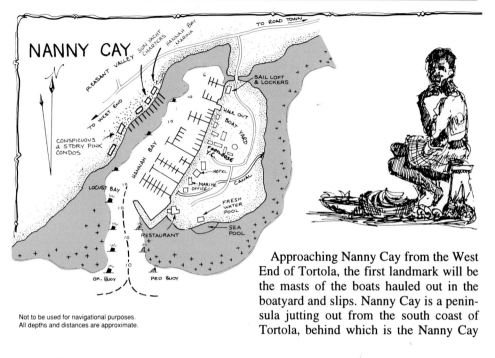

Not to be used for navigational purposes.
All depths and distances are approximate.

Approaching Nanny Cay from the West End of Tortola, the first landmark will be the masts of the boats hauled out in the boatyard and slips. Nanny Cay is a peninsula jutting out from the south coast of Tortola, behind which is the Nanny Cay

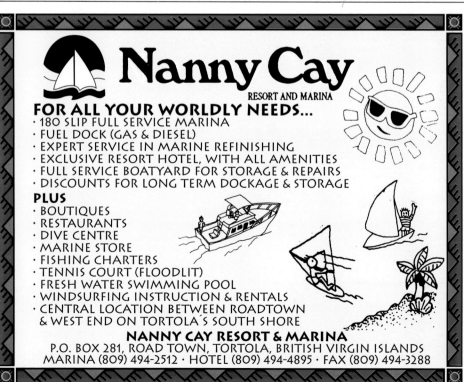

Marine Centre, a full-service marina and boatyard offering a 50-ton lift capable of lifting boats of up to 70 feet.

The marina has 180 slips available and visiting yachtsmen are advised to contact the harbourmaster on VHF channel 16 or 68 for docking instructions. The controlling draft is 9 feet.

Navigation

Head for the southernmost point of Nanny Cay (the Peg Leg Landing restaurant is an easy landmark), until the red and green channel markers are visible. The larger reef is to port and marked by a green buoy. Head between the green and red buoys, leaving the red to starboard. The number of buoys may vary, but the marina does keep the channel marked.

The inner harbour has shoal water on the western shore and is marked with a series of green buoys-do not go west of these buoys. There is *no* anchoring, due to the lack of room. Visiting yachts should tie up to docks A & B (the first docks to starboard upon entering) and check with the harbourmaster.

Ashore

Amenities available within the marina complex, include showers, water, gift shop, laundromat, ice and fuel. Provisions may be purchased from the Gourmet Chandler and storage lockers may be rented through the marina. Blue Water Divers operates a dive shop and conducts diving tours daily.

Please note: Customs and immigration services are no longer available at Nanny Cay Marine Centre. You must clear through one of the other ports of entry.

Two restaurants complement the marina. The Plaza Cafe is open all day. Peg Leg Landing, a rather whimsical restaurant on the point, serves lunch and dinner and overlooks the Sir Francis Drake Channel. It's a great place to eat, with a view from every table.

Nanny Cay, a headquarters for many crewed and bareboat charterers, offers discounted rates for yachtsmen at the hotel, and use of the pool and tennis court. Windsurfing lessons are also available here.

Sun Yacht Charters' new base at Hannah Bay Marina lies to the west of Nanny Cay. Facilities include deep water slips 9 1/2 foot draft, condominiums (conspicuous pink structures with teal green roofs) for short or long term accommodation, swimming pool, showers, water, ice, electricity, telephone, and cable TV hook-ups. Transient yachts are welcome at the facility for short term dockage and use of facilities. Sun Yacht Charters monitors VHF channel 12. There are plans for a provisioning store and laundry facility at a future date.

Just to the west of Road Town is a small harbour that services the Prospect Reef Hotel. It can accommodate vessels up to 40 feet in length and 5-1/2 feet of draft.

Navigation

The harbour entrance has reef on either side. Be sure you know exactly where you are and what to expect, because once in the channel you are committed.

A stone breakwater extends from the shoreline marking the starboard side of the channel. When entering, be prepared to make a "dogleg" to port once you are through the breakwater.

No anchoring is allowed, so tie up alongside the bulkhead and check with the harbourmaster.

Ashore

Prospect Reef offers all the conveniences of a major hotel complex, including an Olympic-size swimming pool, a diving pool and a sea pool, two restaurants, tennis courts, a 9-hole golf course, and provisions at Little Circle. Geared to the needs of tourists and yachtsmen, Little Circle offers an extensive selection of foods and wines.

For those who wish to browse and buy, don't miss On The Beach and the Pink Pineapple, two wonderful shops. This is also the home of Rainbow Visions, which provides a terrific, personalized video service for divers and yachtsmen.

Baskin in the Sun maintains their dive shop operation in the Prospect Reef complex, as well.

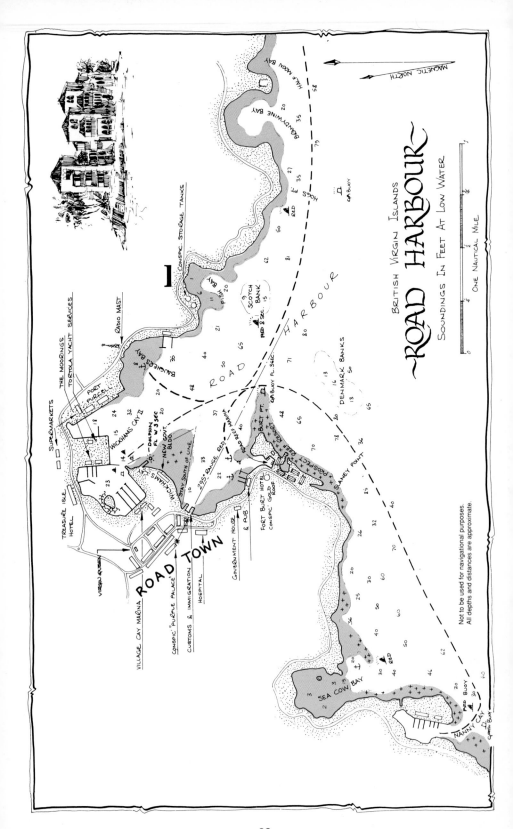

BRITISH VIRGIN ISLANDS

~ROAD HARBOUR~

SOUNDINGS IN FEET AT LOW WATER

ROAD TOWN

ROAD HARBOUR

MAGNETIC NORTH

ONE NAUTICAL MILE

Not to be used for navigational purposes.
All depths and distances are approximate.

HALF MOON BAY
BRANDYWINE BAY
HOGS
CAN BUOY
RED E
RED & SEC.
SCOTCH BANK
FISH BAY
CONSPIC. STORAGE TANKS
RADIO MAST
BAUGHERS BAY
THE MOORINGS
TORTOLA YACHT SERVICES
PORT PURCELL
SUPERMARKETS
WICKHAMS CAY II
WICKHAMS CAY I
TREASURE ISLE HOTEL
VIRGIN QUEEN
VILLAGE CAY MARINA
CONSPIC "PURPLE PALACE" ROOF
CUSTOMS & IMMIGRATION
HOSPITAL
GOVERNMENT HOUSE & PUB
FORT BURT HOTEL CONSPIC. GOLD ROOF
DOLPHIN FL W 3SEC
NEW GOVT. BLDG.
295° RANGE RED / LINE
STAY SOUTH OF LINE
ROAD REEF MARINA
BURT PT.
CAN BUOY FL 3SEC
PROSPECT REEF
SLANEY POINT
DENMARK BANKS
SEA COW BAY
RED
RED BUOY
NANNY CAY
QUEEN BANK

1

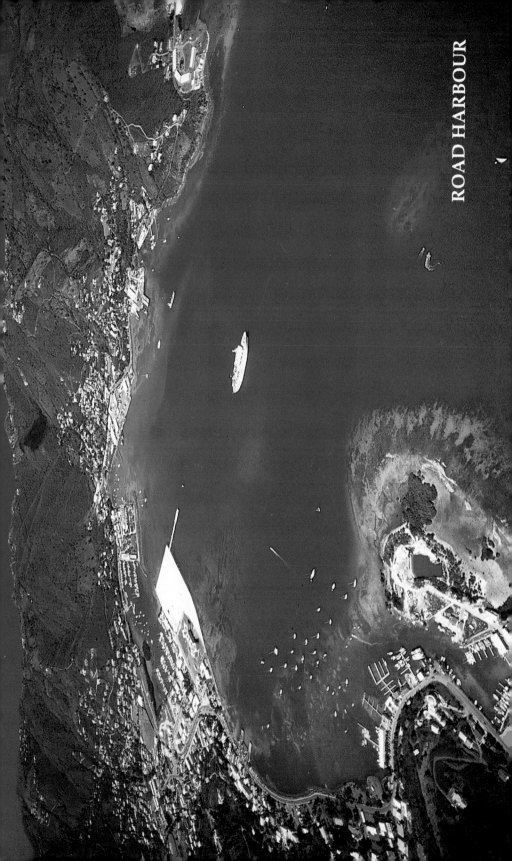

ROAD HARBOUR

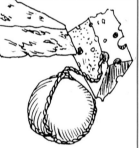

Road Town, the capital of the British Virgin Islands, is the centre of commerce, shipping and social activity. Over the past few years, tremendous development has taken place to enable it to better cope with the steady influx of cruising and charter boats. Now Road Town can boast some of the most sophisticated nautical facilities in the Caribbean chain.

Navigation

Approaching Road Harbour from the west, your first landmarks will be the silver fuel tanks located by Fish Bay on the eastern side of the harbour. The other is the dome-shaped gold roof of the Fort Burt Hotel, located high up on Burt Point, the western side of the harbour entrance.

Locate the green sea buoy (FL Green 3 Sec.) marking the end of the reef, extending east from Burt Point and leave it to port. There is a red conical buoy (FL Red 9 Sec.) marking Scotch Bank on the eastern side of the harbour.

Fort Burt Marina

Once inside the buoys, it is advisable to head for the customs dock (approximately 292 degrees M), until the Fort Burt Jetty is abeam. This will bring you clear of the reef that extends to the north of the mangroves. Anchor to the northeast of the docks about 300 feet out. Check the sketch chart for location of sandbars and anchorage.

Hundreds of sailors have found themselves aground on the sandbar that extends north of the mangroves because they rounded up too quickly. The situation is particularly embarrassing because of the proximity of the local Paradise Pub which overlooks the anchorage.

If you wish to inquire as to services or docking, pull alongside and check with the dockmaster. Fort Burt Marina has recently been updated and refurbished with new docks and slips. They do accept transient boats and offer gas, diesel, water and ice as well as telephone and TV cable hook up and of course, electricity. Call on VHF 12.

For supplies, in addition to The Pub, Island Marine Supply has a well-managed marine chandlery, and Riteway Supermarket operates a grocery in adjacent quarters from which you can resupply.

Road Reef Marina

A line of small green buoys marks the channel to Road Reef Marina, home of Tortola Marine Management, a bareboat charter company. As you enter the channel, keep the green buoys to your port, Fort Burt Marina and Smith's Ferry dock to your right. On the upper right hand corner of the roof of the Pub you will see a day glow orange range marker, this combines with the orange day glow mark on the piling to give you a range to come in to the marina.

There are a couple of shallow patches close to the roadside beneath Fort Burt Hotel, so favour the port side of the channel as you enter the pool of Road Reef Marina. TMM manages the complete marina; most services except fuel are available. Road Reef Marina monitors channel 12, should you require their assistance. In the same complex that houses the marina office is The Marine Division of the Royal Police, the new BVI Yacht Club, the office of VISAR and Island Care Electronics.

The Customs Dock

Being the main port of entry to the British Virgin Islands, all vessels arriving from the U.S. Virgin Islands or other foreign ports must clear with customs and immigration before proceeding to a marina.

Anchor off the town dock, as it is not advisable to lie alongside; apart from the commercial traffic, the surge is often excessive. In landing the dinghy, use a dinghy anchor to keep the stern off.

Wickham's Cay (Moorings/Treasure Isle/ Village Cay/Inner Harbour)

To the north of the government dock is the Wickhams Cay I and II Yacht Harbour and Marine Service complex. Approaching from seaward, you will see the new government administration building and cruise ship dock. There is a quick flashing 3 seconds light marking the dolphin off the cruise ship dock and numerous masts behind a stone breakwater. Head for the masts until you see the outer set of buoys marking the channel entrance. Leaving red to starboard, proceed through the breakwater entrance (80' wide x 10' deep) picking up the second set of markers inside.

The Moorings/Mariner Inn

One of the Caribbean's most comprehensive facilities, the Moorings/Mariner Inn has been developed around the Moorings' charter fleet of 160 yachts. The complex consists of 38 lanai rooms overlooking the harbour, a fresh-water swimming pool, restaurant, gift shop, provisioning store (K-Mark's Gourmet Galley) and service facilities. Underwater Safaris operates its dive shop and tour business at the head of the dock (see dive section).

For docking information it is best to contact the dockmaster via VHF 12.

Upon entering the harbour, there will be three docks. The first, "A" dock, is the one used for visiting yachts and offers finger pier docking for 90 boats. Water is available, as is shore power of both 110 and 220 volts.

Any vessel needing diesel fuel should contact the dockmaster. "B" and "C" docks are reserved for the Moorings/Mariner bareboat and crewed charter fleet.

A short walk will bring you to K-Mark's Gourmet Galley provisioning store. With cruising yachtsmen in mind, the Gourmet Galley has not only practical necessities, but also a variety of fresh fruits and vegetables and fresh-baked items.

Treasure Isle Dock/ Hotel

In the centre as you approach from the breakwater is the Treasure Isle dock, home of the Moorings' crewed charter fleet and Club Mariner small boat activity centre. Treasure Isle Hotel, across the road, is one of Road Town's finer hotels, offering excellent air-conditioned accommodations with telephones. They boast a fresh-water pool with gardenside dining. The staff mem-

THE WILLIAM THORNTON
IN THE BIGHT ON NORMAN ISLAND

bers at Treasure Isle are known for their friendliness, and often remember guests from previous visits.

Village Cay Marina

To your port when entering, Village Cay Marina can accommodate over 100 yachts of up to 150 feet in length. The slips offer metered water and shore power, phone service and cable TV. Shower facilities, laundromat, ice and provisioning are also available. There is also a fresh-water pool, waterfront restaurant and bar.

The Marina Hotel offers air-conditioned rooms and 1- or 2-bedroom condominium rentals, all within short walking distance of the banks, shopping and other conveniences of downtown Road Town.

Near the complex, the Ample Hamper offers custom provisioning services and a fine selection of wine, cheese, paté and various other foods to tempt the palate.

In Columbus Centre you will find outside dining at the Fish Trap seafood restaurant. Also in the Centre are Virgin Island Sailing, Girl Friday, and several

shops. Within a few minutes' walk of the marina are several banking institutions including Barclay's, Chase Manhattan and Nova Scotia, and numerous business offices and gift shops.

The Inner Harbour Marina

Inner Harbour marina is nestled alongside Village Cay to the south. Yachts can pay for their stay by the hour, day or month. The services provided include water, electricity, telephone, and cable TV hookups, and convenient walking distance to the shops of Road Town. BVI Bareboats bases its operations at the marina. The Captain's Table, a congenial restaurant, overlooks the harbour and offers excellent food.

Tortola Yacht Services

Located on Wickham's Cay II behind the Moorings, Tortola Yacht Services, owned and operated by Albie Stewart, has become one of the foremost yacht care centres in the Caribbean. The shipyard has both tami lift and marine railway capabilities up to 80 tons, dry stor-age for up to 40 yachts, an awlgrip refinishing

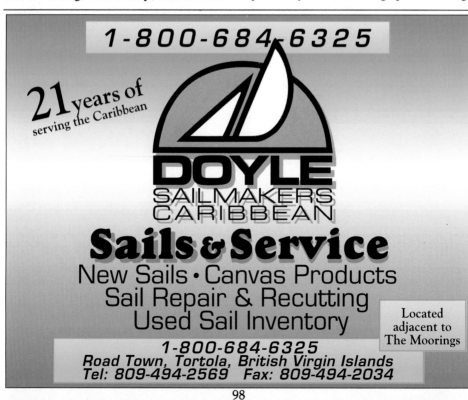

VILLAGE CAY

VILLAGE CAY
MARINA · HOTEL
TORTOLA · B·V·I

RESTAURANT · HOTEL · MARINA

Centrally located in the heart of Road Town

- *Full Service Marina*
    106 slips all with full facilities for boats up to 200ft, security dawn to dusk, 110/220 power, water, cable tv, IDD phone, garbage removal, chandlery, clearing house, fuel, ice, laundry, showers.
    All general services within 5 minutes of marina.
- *Restaurant on the waterfront*
    Open all day 7:30 am – 11:00 pm
    Lunch served 11:00 am – 6:00 pm daily
    Featuring fresh fish, aged meat and daily specials
    Weekly buffet; check local press for details
- *Hotel*
    Recently refurbished rooms with a/c, color cable tv, daily maid service, dry cleaning, laundry and swimming pool.

Village Cay, Wickhams Cay I, Road Town, Tortola, BVI

Tel: (809) 494-2771   Fax: (809) 494-2773

iteam, yacht brokerage and Golden ·Hind Chandlery.

Located conveniently in the immediate vicinity are Nautool Machine & Naucraft Galleries, Omega Caribbean, Doyle Sailmakers, Tradewind Yachting Services, Budget Rent-a-Car, Bon Appetit Delicatessen, Tico Liquors, Al's Marine and Clarence Thomas Plumbing Supplies. Across the street is Riteway Supermarket, carrying all the provisions you may need, and just next door to Riteway, Island Services carries a wide range of books and office supplies.

Baugher's Bay

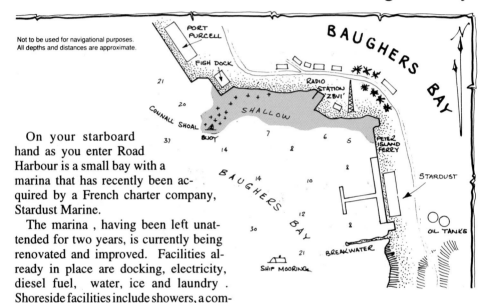

Not to be used for navigational purposes.
All depths and distances are approximate.

On your starboard hand as you enter Road Harbour is a small bay with a marina that has recently been acquired by a French charter company, Stardust Marine.

The marina , having been left unattended for two years, is currently being renovated and improved. Facilities already in place are docking, electricity, diesel fuel, water, ice and laundry . Shoreside facilities include showers, a commissary store, boutique, bistro-bar, restaurant and 10 room hotel.

Visiting yachts are welcome to use alongside docking when available or to use the moorings off the marina.

If you are anchoring off the dock, beware of the numerous coral heads in the area that can cut through nylon anchor line.

There is a landing area inside the breakwater. Do not land your dinghy to the left of the dock, as this area is reserved for the Peter Island Ferry.

FEEL REST ASSURED.

E xperience the peace and tranquility of some of the beautiful ports and lagoons in the Caribbean and Tahiti, and feel rest assured that one of the largest yacht charter companies in the world is backing you up.

Tortola • St. Martin • Guadeloupe • Martinique • Union *(Grenadines)* • Tahiti

Bareboats and Crewed Yachts

2280 University Drive, Suite 102 • Newport Beach, California 92660 U.S.A.
(714) 650-0889 • FAX: (714) 642-1318

Call 1-800-634-8822 *US & Canada*
or contact your Yacht Charter Broker

formerly

When going ashore in Road Town, it is important to observe the local dress code, which prohibits swimwear, brief attire and shirtless males. In order to avoid embarrassment, please cover up.

The BVI Tourist Office and Information Service is located at the east end of the waterfront, across the street from the new government building. The Immigration office is located across the street from the Customs building, west of Banco Popular Bank. When the new government administration building is complete, it will house most of the different government departments.

Road Town has some beautiful old West Indian buildings, complete with red tin roofs and Victorian dado work around the porches. A walk down Main Street east from Peebles Hospital will reveal all sorts of delights tucked away behind newer buildings or squeezed shoulder-to-shoulder along Main Street.

Most of the shops are clustered along Main Street from Sir Olva Georges Square to the bottom of Joe's Hill.

A visit to the Philatelic Bureau of the post office across the street from the Square should be a must-stop for anyone who would like to take home a collection of the exotic, colourful stamps of this tropical country.

You may wish to get caught up on the news at home with a *New York Times* or a magazine from Esme's Shoppe on the Square. Get yourself a fresh-baked treat at Sunrise Bakery while you read your newspaper. Visit the Virgin Island Folk Museum, situated in a quaint, West Indian building, and examine the artifacts from days gone by.

Handcrafted silver jewelry is a specialty of Samarkand, across from the colourful clothes of Bonker's Gallery Boutique. The Sea Urchin features island sports and beachwear, while Kaunda's Kysy Tropix carries video tapes, cassettes, cameras and that extra roll of film you may need by now.

Kids In De Sun will help you outfit your children for life in the tropics. You can get your crew matching, embroidered shirts at Personal Touch. Ooh La La carries toys, games and assorted frivolities. Caribbean Handprints specializes in silk-screened clothing and accessories.

Across the street is the Pusser's Company Store and Pub. This is a delightful, air-conditioned pub where you can cool down with a beer or lemonade and a deli sandwich or pizza. If you haven't tried a Pusser's Painkiller, this may be the time!

The Company Store carries a unique line of Pusser's own sports and travel clothing, watches and chronometers, luggage and nautical accessories.

Around the corner you will find Flaxcraft, which features hand-crafted gold, silver and coral jewelry. The Carifta Shop carries an assortment of clothing and accessories for women. Don't miss Sunny Caribbee Herb and Spice. Situated in a delightful old West Indian House, the shop carries specially packaged herbs and spices from the islands.

Another great memento to bring home is a coral sculpture from the Courtyard Gallery. The exquisitely carved birds, fish and shells of the islands are sure to please. Little Denmark, another unique gift shop. Housed in an old West Indian building, perched above a huge boulder, is Smith's Gore real estate company.

Her Majesty's Prison is a somewhat interesting edifice, and one we hope you'll never have to see from the inside. St. George's Anglican Church is another lovely landmark worth a visit.

Continuing past the church, you will find Joe's Hill Road, which leads up to Mount Sage or over to Cane Garden Bay. Past that is Sunday Morning Well.

If you're still feeling energetic, be sure to stop at the J.R. O'Neal Botanical Gardens, across from the police station by the tamarind tree. It is a refreshing stop away from the hustle and bustle of Road Town. The gardens feature a beautiful, exotic variety of lush, tropical plants.

Coming in to Road Harbour from the sea, you will see an old, purple Victorian building with white trim. This is the Bougainvillea clinic, affectionately known to the locals as the "Purple Palace." Dr. Tattersall, who specializes in plastic surgery, is well known for both his surgical skills and his sailboat racing skills.

BOAT BUILDING IN THE VIRGINS

Because of the scattered formation of the Virgin Islands, the inhabitants, by necessity, became expert boat builders, specializing in small, light craft that were ideal for these sheltered waters.

The unique skills that the West Indians learned from the 18th-century Navy have been preserved, virtually unchanged, to the present day, and "Tortolan Sloops" are still launched with regularity.

This lovely curve of a bay is carved out to the east of Road Harbour and provides a comfortable overnight anchorage in the usual east / southeast moderate trade winds, but can have a surge if the wind moves around to the south.

Brandywine Bay is tucked in behind a reef that extends out from both sides of the land. The opening between the two sections of reef is wide and safe for entry in the center between the two reefs, with a depth of at least 10 feet. The entrance is easy enough to see in reasonable light. As a landmark to locate Brandywine Bay, look for the "Greek temple" - an imposing building with a columned facade, situated on top of the headland, immediately to the east of the bay.

Anchoring

Brandywine Bay Restaurant, situated on the headland to the east of the bay, in front of the Greek temple, and overlooking the Sir Francis Drake channel, maintains three moorings for dinner guests. These moorings are located in the center of the bay directly in line with the entrance to the bay. The southern-most mooring is in the deepest water, while the mooring closest to the northern shore is in approximately 7- 8 feet of water. The restaurant monitors VHF Channel 16 after 2 p.m., and is available by telephone all day for reservations and instructions for mooring. If you choose to anchor, select a spot in the center of the bay to the east or west of the line of moorings, where shoal water that extends from all shores. If there is a surge, usually caused by a southerly wind or generally very rough local conditions, you may want to use a stern anchor in order to keep the bow of your boat facing the entrance of Brandywine Bay.

Ashore

As you face the row of apartments on the water edge on the eastern side of the bay, the dinghy dock is located about 50 yards to their right. Once ashore, follow the pathway to the left of the dock to where it meets the concrete road on Brandywine Estate, and then it's just a short walk up the hill to the restaurant.

For dinner only, Brandywine Bay Restaurant offers al fresco dining on cobblestone terraces. Davide and Cele Pugliese are your hosts in this international restaurant with a distinctive Florentine flair. Dinner reservations are requested.

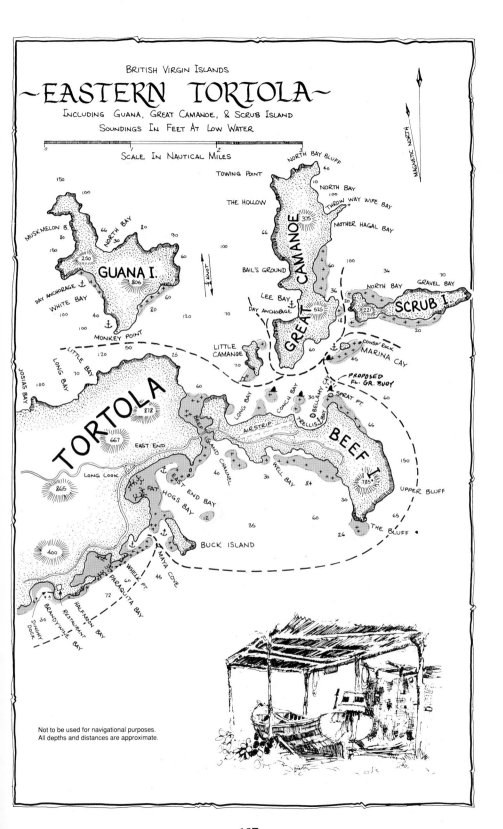

British Virgin Islands

~EASTERN TORTOLA~

Including Guana, Great Camanoe, & Scrub Island

Soundings In Feet At Low Water

Scale In Nautical Miles

MAGNETIC NORTH

NORTH BAY BLUFF

TOWING POINT

THE HOLLOW

NORTH BAY

THROW WAY WIFE BAY

MOTHER HAGAL BAY

150

100

MUSKMELON B

NORTH BAY

GUANA I.

806

DAY ANCHORAGE

WHITE BAY

MONKEY POINT

GREAT CAMANOE

BAIL'S GROUND

LEE BAY

DAY ANCHORAGE

525

NORTH BAY

GRAVEL BAY

SCRUB I.

221

CONSP' ROCK

MARINA CAY

LITTLE BAY

LONG BAY

JOSIAS BAY

LITTLE CAMANOE

PROPOSED FL. GR. BUOY

TORTOLA

818

667

EAST END

LONG BAY

CONCH BAY

BELLAMY CAY

TRELLIS BAY

SPRAT PT.

AIRSTRIP

BEEF I.

735

150

UPPER BLUFF

866

LONG LOOK

FAT HOGS BAY

EAST END BAY

REEF ISLAND CHANNEL

WELL BAY

THE BLUFF

BUCK ISLAND

400

WHELK PT.

MAYA COVE

PARAQUITA BAY

HALF MOON BAY

RESTAURANT BAY

BRANDYWINE BAY

DINGHY DOCK

Not to be used for navigational purposes.
All depths and distances are approximate.

107

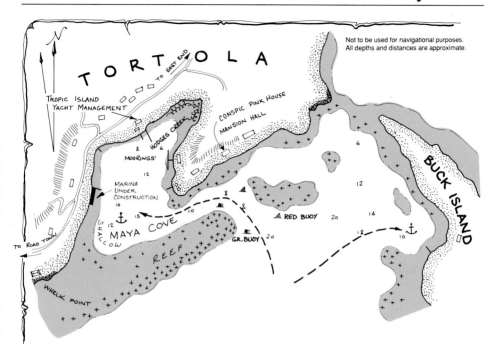

Not to be used for navigational purposes.
All depths and distances are approximate.

Anchoring

Maya Cove, or Hodges Creek, as it is shown on the charts, is approximately a half mile west of Buck Island on the southeastern shore of Tortola. Sheltered by the reef, it is always cool and free of bugs.

Tropic Island Yacht Management operates its fleet of yachts from this protected haven.

Navigation

If you are approaching Maya Cove from the west, it is well to remember that the reef extends from Whelk Point to the buoyed entrance and the northeastern end of the reef. Entry should be attempted only under power.

Now that the cove is so well buoyed, it has become redundant to put in a range on which to enter. The buoys are easy to see and are located under a promontory of land approximately 75–100 feet high. The channel is marked with two sets of red and green buoys. Proceed through the centre leaving the red buoy to starboard. At the second green buoy you will be making a turn to port, which will lead you to the harbour.

Anchoring

It is imperative when anchoring that you do not obstruct the channel after entering.

The main anchorage is to the south of the channel in 7–12 feet of water with a sandy bottom. Don't go too far back into the southwestern corner of Maya Cove, as it shoals off rapidly. A new marina in the western section of the bay has been started. The completion date and list of facilities are not yet available.

Ashore

Tropic Island Yacht Management operates a fleet of yachts, as well as a restaurant and boutique for your shopping pleasure. Visiting yachtsmen are welcome and may purchase ice, water, fuel and showers, and use the USA-direct telephones. Underwater Safaris has a direct hotline available from here. Moorings can be paid for ashore.

On the dock is a restaurant open for breakfast, lunch and dinner. The gift shop is at the head of the dock. This is a lovely spot to sip a drink and listen to the waves break on the outside of the protecting reef.

There is a small anchorage in 7-10 feet of water on the western shore of Buck Island. Very few yachts anchor here. In certain sea conditions it can be very rolly, but most of the time is an ideal anchorage.

Take care not to go too far toward the northwest tip of the island, as the bottom shoals rapidly. There is no passage between Buck Island and Tortola except by dinghy with the engine tilted up.

Fat Hog's Bay

Fat Hog's Bay is located north of Buck Island between Beef Island Channel and Maya Cove. This beautiful, well-protected anchorage is conveniently situated in the middle of the cruising grounds and is perfect for overnight anchoring.

Navigation

Fat Hog's Bay is easily accessible from Sir Francis Drake Channel by leaving Buck Island to port and going between the green can (leave to port) and Red Rock. Head directly to the Seabreeze Marina dock or pick up a mooring. Average depth from Red Rock to Seabreeze is 8 feet with good holding ground and excellent protection behind the reef. Call ahead on channel 12.

Ashore

Facilities include water, ice, fresh-water showers, fuel dock, overnight dockage for boats up to 51 feet and mooring buoys. Visitors may stop in at The Bistro for a light snack, full meal or refreshing drinks. There is also a boutique at the marina selling anything from postcards to island prints. Hotel accommodations are also available at the marina.

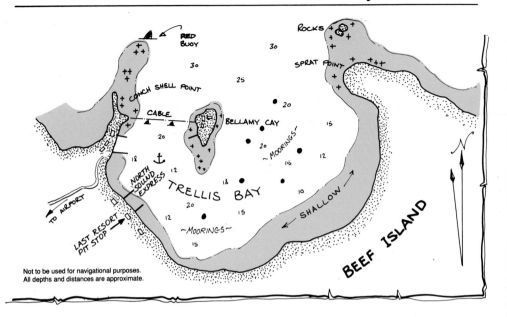

Not to be used for navigational purposes.
All depths and distances are approximate.

Located on the north shore of Beef Island, Trellis Bay was once a major anchorage in the BVI, with a hotel, large marine railway and jetty. The railway and hotel have since been abandoned, and the jetty is now used by the boats servicing Marina Cay. The anchorage is well protected even in adverse weather conditions, and its proximity to the airport makes it ideal for embarking and disembarking passengers.

Navigation

Entering Trellis Bay from the north, stay to the east of Conch Shell Point to avoid the submerged rocks. These rocks are marked by a red buoy, which should be left to starboard as you enter the bay.

If entering from the east, take care to locate the two rocks to the north of Sprat Point. Leaving them to port, enter Trellis Bay halfway between Bellamy Cay and Sprat Point.

Anchoring

Good anchorage is available off either side of Bellamy Cay in 10–20 feet of water. Do not anchor within 200 feet of the western shore of the bay to leave a channel for the frequent ferry boats and cargo vessels. The

111

Trellis Bay

holding ground is excellent in some places but poor in others. New moorings are a great addition to Trellis Bay. Beware of underwater obstructions in areas less than 10 feet deep (in the eastern and southern parts of the bay). The area south of Sprat Point is shoal and should be avoided. A sandbar extends due south of Bellamy Cay; take care when passing over in the dinghy.

All vessel captains should note that an underground telephone cable marked by three buoys runs from Conch Shell Point to the building on Bellamy Cay; take care not to pick it up with the anchor.

Ashore

The Last Resort on Bellamy Cay is an absolute must on a cruise around the Virgins. Run by Englishman Tony Snell, his wife Jackie and donkey Vanilla, the Last Resort offers excellent value in buffet-style food and Tony's own brand of entertainment. You will find this evening of hilarity and song unforgettable. Ashore is their gift shop, the Pit Stop, where ferry service to Bellamy Cay is available for those driving to Trellis Bay.

The Conch Shell Point Restaurant can be reached leaving your dinghy by the dock past the public phone, and walking up the small path to the right. Owned by the Dawson family, this restaurant has an excellent reputation for both the food (West Indian and continental) and the service.

For those who wish to learn to windsurf, the BVI Boardsailing School is located on the beach to the south of Bellamy Cay. Windsurfing has become increasingly popular in the Virgin Islands. The steady

winds combined with the consistency of the weather provide an excellent learning environment.

Located on the south shore of Trellis Bay is the Beef Island Guest House with bar and snack bar De Loose Mongoose. Drinks, lunch, snacks and ice cream are available from 8 a.m. to 7:30 p.m. Try their rum punch called the "No-see-um."

Anouk's Designs Workshop, next to the boardsailing school, offers a variety of handcrafted costume jewelry. Ask Anouk and Guy to show you how they create their crafts.

On the beach near the government dock is Flukes Designs workshop and gallery. You are welcome to visit the artists at work, handpainting T-shirts, pictures and maps. Other local crafts are also on display.

If you find you are running out of anything, provisions are available at the brightly coloured Trellis Bay Market. The North Sound Express ferry shuttles guests to North Sound from their dock here convenient to the airport.

Eastern Tortola and the Camanoe Passages

When sailing around Tortola from the north side, several passages are available. The passage between Monkey Point on the southern end of Guana and Tortola is plenty wide and free of hazards. The large rock on Monkey Point is your landmark.

Once through, you may either bear off to starboard and negotiate the channel between Little Camanoe and Beef or continue due east, leaving Little Camanoe to starboard, making the transit between Little Camanoe and Great Camanoe.

The latter should be negotiated in good light and then only under power. There is a small reef on the northeast tip of Little Camanoe and the seas are usually breaking, making it easy to identify. When the ground seas are up during the winter months, the surf breaks heavily on this reef.

The channel, though narrow, carries adequate depth and is free of reef or other hazards. Once clear of the channel, the entrance to Marina Cay to the northeast and Trellis Bay to the southeast are before you.

The passage between Little Camanoe and Beef Island should be negotiated only in good light. Be sure to avoid the reef area that extends from the southwest tip of Little Camanoe. Another hazard in this area is the middle ground or reef that lies two thirds of

the distance between the southwest tip of Great Camanoe and the rocks on the eastern end of Long Bay.

A red nun buoy marks the rocks that lie 100 yards off the westernmost point of Trellis Bay. This buoy should be left to starboard; from here you have good water to enter Trellis Bay or continue to the East.

Anchorages

All the anchorages listed below are recommended as daytime stops only. During the winter when the northerly ground seas are running, none of these are recommended even as comfortable lunch stops.

Tortola / Little Bay

If there is no surf on the beach, this anchorage is a delightful stop. Anchor well off, make sure your hook is well set, then dinghy ashore.

Guana Island, White Bay/ Monkey Point

White Bay is on the southwest shore of Guana Island and is easily spotted by its long white beach. The anchorage is 20–25 feet deep, and care should be taken not to swing into the coral heads inshore. The island was named for the rock formation to the north of White Bay, which resembles the head of an iguana.

This island is private, so exploring ashore is not permissible. Another day stop is in the small cove to the west of Monkey Point. The snorkeling is good and there is a small beach facing east. Power in slowly and drop anchor in 15–20 feet, taking care not to foul the coral heads.

Great Camanoe/Lee Bay

Another little bay used infrequently is Lee Bay on the west coast of Camanoe. The anchorage is deep—35 feet—but the snorkeling is good.

VIRGIN ISLANDS SEARCH & RESCUE IS ...

- **SAVING LIVES** of people in distress at sea.
- **RENDERING ASSISTANCE** as necessary to vessels and persons in distress at sea.
- **ASSISTING INTERNATIONAL ORGANIZATIONS** in the search for missing vessels, aircraft, and people.
- **TRAINING AND EDUCATING** the public in safety at sea.
- **HELPING COORDINATE** the response of the private and government sectors in the BVI in the event of a marine, air, or natural emergency under the guidelines established by the National Emergency Committee.

MEMBER'S BENEFITS AND ANNUAL DUES

Individual - $25   Receives semi-annual newsletter and decal
Family - $40   Receives semi-annual newsletter and decal
Benefactor - $250   Receives semi-annual newsletter, decal and VISAR burgee
Life Member - $500   Receives semi-annual newsletter, decal and VISAR burgee

To become a member or for more information, contact:

VIRGIN ISLANDS SEARCH & RESCUE LTD.
P.O. Box 3042, Road Town, Tortola
British Virgin Islands   (809) 494-4357

Don't Miss Marina Cay...

Recently refurbished, this special island in the BVI offers you secure moorings in a sheltered lagoon, magnificent snorkeling and much more...

● *Casual Dining on the Beach* with your choice of grilled lobster, fish, chicken, steak or the Chef's Special of the Day.

● *A Full Service Fuel Dock, providing Ice, Water, a Launderette and Spotless New Showers* for visiting yachtsmen.

● *Secure Moorings* in the quiet protection of the lagoon.

● *A PUSSER'S Company Store* with one of the best selections of tropical sports & travel clothing and unique accessories for which PUSSER'S has become known.

● *Enjoy a drink at The Sunset Bar,* on the very top of Marina Cay with a splendid 360 degree view of the surrounding islands.

● *Book One of our Six Rooms for a Night's Rest Ashore,* or stay longer if you wish. You'll enjoy our lodgings, perched high over the beach with a spectacular view of the lagoon and the Sir Francis Drake Channel.

● *Some Marina Cay History:* Inhabited occasionally by fishermen, in 1936 Marina Cay became the home of American author Robb White and his bride Rodie. Called to war in 1941, he never returned to the island, but his house still stands and is open daily to visitors. He later wrote the book *"Two On The Isle"*, which became a 1950's movie (and was actually filmed on Marina Cay) starring Sidney Poitier and John Cassavettes.

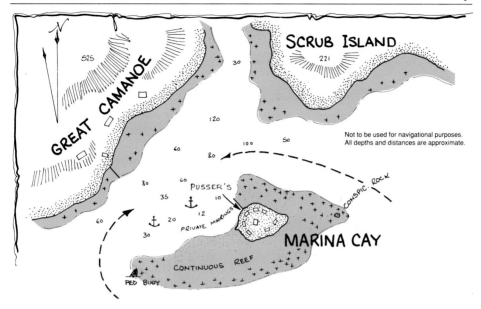

Marina Cay, nestled behind a reef and lying between the islands of Camanoe and Scrub, is easy to enter and provides the visiting yachtsman with good holding in an all-weather anchorage. For those who have read Robb White's book *Our Virgin Island*, it was Marina Cay of which he wrote.

Navigation

Approaching Marina Cay from the east, you have two choices. The recommended route is to go around the north end of the island. There is good water up to the large rock that marks the northeast end of the reef. Leave it to port and pass between Marina Cay and Scrub Island into the anchorage.

Alternatively, approaching from the west, you should favour the southern tip of Great Camanoe. There is a temporary marker marking the southwest end of the reef—the BVI government proposes to have a new red buoy in place sometime in the near future, which you may see. Leaving it well to starboard, you will enter the anchorage. The reef extends south and west of Marina Cay and is highly visible in good light.

If the light is good, it is also possible to approach Marina Cay from the north be-

tween Scrub Island and Great Camanoe. There are reefs lining either side of the channel and you should favour the Great Camanoe side when entering. This anchorage should be negotiated only in good light under power.

Anchoring

Several fully maintained moorings are in place, and should be paid for ashore. The holding ground is reasonable for anchoring.

There is excellent snorkeling behind Marina Cay along the shore of Great Camanoe, and plenty of dinghy exploring around the adjacent islands.

Ashore

Marina Cay has been recently refurbished with a full service fuel dock, offering ice, water, laundry facilities and showers for yachtsmen, as well as the moorings.

Ashore you will find a Pusser's Company store stocked with their unique clothing and accessories. The Sunset Bar ,at the highest point of Marina Cay is a great place for a drink with a spectacular view. The beach offers casual dining at the grill. The island even boasts six rooms for those wanting some time ashore.

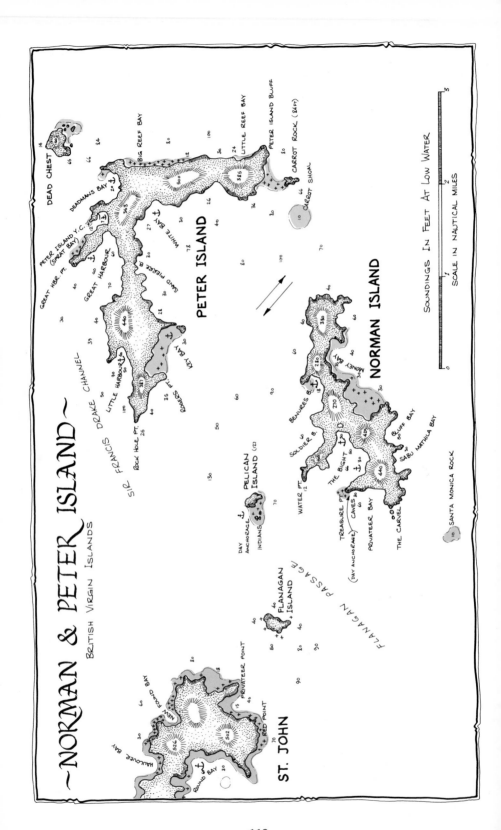

~NORMAN & PETER ISLAND~

British Virgin Islands

PETER ISLAND

NORMAN ISLAND

ST. JOHN

Soundings In Feet At Low Water

Scale in Nautical Miles

Norman is the first island of any size that, together with the islands of Peter, Salt, Cooper and Ginger, form the southern perimeter of the Sir Francis Drake Channel. Often referred to by the locals as "Treasure Island" after the pirates, legends of Norman Island are resplendent with stories of buried treasure. A letter of 1750 stated, "Recovery of the treasure from *Nuestra Senora* buried at Norman Island, comprising $450,000 dollars, plate, cochineal, indigo, tobacco, much dug up by Tortolians."

The main anchorage on Norman Island is the Bight, an exceptionally well-sheltered anchorage.

Navigation

On making an approach to the Bight, the only hazard is the Santa Monica Rocks, which lie to the southwest of the Carvel Point. There is in excess of 6 feet of water over them, but watch out for sea swells. If your approach brings you by Pelican Island, remember that you cannot pass between the Indians and Pelican.

The entrance to the Bight is straightforward and without hazard. Enter between the headlands, keeping in mind that there is shoal water just off both points.

Anchoring

The best anchorage is well up in the northeast corner of the bay. You will need to get far enough in to anchor on the shelf in 15–30 feet of water. The wind tends to funnel down through the hills, giving the impression that the weather is much heavier than it is once you are outside of the bay.

If the anchorage is crowded, an alternative is to move into the area forming the southeast section of the bay.

Ashore

A dinghy trip to Treasure Point and the caves for snorkeling and exploring is a

must. Take your flashlight and dinghy anchor. Good snorkeling also exists on the reef at the eastern end of the harbour just south of the beach.

If you are in the mood for a hike, take the track from the pebble beach to the top of the hill. It should be negotiated only with adequate shoes and clothing to protect you from the brush. Caution is also advised when encountering the local population of wild cattle: Stay clear of them.

The William Thornton, a 1915 black Danish Baltic Trader sailing vessel, has been converted into a bar-restaurant with dinghy dock and is situated in the southeast corner of the Bight. Yachtsmen are very welcome to discuss buried treasure over a drink or a meal.

Other Anchorages

To the west of Water Point (the northernmost point) is a small cove which provides an excellent lunch stop. Approach the anchorage under power and work up to the western end of the bay. Anchor in 25-30 feet of water with plenty of swinging room, as you are likely to be backwinded. If other vessels are anchoring in the bay, it may prove prudent to use a second anchor to reduce the amount of swing.

Treasure Point

Providing there is not much sea running, a delightful daytime stop can be had by anchoring approximately 300–350 yards south of Treasure Point. You will have to anchor in 30–40 feet of water, avoiding damaging the coral bottom. Make sure the anchor is well set before going ashore. You are also likely to be backwinded, so don't be surprised if you end up lying stern to the caves. National Parks Trust moorings are available here for your use with a permit.

The snorkeling is excellent along the mouths of the four caves and two caves are large enough to take the dinghy in. *Caution*: Do not use the outboard engine in this area as there are always swimmers in the water—use the oars.

Benures Bay (or Benares Bay)

When the wind moves around to the south, there is a protected anchorage on the north coast of Norman called Benures Bay. Anchor up in the northeast corner as close to the pebble beach as possible. The bottom is sand and the holding is good. Snorkeling on the western end is pristine.

Pelican Island/The Indians

This should be considered a daytime stop only, but well worth the effort. Do not attempt to sail between Pelican Island and the rocks to the west called the Indians. Approach them from the north and anchor midway between in 10-15 feet of water.

A reef extends between the two and provides excellent snorkeling as does the area immediately around the Indians. As part of the National Parks Trust, this area is protected. You will find National Parks Trust moorings available for use with a permit.

PETER ISLAND

Sailing to the east, the next island is Peter. Captain Thomas Southey wrote his impressions of the island in his chronological history of the West Indies over 100 years ago:

"In May (1806) the author with a party visited Peter's Island, one of those which form the bay of Tortola, a kind of Robinson Crusoe spot, where a man ought to be farmer, carpenter, doctor, fisherman, planter; everything himself."

Little Harbour

There are several good overnight anchorages on Peter Island, the westernmost of which is Little Harbour. Although it doesn't look it on the chart, Little Harbour is a well-protected overnight stop with good holding ground.

When approaching, the first landmark is a white house on the northwest point, which forms the east side of the harbour. This is a private home, and it is important when an-

BVI NATIONAL PARKS TRUST

The British Virgin Islands are currently experiencing rapid development, making it ever more vital to protect the area's wildlife, scenery and areas of natural and historic significance.

The National Parks Trust manages the Territory's parks and protected areas, and works to save the endangered species and reforest Sage Mountain and Gorda Peak. Other activities of the Trust include establishing the Botanical Gardens in Road Town and preserving the historic Copper Mine on Virgin Gorda.

You can assist in this essential work by becoming a Friend of the National Parks Trust. Your donation will enable the Trust to undertake scientific research, conserve wildlife, manage parks and establish protected areas. By joining you will learn more through the Trust's newsletter, bulletin updates and special tours.

Membership dues are $20. Please make your membership check out to:

Friends of the National Parks Trust
Ministry of Natural Resources
Road Town, Tortola • British Virgin Islands

choring in the bay to respect the privacy of the homeowners.

Do not pick up or foul any of the moorings as they are private. Try to keep noise to a reasonable level and do not go ashore as the entire bay is private.

Anchoring

The best spot to anchor is well up in the western reaches of the bay, in 15–25 feet over a sandy bottom. You will be back-winded, so check your swinging room relative to other vessels and use two anchors if necessary. If the anchorage is crowded, anchor close to shore on the southern coast of the bay in order to stay in 25–35 feet of water. The centre drops off rapidly.

Great Harbour

Great Harbour is considered too deep to make a worthwhile anchorage; however, if you can spend the time, there are two shallow areas and the rewards are those of private seclusion.

It is important not to get in the way of local fishermen who run their nets out into the bay each afternoon. For this reason, it is recommended that you find the 3 Fathom Spot on the northwest shore, about one-third of the way in from the point. While the fishing is going on, the least amount of activity in the bay the better. After the fishermen have gone, you can bring the boat in closer to shore.

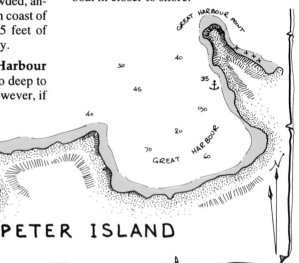

Not to be used for navigational purposes.
All depths and distances are approximate.

PETER ISLAND

Sprat Bay

Peter Island Yacht Harbour

Sprat Bay is easy to spot from the channel by the row of roofs that comprise the accommodation section of the Peter Island Hotel and Yacht Harbour. The entire bay, Deadman's Bay and several beaches on the south coast are part of the complex.

Docking space is available, as are water, fuel, ice, showers, etc. The marina stands by on VHF channel 16. Dinner reservations should be made in advance.

Navigation

When making your entrance to Sprat Bay, it is important to familiarize yourself with the location of the reefs on either side of the channel. The main reef extends north and slightly west of the main bulkhead, so do not get too close to the west-

ern shore.

Entering on a heading of 165 degrees magnetic, you can either tie up to the dock, which requires dropping an anchor and lying to the dock stern-to, or anchor behind the dock in 6–12 feet of water. Do not go too far into the southern end of the bay, as it is shallow. Six moorings are now located in Sprat Bay, which gives more room than if boats were anchored there. After picking a moorings up, check with the dockmaster ashore.

Ashore

The Peter Island Yacht Harbour and Hotel complex was originally built by Norwegians and was done in excellent taste. The 40-unit hotel and restaurant

122

extends along the bulkhead. Reservations for breakfast, lunch and dinner should be made at the front desk, and yachtsmen are requested to adjust their attire to suit the tone of the hotel.

Dive BVI has a base here for those interested in diving and/or airfills. The Beachbar and Deadman's Bay are favourites of yachtsmen. In season, they often hold beach barbecues with bands and dancing.

There are numerous walks to take, but be sure to take the short walk to the top of the hill to the eastern side of the harbour for a delightful, panoramic view of the channel and Dead Chest Island.

Deadman's Bay

The easternmost anchorage on Peter Island, Deadman's Bay is a beautiful day stop, but you will feel the effects of the surge that makes its way around the northeastern point.

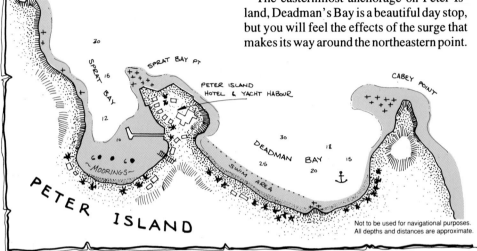

Not to be used for navigational purposes.
All depths and distances are approximate.

123

Move right up into the extreme southeastern corner when anchoring. The bottom is grassy and it is sometimes difficult to get the anchor set, but the snorkeling is excellent and the ideal, white sand beach is fringed with palm trees.

The beach to the west is for the use of hotel guests only, and yachtsmen are requested to respect the line of buoys designating the swimming area.

The South Coast of Peter Island

There are two anchorages on the south side of Peter that are worthy of mention, but some regard to sea and weather conditions should be noted when planning the anchorage.

White Bay

Named for the white sand beach, White Bay is a reasonable anchorage when the ground seas are not running. Anchor close to shore, but be careful of backwinding.

Key Point

There is an excellent anchorage to the west of Key Point. Make your approach from the south, favouring the key side in order to clear the rock on the west side of the entrance. Anchor between the point and Key Cay in 18 feet of water.

The snorkeling is excellent and the anchorage is open to the prevailing breeze, keeping it free from bugs.

SALT ISLAND

Named for the island's three evaporation ponds, Salt Island was once an important source of salt for the ships of Her Majesty, the Queen. The island and its salt ponds, although belonging to the Crown, are operated by the local populace. Each year at the start of the harvest, one bag of salt is accepted by the Governor as annual rent. In 1845, a barrel was quoted at one shilling and, although inflation has taken its toll, salt is still sold to visitors.

The settlement just off Salt Pond Bay, is deserving of a visit.

Local Salt Islanders will be pleased to show you around the salt ponds and explain how the harvesting is done.

Anchoring

Both of the Salt Island anchorages are affected by a surge and consequently should be considered day anchorages only.

Salt Pond Bay is clear of hazards, but the prudent skipper is advised to ensure that his anchor is well set before going ashore. Anchor in 10-20 feet of water.

Lee Bay is another alternative for those wishing to dive the *Rhone*. Located on the west shore, Lee Bay is not very well protected.

Moorings are available here for boats under 50 feet to pick up in order to dinghy over to the *Rhone*. Anchoring over the *Rhone* is strictly forbidden and is protected by the National Parks Trust. Constant anchoring by boats has destroyed the coral.

The National Parks Trust has installed moorings for the use of permit holders *only*, at the site of the *Rhone*.

It is suggested that you dinghy over from Lee Bay, drop off snorkelers and use the dinghy mooring line available.

Watch out for divers!!

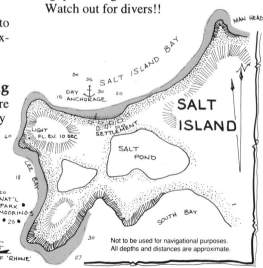

Not to be used for navigational purposes.
All depths and distances are approximate.

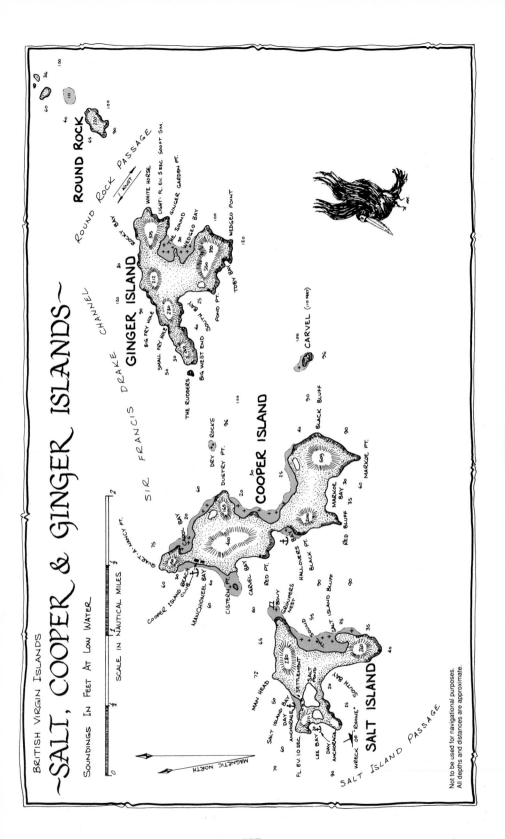

British Virgin Islands

~SALT, COOPER & GINGER ISLANDS~

Soundings In Feet At Low Water

SCALE IN NAUTICAL MILES

ROUND ROCK

ROUND ROCK PASSAGE

1 KNOT

SIR FRANCIS DRAKE CHANNEL

GINGER ISLAND

BIG FRY HOLE
SMALL FRY HOLE
THE RUDDERS
BIG WEST END
SOUTH
POND PT.
TOBY BAY
WEDGED POINT
NEDGEO BAY
THE SOUND
GINGER GARDEN PT.
WHITE HORSE
LIGHT. FL. EV. 5 SEC. 50 FT 5M.

COOPER ISLAND

QUART-A-NANCY PT.
CAROL BAY
COOPER ISLAND BEACH CLUB
MANCHIONEEL BAY
CISTERN PT.
CARVEL BAY
RED PT.
BLACK PT.
HALLOVERS
DRY ROCKS
DUSTZY PT.
MARKOE BAY
RED BLUFF
MARKOE PT.
BLACK BLUFF

CARVEL (110 FEET)

MAGNETIC NORTH

MAN HEAD
SALT ISLAND BAY
DAY ANCHORAGE
SETTLEMENT
SALT POND
LEE BAY
DAY ANCHORAGE
WRECK OF "RHONE"
SOUTH BAY
SALT ISLAND BLUFF
THE SOUND
GROUPERS NEST

SALT ISLAND

SALT ISLAND PASSAGE

FL. EV. 10 SEC.

Not to be used for navigational purposes.
All depths and distances are approximate.

125

Salt Island

Jim Scheiner

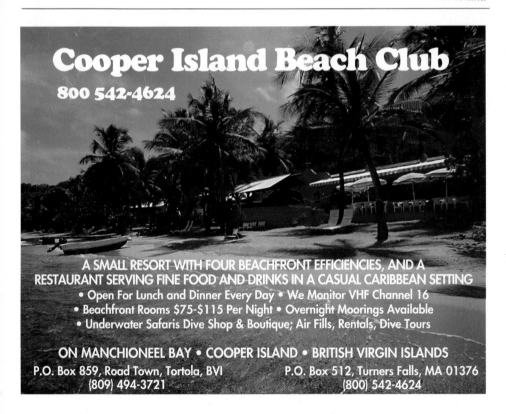

As you sail between Salt and Cooper Islands, you will see a rock off the northeast point, marked by a green buoy with a red stripe. You can go to either side of the marker as there is 20 feet of water.

The principal anchorage on Cooper Island is Manchioneel Bay located on the northwest shore. When approaching the bay from the north, around Quart-O-Nancy Point, you will be on your ear one minute and becalmed the next. The point shelters the wind entirely, and we would recommend lowering sail and powering up to the anchorage.

Anchoring

There are several maintained moorings off of Cooper Island that are available for any vessel's use at the cost of $15 per night. You may pay ashore at the Beach Club.

If you are anchoring, the bottom is covered in patches of sea grass and, consequently, it is sometimes difficult to get the anchor set.

You can anchor almost the entire length of the beach in 10–25 feet of water, but it is advisable to minimize swinging room.

Ashore

There is a good, sandy beach fringed with palm trees. To the right of the main jetty is the Cooper Island Beach Club, run by Steve Pardoe and Toby Holmes. The menu is varied and the setting unique. Both lunch and dinner are served daily.

Don't miss Underwater Safaris' boutique and air-fill station. Underwater Safaris also runs a boat between Cooper Island and the Moorings dock. Call by phone or VHF 16 by 5:30 p.m. for reservations.

Four new beachfront efficiencies are available at very reasonable rates.

For some excellent snorkeling, take the dinghy to the South of Manchioneel Bay to Cistern Point.

Caution:

Manchioneel Bay is named for the tree that grows there which produces a small,

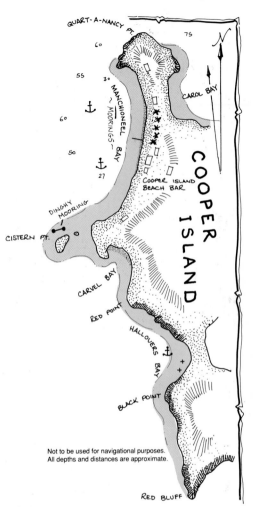

Not to be used for navigational purposes.
All depths and distances are approximate.

green apple. *Don't eat the apples from the manchioneel tree— they are poisonous!*

Other Anchorages

If the sea conditions are light, there are two day anchorages just to the south of Manchioneel Bay: Carver Bay under Cistern Point; and Haulover Bay.

By tucking yourself up in the southeast corner of the bay, the surge will be minimal. The island of Ginger has no tenable anchorages.

British Virgin Islands

~VIRGIN GORDA~
(SOUTH)

SOUNDINGS IN FEET AT LOW WATER

SCALE IN NAUTICAL MILES

Not to be used for navigational purposes.
All depths and distances are approximate.

128

VIRGIN GORDA

panorama
British Virgin Islands

The "Fat" Virgin, as Columbus irreverently called it because of its resemblance from seaward to a fat woman lying on her back, was once the capital of the British Virgins with a population of 8,000 persons. The island is approximately 10 miles long with high peaks at the north and central areas. All land over 1000 feet high on Virgin Gorda has been designated National Parks land to preserve its natural beauty.

Laurence Rockefeller has built the Little Dix Bay Hotel, another of his fine resorts, and also the Virgin Gorda Yacht Harbour in St. Thomas Bay.

The Baths

When planning a trip around the islands, it is essential to include the Baths. Located on the southwest tip of Virgin Gorda, the Baths are a most unusual formation of large granite boulders. Where the sea washes in between the huge rocks, large pools have been created, where shafts of light play upon the water, creating a dramatic effect. The beach adjacent to the Baths is white and sandy and the snorkeling excellent.

the slot in the rocks and follow the trail. Do not leave valuables in your dinghy! There is excellent snorkeling around the point from the Baths south to Devil's Bay, but the beaches to the north are private. A fabulous new trail leads inconspicuously between the Baths and Devil's Bay. Wear reef shoes—it can be slippery, but is well worth the challenge.

Navigation

When approaching from the Sir Francis Drake Channel, the first landmark will be the large rock formations. There are fine, white sandy beaches of varying sizes and the Baths are located at the second beach from the westernmost tip of Virgin Gorda. If there is a ground sea running, it is advisable to keep sailing into the Yacht Harbour and take a taxi to the Baths.

Anchoring

It is possible to anchor all along the coast, but the preferred spot for landing people ashore is directly out from the beach in 30–35 feet of water. The bottom is rock and coral, so check your anchor with a snorkel prior to going ashore. If anchoring further north, be mindful of Burrows Rock, which extends 200 feet out from the small headland at the south end of Valley Trunk Bay.

Ashore

If there is any sea at all, landing a dinghy can prove tricky. Take ashore only those articles that you don't mind getting wet, and wrap cameras and valuables in plastic bags. The entrance to the Baths is unmarked but at the southern end of the beach under the palm trees. Make your way in between

Not to be used for navigational purposes.
All depths and distances are approximate.

Virgin Gorda Yacht Harbour

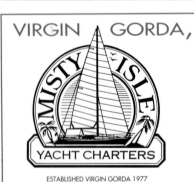

132

Spanish Town / Virgin Gorda Yacht Harbour

Once the capital of the BVI, Spanish Town is still the major settlement on the island. Although opinions vary, it is commonly thought that Spanish Town is so called for the number of Spanish settlers who came to mine the copper at Copper Mine Point early in the 16th century. The mines were still working until 1867, and it is estimated that some 10,000 tons of copper ore were exported.

The Virgin Gorda Yacht Harbour is located in the middle of Spanish Town (or "The Valley") and is the hub of shopping and boating activity on the south end of the island. Misty Isle Yacht Charters makes its home in this marina complex.

Navigation

To enter the Yacht Harbour, you should familiarize yourself with the location of the reef that parallels the shoreline. Approach the harbour on a line with the prominent jetty in St. Thomas Bay. The first buoy will be on your port hand and be green. Immediately to starboard, you will notice a red buoy. Leave it to starboard, as you would with the U.S. system of red right returning.

As you round the red buoy, you will turn approximately 90 degrees to starboard and pass between two more sets of buoys before entering the harbour. Once inside, you may dock at the fuel dock or pull into a slip and seek the dockmaster.

There is no anchoring inside the yacht harbour.

Ashore

Virgin Gorda Yacht Harbour is owned and operated by Rock Resorts. The manager of the complex is Lee Beauchamps.

Customs and immigration services are available dockside from 0830 to 1630 weekdays and from 0900 to 1230 on weekends.

The complex offers such facilities as a bank, drug store, bakery, gift shops and markets. The Ship's Store is a complete chandlery with a full line of marine equipment and accessories.

This full-service marina offers dockage for 110 vessels carying a maximum draft of 10 feet. It also operates a full-service boatyard and dry storage facilities adjacent to the harbour.

The boatyard offers complete services including awlgrip and osmosis treatment for boats. The lift has 60-ton capability and can handle vessels up to a 22-foot beam and 10-foot draft. The boatyard manager is Keith Thomas.

For a lunch or dinnertime stop, the Bath and Turtle offers excellent food.

For divers, Dive BVI operates a full-service dive shop here, offering daily tours

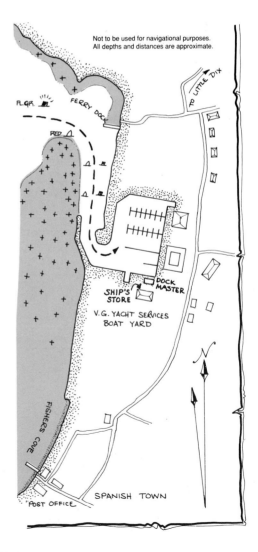

Not to be used for navigational purposes. All depths and distances are approximate.

as well as rendezvous dives from the yacht harbour.

Little Dix Bay Hotel is a taxi ride away and those wishing to look around the grounds are welcome for drinks and luncheon. Reservations are required for dinner. Jackets are not required, but shorts are not allowed in the dining room after 6 p.m. — appropriate casual attire, please.

Chez Michelle, a 5-minute walk from the Yacht Harbour, is known for its excellent dinners served from 6:30-9:30 p.m. Further up the road to the north is the Olde Yard Inn, specialising in seafood and French desserts. Visitors will be duly impressed by not only the food, but the lovely garden gazebo.

While here, don't miss a trip to Copper Mine Point on the southeast tip of Virgin Gorda. The Fischer's Cove restaurant on the beach serves breakfast, lunch and dinner in casual surroundings and is a 5-minute walk from the marina.

To experience the sunset, visit the Mad Dog Bar located at the roundabout to the Baths. The quaint, West Indian-style building with continuous cool breezes reflects the peacefulness of the island.

When leaving the yacht harbour and St. Thomas Bay and heading north to Gorda Sound, be sure to give Colison Point a wide berth, as the rocks extend well out from the land into the water.

134

During the summer months or when the ground seas are down, there is a very nice daytime anchorage in Savannah Bay. To enter the bay, just north of Blowing Point, you must have good light in order to see the reefs. The entrance between the reef is at the southern end of the bay.

Watch for the small reef that extends from the headland on your starboard hand and work your way around the coral heads that comprise the centre reef. Once inside, you can anchor in 15-25 feet of water and the snorkeling is excellent.

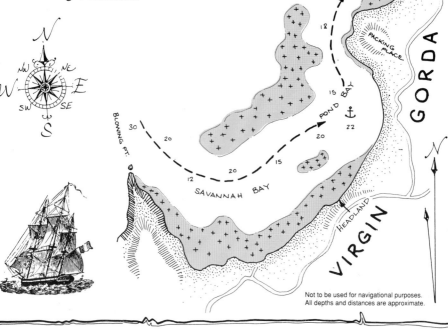

Not to be used for navigational purposes.
All depths and distances are approximate.

Long Bay is another day anchorage that is tenable only when there is no ground sea. Located just to the southeast of Mountain Point, this anchorage is easy to approach, and anchoring is on a sandy bottom in 15-25 feet of water.

The Dogs

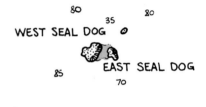

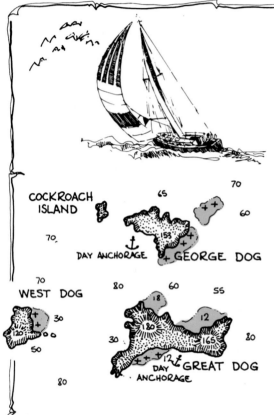

Great, George, West and Seal Dogs lie to the west of Virgin Gorda, and have good water all around them. They are all in a protected area of the National Parks Trust. It is not possible to sail or power between West and East Seal Dogs. If there is no sea running there are two good daytime anchorages in the lee of Great Dog and George Dog.

On George Dog, the best anchorage is in the bay to the west of Kitchen Point. You will have to anchor in 25-35 feet of water and will probably be backwinded, so check your anchor carefully.

Great Dog

Depending on the weather, there are two possible anchorages. The most common one is on the south side of the island. Here you will have to anchor in 20-30 feet of water on a rocky bottom. The second spot is off the beach on the northeast coast.

The snorkeling is excellent in both locations, but don't anchor here during ground seas.

WELCOME
CRUISING YACHTSMEN

Visit The Bitter End Yacht Club
"A world class sailing resort!"

Join us for a meal...a day...overnight. We've everything for your enjoyment.

Excellent deep water anchorage. 70 moorings. Garbage pickup available. Deep draft dockage at our Quarterdeck Marina for yachts up to 100 ft. 110V hookups, or 220V metered. Showers on dock. Ice. Water. Gas.

Yachtsman's favorite rendezvous. Clubhouse Steak and Seafood Grille. English Carvery. Champagne breakfasts. Club lunches. Gourmet dinners. English Pub at the Emporium, draft beer and sandwiches. **NEW** entertainment. Disco with Jimmy the DJ. Reggae with our own Steel Band. Eldon John twice weekly with mellow calypso guitar. Free TV and video movies nightly!

Shopping ashore. Browse and shop the Reeftique, "smartest little shop in the BVI." Gear, coverups, gifts. **NEW** Captain B's Trading Post. Film, charts, snorkeling gear, Caribbean art. The Emporium...stock your larder, liquor package store. Wines, staples, fresh vegetables and fruit, eggs, ice cream, our famous Entrees to go!

Activities! Rent our day sailers and sailboards. Book scuba with famed Kilbrides. Daily snorkeling trips. Excursions to Anegada. View deep in submersible Flipper. Freshwater swimming pool with bar and luncheon service. Two beautiful beaches.

Luxury Accommodations. A full resort, 50 duplex cottages, fleet of charter boats.

Come see us when island cruising. Register for a Bitter End Decal and pick up a copy of our latest North Soundings newspaper.

 ## The Bitter End Yacht Club
North Sound, Virgin Gorda, BVI
Marina dockage or dinner reservations: 494-2746
or Standby VHF Channel 16

137

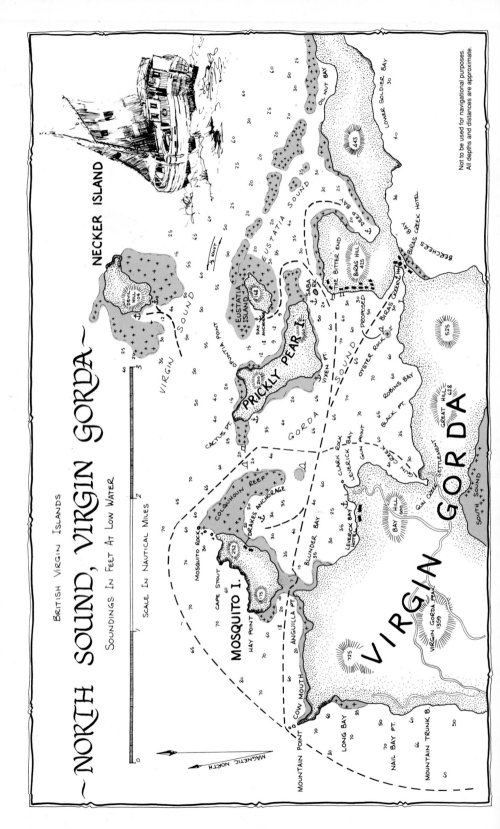

British Virgin Islands

~NORTH SOUND, VIRGIN GORDA~

Soundings In Feet At Low Water

Scale In Nautical Miles

NECKER ISLAND

Not to be used for navigational purposes.
All depths and distances are approximate.

EUSTATIA SOUND

EUSTATIA ISLAND

OIL NUT BAY

LOWER SOLDIER BAY

DEEP BAY

THE BITTER END

SABA

BRAS HILL 425

BRAS CREEK HOTEL

BEECHES CREEK HOTEL

PROPOSED

OYSTER ROCK

VIXEN PT.

GORDA SOUND

ROBINS BAY

BLACK PT.

GREAT HILL 628

525

PRICKLY PEAR I.

OPUNTIA POINT

CACTUS PT.

COLQUHOUN REEF

DRAKES ANCHORAGE

MOSQUITO ROCK

BLUNDER BAY

CLARK ROCK

LEVERICK BAY

GUN POINT

CLEEK

GUN CREEK

SETTLEMENT

BAY HILL

SOUTH SOUND

MOSQUITO I.

CAPE STOUT

HAY POINT

ANGUILLA PT.

COW MOUTH

MOUNTAIN POINT

LEVERICK BAY HOTEL

VIRGIN GORDA PEAK 1359

725

LONG BAY

NAIL BAY PT.

MOUNTAIN TRUNK B.

VIRGIN GORDA

VIRGIN SOUND

MAGNETIC NORTH

138

VIRGIN GORDA
Approaches to North Sound

North Sound

Located at the northern end of Virgin Gorda, the Sound is a large bay protected all around by islands and reefs. It is an ideal place to spend several days exploring the reefs and relaxing.

There are numerous restaurants and marina complexes here to suit all tastes.

Navigation
Northern Entrance Via Calquhoun Reef

When making your approach to the Sound from the north, you will easily be able to recognize Mosquito Rock just to the north of the tip of Mosquito Island.

Leaving the rock well to starboard, head for the green can buoy that marks the port side of the channel when entering. This will keep you clear of both reefs. Leaving the green can to port, you will proceed past a red cone or nun to starboard.

If you are proceeding to Drakes Anchorage, there is another red buoy marking the lower end of the reef. It is imperative that you leave it to starboard in order not to find yourself aground. Once past the buoy, you can proceed directly to the anchorage with clear water.

If you are heading for Bitter End or Biras Creek, continue into the sound past the sandspit on Vixen Point and then head for the cottages on the hill that comprise the accommodations at Bitter End.

There is one other navigational hazard in the sound and that is Oyster Rock, which is to the west of the Biras Creek anchorage. The rock will be marked with the new "B" International System lateral marker, a red cone buoy with a green band. This is on the list of proposed buoys in the BVI.

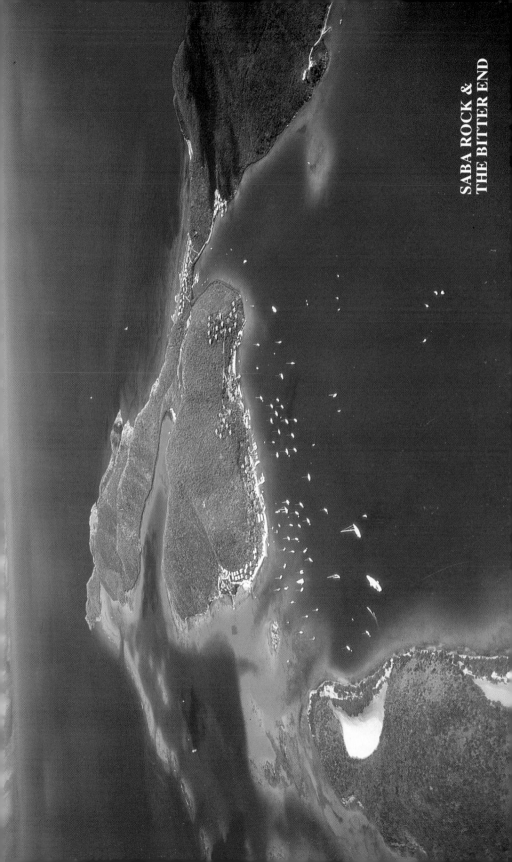

SABA ROCK &
THE BITTER END

LEVERICK BAY

RESORT & MARINA

- 10 Slips & 36 Moorings
- 110 & 208 Volt Electricity
- Fuel, Fresh Water & Ice
- Freshwater Showers & Laundry Facilities
- Fresh Water Swimming P & Tennis
- PUSSER'S Restaurants, B & Company Store
- Full Service Dive Shop
- Supermarket
- Spa
- Caribbean Arts & Crafts
- Water Sports Instruction Equipment Rental

VIRGIN GORDA VILLA RENTALS

- Air-conditioned Guest Rooms
- Air-conditioned Condominiums
- Individually Styled Villas, Many With Pools at Leverick Bay and Around the Island
- All Resort Facilities Available to Villa Guests

1-809-49-57421

Dial ISLAND FAX (404) 399-3077
Select Code #1130...For More Information.

Anguilla Point Entrance

This entrance is tricky but, in fact, can carry 6 feet; however, it is recommended that vessels of over 5-foot draft should use the northern approach, and *bareboat charters not use this entrance at all.* During ground seas and heavy swells, it is always advisable to use the northern passage.

Entrance from the west is recommended under power only. There is a reef extending from Hay Point on Mosquito Island, so make sure your course is laid a little south of east, or approximately 95 degrees magnetic, which should bring you in half way between Anguilla Point to starboard and Mosquito Island to port.

In order to stay in the deepest water, lay a course from the centre of the cut to Gnat Point southeast until you clear the sandbar.

When leaving the sound, there is a range that can be utilized. By placing the tip of Anguilla Point in the "Cows Mouth," a hollow in Mountain Point, follow it until clear of the point and shoal water to starboard and then head for Seal Dog Rocks.

Drake's Anchorage, Mosquito Island

Located on the east shore of Mosquito Island under Colquhoun Reef, Drakes Anchorage has long been one of the favourite North Sound stops. Anchor off the docks in 15-20 feet of water. The holding ground is good and the prevailing wind keeps the anchorage cool and bug-free.

Ten moorings installed and maintained by Moor Seacure are available for use. Payment may be made at the restaurant. Ashore, you will find an informal hotel and restaurant featuring West Indian and French cuisine. Call on VHF 16 for reservations.

Visitors are reminded that this is a private island and the facilities are reserved for the guests; however, you are very welcome at this superb restaurant. There is excellent snorkeling on the reef west of Anguilla Point.

Leverick Bay

Located on the northern shore of Virgin Gorda, Leverick Bay is the newest recre-

ational centre here. The resort has restaurants, gift shops, food market, women's body salon, pool, beach, and full-service marina with fuel, ice, water, showers and laundromat. A fuel fill-up of 25 gallons will get you a free bottle of Pusser's Rum. Pussers Company Store and the elegant Terrace Restaurant with Victorian-style bar offer a great view of North Sound and the surrounding islands. The Beach Bar adjacent to the pool area serves pizza, hamburgers, shepherd's pie, ice cream and frozen tropical drinks, as well as breakfasts.

Weekends are fun at Leverick Bay with a band on Saturday and a beach barbecue, volleyball and steel band music on Sunday.

Gun Creek

To the east of Leverick Bay around Gnat Point, Gun Creek provides a protected anchorage. Ashore, there is the native settlement of Creek Village and well worth the time to explore.

Biras Creek

A very protected anchorage fringed by mangroves, Biras Creek has been developed by Norwegian interests who have built a resort complex at the head of the harbour. There is dockage available; moorings are also for rent from the harbourmaster. Biras Creek Hotel is noted for its fine cuisine; dinner reservations are required.

Bitter End

Located on John O'Point, the Bitter End is a recreation centre resort hotel, with restaurants and marina with overnight dockage, guest rooms and moorings. Visiting yachtsmen are welcome to pick up a moor-

ing for $15 per night. Garbage pickup from your boat is available for a nominal fee..

If you are anchoring, please keep clear of the moorings (garbage collection may be available for anchored boats as well). There is room behind the moorings and to the northwest of Saba Rock.

There are two sets of buoys marking the approach for the North Sound Express ferry boat. Avoid anchoring near this channel to keep it clear for ferry traffic.

Visitors are welcome at the clubhouse restaurant for breakfast, lunch and dinner and may join the activities, windsurfing rentals and Anegada excursions, book dive trips, and use the beach, bar, gift shop and Emporium bakery-deli with its English Pub and complete package store.

Dinner reservations are required and may be made via VHF channel 16. Mary Jo Ryan is your hostess. The Bitter End is also headquarters of the Nick Trotter Sailing School.

Saba Rock

Saba Rock is the home of Bert and Gayla Kilbride. The Kilbrides have turned their former home into the Pirate's Pub, an informal place which welcomes yachtsmen to have a drink and swap stories, followed up with some barbecued ribs or chicken. The Pub is open daily from 10 a.m.

All diving trips should be booked through the Bitter End Yacht Club.

Eustatia Sound

It is not recommended to take your vessel east of Saba Rock owing to the reefs and

numerous coral heads. It does, however, offer good exploring by dinghy and the snorkeling is excellent.

Take the dinghy around to Deep Bay or Nut Bay or take the dinghy anchor and snorkel the reef extending to Eustatia Island, which is private.

Necker Island

There is a day anchorage on the northeast shore of Necker, but it must be approached from the south (see sketch chart) in order to pass through the reef. Once again, the snorkeling is excellent! Do not go ashore, however: this is a private island.

ANEGADA, The Drowned Island

In contrast to the mountainous volcanic formation of the remainder of the Virgin Islands, Anegada is comprised of coral and limestone, and at its highest point is 28 feet above sea level. Created by the movement between the Atlantic and Caribbean plates, which meet to the northeast of the island, Anegada is 9 miles long and fringed with mile after mile of sandy beaches.

Horseshoe Reef, which extends 10 miles to the southeast, has claimed over 300 known wrecks, which provide ex-citement and adventure for scuba diving enthusiasts who descend on them to discover their secrets. The reef also provides a home for some of the largest fish in the area, including lobster and conch. The numerous coral heads and tricky currents that surround the island, along with the difficulty in identifying landmarks and subsequent reef areas, make it off limits to many charter companies.

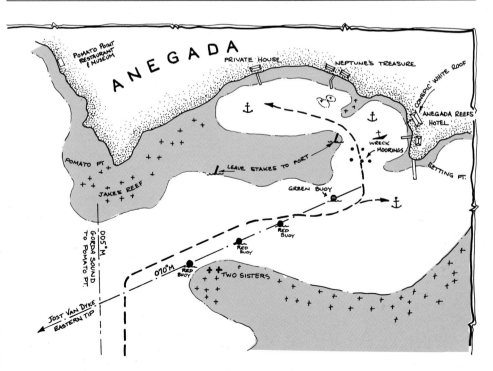

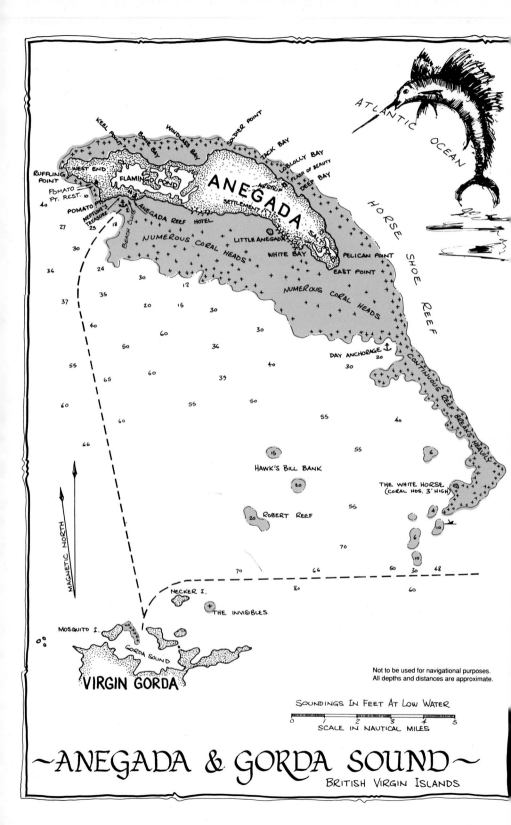

ATLANTIC OCEAN

RUFFLING POINT
KEEL PT.
BONE BAY
WINDLASS BAY
SOLDIER POINT
JACK BAY
LOBLOLLY BAY
FLASH OF BEAUTY
DEEP BAY
WEST END
FLAMINGO POND
AIRSTRIP
ANEGADA
SETTLEMENT
HORSE SHOE REEF

POMATO
PT. REST. 10
40
POMATO PT.
NEPTUNE'S
TREASURE 25
27
18
ANEGADA REEF HOTEL
BEACH CLUB
ANEGADA REEF
NUMEROUS CORAL HEADS
LITTLE ANEGADA
WHITE BAY
SALT
PELICAN POINT
EAST POINT
NUMEROUS CORAL HEADS
CONTINUOUS REEF BREAKS HEAVILY

30
36
24
30
12
37
35
20
15
30
40
60
30
50
36
55
65
60
39
DAY ANCHORAGE 20
30
60
55
50
60
55
40
66
55
6
HAWK'S BILL BANK
15
20
THE WHITE HORSE
(CORAL HDS. 3' HIGH)
20
ROBERT REEF
55
4
10
6
70
10
MAGNETIC NORTH
70
66
50
30
48
NECKER I.
80
60
THE INVISIBLES
MOSQUITO I.
GORDA SOUND

VIRGIN GORDA

Not to be used for navigational purposes.
All depths and distances are approximate.

SOUNDINGS IN FEET AT LOW WATER

0   1   2   3   4   5
SCALE IN NAUTICAL MILES

~ANEGADA & GORDA SOUND~
BRITISH VIRGIN ISLANDS

ANEGADA
West End

Navigation

Because of its profile and surrounding coralheads, Anegada should be approached only in good weather conditions and with the sun overhead in order to see the bottom. Leave North Sound between 8 - 9:30 a.m. to arrive at the west end of Anegada with good light to see the reefs. Steer a course of 005 degrees magnetic which will take you from Mosquito Rock to Pomato Point. The 1-2 knot current will set you down to the west. Approaching the island, you will see coral patches, but if you are on course, they will have 10 - 20 feet of water over them. Owing to the low elevation of the island, the palm trees and pines will be sighted first. Do not turn off course until you have identified Pomato and Setting Points and located the red buoy marking the entry into Setting Point. When in line with the eastern tip of Jost Van Dyke head in towards Anegada steering 050 degrees magnetic (no need to go further west).

Keep to port of the first red buoy, maintaining 070 degrees, from the reds (3 of them) keeping all reds to your starboard until you approach the green. Go east (leave the green buoy to port) of the green and as you come around the green, steer into the anchorage on 015 degrees magnetic. If in doubt call Anegada Reef Hotel or Neptune's Treasure on VHF channel 16 for assistance.

Anchoring

Yachts drawing over 7 feet should anchor off the commercial dock which is in line with the green buoy in 10 - 15 feet of water. All others can make their way into the inner harbour, watching out for the coral heads that extend out from the small headland between the hotel and Neptune's Treasure and the coral off the dock (see chart). Drop the hook in 8 - 12 feet of water on a good, sandy bottom. If picking up a mooring buoy, the outer buoys are for boats of 7 foot draft and the inner ones for 6 feet and less. Please go into the hotel straightaway and pay the appropriate mooring fee. If anchoring do not foul the area for boats wishing to pick up moorings.

Ashore

Anegada has a lot to offer the visiting yachtsman. The hotel rents bicycles and vehicles and operates a taxi service which takes guests across the island to the great snorkeling beaches of Loblolly Bay. Flamingos, recently reintroduced to Anegada, may be seen on the salt ponds, and a nature trail has been opened around the Bones Bite area where you may spot some iguanas, also look for the wild orchids on the west end of the island.

If you want dinghy fuel, you can walk through the hotel gate to Kenneth's Gas Station. Ice is available at the hotel and there is also a fishing tackle shop which sells bait, lures, rods, etc. for the enthusiastic fisherman, who wishes to fish the bonefishing flats. There are several bars and restaurants in the village, known as the Settlement and on some of the beaches. However, most of the beaches are deserted and you need to take some cold drinks with you.

In the evening, a dinghy pulls into Setting Point anchorage selling delightfully

fragrant fresh breads and cookies to the boats at anchor.

The Anegada Reef Hotel is owned and managed by Lowell Wheatley and Susan Robinson. There are 20 units and an informal bar on the beach. Dinner is served by reservation, VHF 16. The food is excellent, and barbecued lobster is one of the house specialties. A 46-foot sportsfisherman is available for charter for those wishing to try some deep sea fishing. The hotel has a compressor for airfills, and tanks can also be rented.

Neptune's Treasure, a little farther along the beach, also serves dinner, specializing in lobster, conch and local grouper; accommodations are now under construction.

Try the Anegada Beach Club for seafood and lobster, also located in the Setting Point anchorage.

Snorkeling on and around the reefs of the north side of the island is spectacular and worth the ride. It is a good idea to take along liquid refreshment as well as a good sun block and a T-shirt. Loblolly Bay is a fabulous place to snorkel. Lunch is served there daily at the Flash of Beauty or the Big Bamboo.

Note: The BVI Government has declared Horseshoe Reef off limits for anchoring, fishing or collecting conch, in hopes that the environmental holiday will help the sealife proliferate.

UNITED STATES VIRGIN ISLANDS

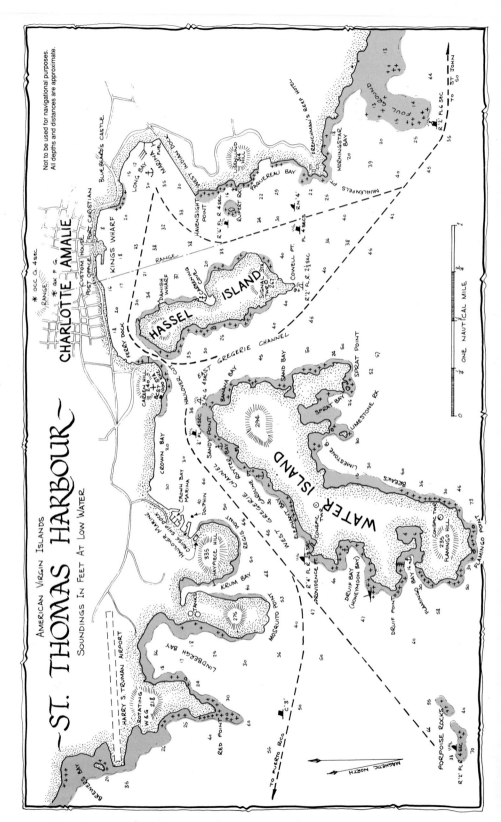

ST. THOMAS HARBOUR
U.S. Virgin Islands

Charlotte Amalie/ St. Thomas Harbour

Named after a Danish Queen, Charlotte Amalie is the capital city of the U.S. Virgin Islands and a major seaport. Used extensively over the centuries as a haunt of pirates and privateers, St. Thomas was declared a freeport by the Danes; thus, enabling the sale of goods, livestock and ships acquired in honest trade or under the flag of piracy.

The town still has many of the original Danish buildings and mansions on the hillside overlooking the harbour. Picturesque alleys and stairways will lead you from large mansions to traditional West Indian houses surrounded by gardens.

Sheltered in all weather, St. Thomas harbour tends to have a surge, especially when the wind moves around to the south, making it uncomfortable for small boats. Since it is a commercial harbour, swimming is not recommended.

Navigation

If you are making your approach from the east, you will pass the red nun buoy marking Packet Rock, which lies due north of Buck Island. It is best to stay well off the coast.

Another red nun "R.2" marks the shoal ground that lies to the south east of the harbour entrance. You will also be able to see the Frenchman's Reef Hotel that sits atop Muhenfels Point.

As you continue in, you will pick up RN'4' and R6 marking Rupert Rocks. Leaving them to starboard, you can head directly for the anchorage.

Once inside the harbour, you will note several buoys off the West Indian dock. These designate the turning area for the many cruise ships that come and go on a daily basis and the anchorage lies to northeast of them.

Anchoring

The traditional anchorage for yachts is off the Yacht Haven Marina and Hotel complex. Take care not to foul any of the private moorings that have been laid down by the charter yachts operating out of the harbour. If you wish to tie up to the dock, contact the dockmaster via VHF or pull up to the fuel dock for slip assignment.

It is not recommended to tie up to quay in Charlotte Amalie as the surge is both dangerous and uncomfortable.

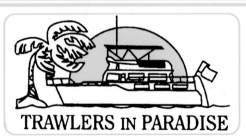

Ashore/
Yacht Haven Marina and Surrounding District

Customs clearance can be carried out wharfside at the ferry dock at the west end of the harbour; the hours are from 8 a.m.-5 p.m., Monday through Saturday. Of course, these hours are subject to change. If you have all U.S. citizens aboard, you may call 774-5539 to request clearance by phone. Your request may be denied, but it may be worth a shot to save you some time.

The Yacht Haven Marina and hotel complex offer many facilities for the visiting yachtsman, including fuel, dockage, showers, water, electricity, cable TV and laundry. Should you require any equipment for your vessel, Island Marine is located at the base of the pier .

For food and drink, several restaurants and bars and a small market, the Fruit Bowl are located within the complex.

V.I. Canvas features canvas goods, repairs, boat cushions and bags. Across from them is a clothing boutique. Underwater Safaris can service your diving needs. Within walking distance are two large supermarkets, Pueblo and Grand Union, for provisions. Many other shops and restaurants line the area, servicing the cruise ship passengers.

The Yacht Haven Marina office is a good source for directions and information. Yacht Haven is home to many charter yachts. The Virgin Island Charter Yacht League is based on the premises.

A new cable car is near completion at Paradise Point. It will carry you to the top of the hill presenting you with incredible vistas of Charlotte Amalie and the harbor. You can get a variety of tropical drinks and food as you gaze out on this spectacular view.

Charlotte Amalie

Main Street with its Danish buildings and stone alleys is laced with shops and restaurants. Known as a free port, St. Thomas bustles with shoppers from the cruise ships, and visitors from all parts of the Caribbean and many other parts of the world.

U.S. citizens are allowed a $1200 duty-free exemption on imports purchased in the USVI. Excellent values can be found on such luxury items as perfumes, camera gear, liquor, jewelry and other treasures.

Many attractive gift shops offering attractive prices line Main Street. Be sure to stop in at A.H. Riise's, Cardow's, Royal Caribbean, Little Switzerland, Brummey's Gem Shop and Columbian Emeralds, all in the Main Street area.

Charlotte Amalie has many historical buildings steeped in the myriad of cultures that preceded that of the U.S. A tour of the town will take you through many fascinating labyrinths of old stone buildings and wooden houses.

The Hospitality Lounge on Tolbod Gade, one building up from the waterfront, is a good place to rest your feet and get your bearings. A checkroom for parcels is provided, along with a hostess or host from 9 a.m. to 5 p.m., Monday through Saturday. The Tourist Board of the Virgin Islands maintains an office in that same area near the waterfront across from Emancipation Park, as well as another office at the West Indian Company Dock.

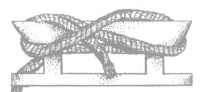

159

Market Square, just west of the busy shopping district of Main Street, was a slave market in earlier days, and later became a market for local farmers. Note the wrought iron roof, which came from a European railway station at the turn of the century.

The second oldest synagogue in the United States is located on Crystal Gade. It is open from 9 a.m. to 4 p.m., Monday through Friday, and 8:30 to 11:30 a.m. on Saturday. The sand floors in the synagogue are characteristic of Sephardic Carib Synagogues.

On Norre Gade stands the Frederick Lutheran Church, the official church of the Danish Virgin Islands. It was rebuilt in 1826 after a fire. You may visit the church Monday through Saturday from 8 a.m. to 5 p.m., and on Sunday from 8 a.m. to noon.

Above Main Street is the Governor's House and other government buildings, painted with traditional bright red roofs to be easily spotted from sea. This lovely building has housed both the governor's residence as well as his offices. The spacious second-floor reception room can be viewed by appointment.

Bluebeard's Castle tower guarded the harbour and the Danish settlers, with the help of Fort Christian and Blackbeard's. The hotel and grounds command an excellent view of the harbour.

Charlotte Amalie offers a central location from which to either rent a car, join a tour or hire a taxi to tour the island. Remember if you will be renting a car to drive on the left hand side of the road.

There are many beautiful beaches that should be visited, some with restaurants and dressing rooms. Magen's Bay Beach is located on the north side of the island in the curve of a sparkling bay. Small sailboats and snorkeling gear can be rented. There is a nominal charge for admission. Hull Bay Beach, also on the north shore, offers some wave action for surfing and a snack bar.

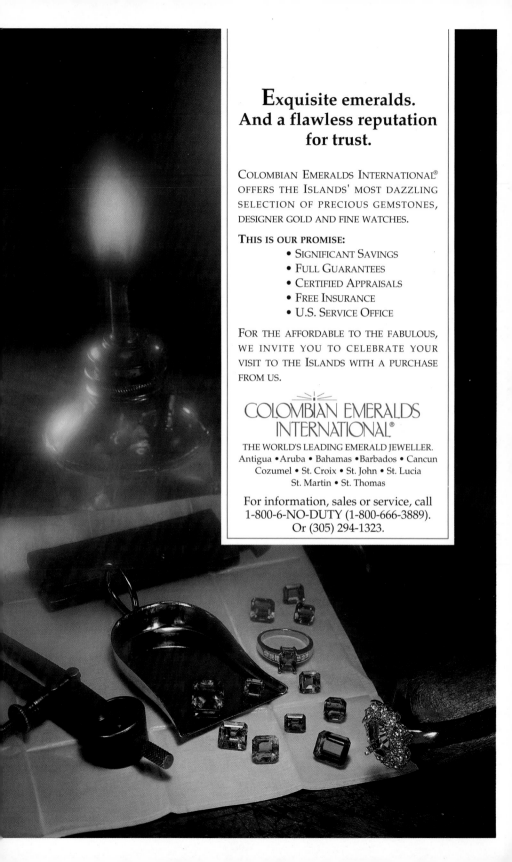

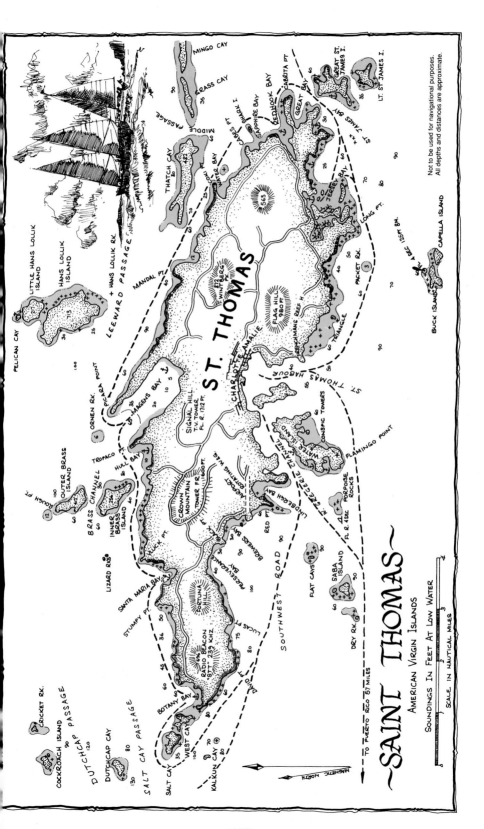

Not to be used for navigational purposes.
All depths and distances are approximate.

~SAINT THOMAS~

AMERICAN VIRGIN ISLANDS

SOUNDINGS IN FEET AT LOW WATER

SCALE IN NAUTICAL MILES

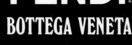

Bordeaux and Stumpy beaches are on the western end of the north shore, but are accessible only by a somewhat rough road.

Brewers Beach is near the College of the Virgin Islands and the Airport. Chaises may be rented and there is a restaurant nearby.

Morningstar Beach, next to Frenchman's Reef Hotel is close to Charlotte Amalie, and offers dressing rooms and a restaurant.

Windsurfers can be rented at Secret Harbour Beach. Coki Beach is a great outing to combine with a visit to Coral World, a full marine park with a fascinating underwater tower. Lockers may be rented while you swim and showers are available for rinsing off. A restaurant and bar are also located on the premises, along with several shops. There is an admission charge.

These are just some highlights of the sights to see in St. Thomas. Pick up one of the tourist publications, such as *Here's How, St. Thomas This Week* or *V.I. Playground,* or pay a visit to the Tourist Board of the Virgin Islands for more details of what to see and where to go.

Further to the west in what is still known as the Sub Base, is the Island Marine chandlery store. Island Marine is the supply headquarters for other stores, as they keep a very comprehensive inventory on hand.

Crown Bay

Located immediately west of the Charlotte Amalie Harbour and north of Water Island is the Crown Bay Marina. Enter via West Gregerie Channel or East Gregerie channel; both channels are well marked. Avoid the reef extending northward from Water Island. The reef is well marked by a lighted tower.

While in Gregerie Channel, approach Crown Bay Marina by leaving the cruise ship dolphin piling to port. The entrance to Crown Bay Marina is immediately north of the northernmost cruise ship dock.

You will find ample maneuvering room inside the basin and you will carry in excess of 17 feet of depth throughout, except between D and E docks, where the controlling depth is 12 feet.

Upon entering, the fuel dock lies hard to starboard. Crown Bay can be reached on VHF 16 or call 809-774-2255.

164

The facilities at the marina are exceptional and designed to meet the needs and requirements of the charterboat industry. 96 slips are available from 25 to 170 feet, with draft in excess of 20 feet, and offering telephone and water hookups. Gasoline, diesel fuel and water are available at the fuel dock through high-volume dispensers. Security is provided 24 hours a day. Tickle's Bar and Restaurant provides casual dining and drinks. Marine Warehouse has a shop located here to purchase bits and pieces to keep your boat in good working order. Don't miss a trip on the Atlantis Submarine berthed at Crown Bay. Call for details, it is two very interesting hours viewing life beneath the sea. The marina is conveniently located just five minutes away from the airport.

166

Sugar Reef Marine Services

Located on the east end of Crown Bay under the radio tower is the Sugar Reef Marine center. The marina offers complete facilities for yachtsmen, including fuel, ice, water, showers, laundry, provisions and dockage for vessels up to 13-foot draft.

A delightful restaurant and bar look out to sea from the dock. Call E-Z Shopper on VHF 16 for information.

Haulover Marine Yachting Center

On the western side of Crown Bay is the Haulover Marine Center, providing a complete repair facility including yacht repairs, painting, fiberglass work, electrical and carpentry shops.

Banks Sails have their loft here, and air conditioning and refrigeration, and diesel repairs are also available. Island Rigging can help with all of your rigging requirements and Virgin Island Power Systems sells and repairs generators.

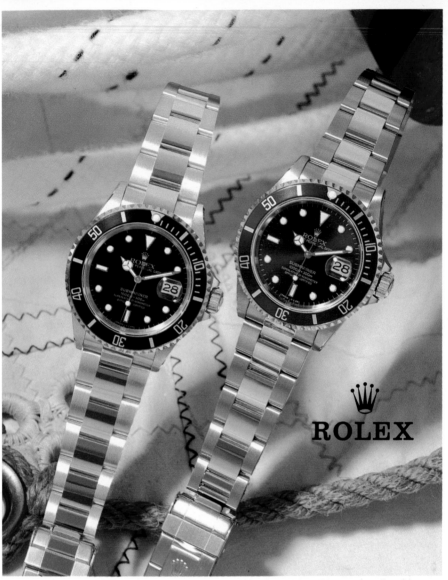

Rolex Submariner Date. Chronometers in 18 ct gold and in steel and gold.
Guaranteed waterproof to a depth of 300 meters.

WATER ISLAND

Water Island is among the largest private islands in the USVI. The island, once a military base, is owned by the U. S. Department of the Interior, and is leased to a private individual.

Water Island is two-and-one-half miles long and one-half mile wide. It can be reached via the ferry that leaves from the Sub Base on St. Thomas.

Water Island divides the east and west Gregerie channels. On the southernmost part of the island is an old lookout tower on top of Flamingo Hill.

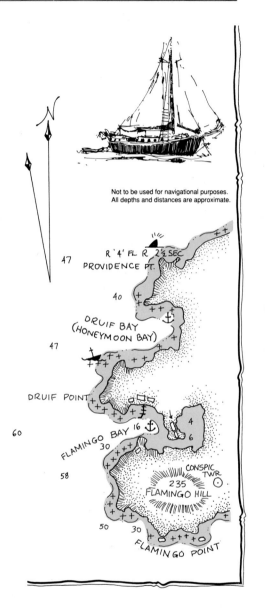

Not to be used for navigational purposes.
All depths and distances are approximate.

Flamingo Bay

Flamingo Bay is a daytime anchorage in Water Island and the location of the Flamingo Bay Marina, which is for the exclusive use of hotel guests. The bay can develop a surge and therefore is not recommended for overnight anchorage.

Sea Cliff Beach Resort overlooks both the bay and the marina. It is a full resort offering beach, pool, restaurants and shops.

Honeymoon Bay

Honeymoon Bay, or Druif Bay, slightly to the north of Flamingo Bay, is a favourite anchorage in normal weather. A beautiful white sand beach attracts swimmers. A beach bar, restaurant, and dining deck can be found ashore under the palms.

The designated swimming area is well marked so you can avoid motoring through. Dinghies may be beached on either side. The anchorage has a sandy bottom in 15 to 20 feet of water. Good snorkeling can be found along the southern shore.

HASSEL ISLAND

Hassel Island, just minutes from the Charlotte Amalie waterfront, is under the domain of the National Parks Service. You can still see some 18th- and 19th-century fortifications, as well as some private homes and a shipyard.

The park has a limited trail system at this time, amongst the cactus and orchids. Green iguanas can be spotted from time to time. There is a small anchorage in the Careening Cove on the eastern side of the island, often full of local boats.

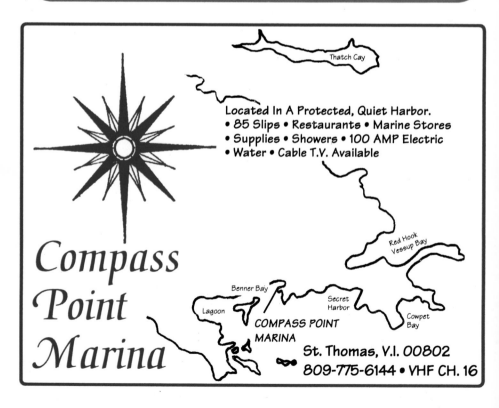

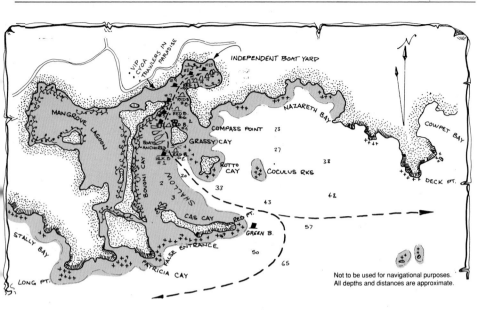

Not to be used for navigational purposes.
All depths and distances are approximate.

Yachts drawing up to 7 feet have access to the Lagoon, the best hurricane shelter on the island of St. Thomas.

Navigation

When making your approach to the Lagoon, it is imperative that you not confuse it with the tricky "False Entrance" to the west. As its name implies, there appears to be a direct passage when approaching from the south or west, and boats at anchor can be seen at the head of the bay, but *beware:* There is a reef extending all the way across the false entrance.

A good rule of thumb would be to say: If you can't see a green can buoy on the port side of the channel, don't go in! The channel into the Lagoon is well marked and provides no problems once you have identified Rotto Cay and its relationship to other landmarks. Leaving the green buoy on the tip of Cas Cay to port, and Coculus Rocks to starboard, proceed to Grassy Cay. You will pick up a green buoy on your port hand and red nun marking the southern tip of Grassy Cay. Leave it to starboard. Take Grassy Cay to starboard by 25 feet, and round the red buoy on the northwest side. Leave the anchored boats to port and follow the channel. The channel is marked with red and green buoys and is easily followed leaving the red nuns to starboard when entering from the sea.

Ashore

Independent Boat Yard provides a full-service boat yard, complete with a 30-ton travel lift and 15-ton crane. The boatyard maintains a group of private contractors to accommodate boats requiring services, including: a wood shop; fiberglass shop; machine shop; electrical shop; paint shop; Island Rigging; Tim Peck Enterprises, which does awl grip work; and Mace of Arts, which does boat lettering.

Bottoms Up, a bar and grill, serves breakfast, lunch and dinner daily. For those requiring marine supplies, Island Marine is also on the premises.

The Marina has expanded to include 85 slips, with full services for both transients and live-aboards. Marina employees standby on VHF channel 16 from 8 a.m. to 5 p.m. weekdays. Pieter Stoeken is the manager of Independent Boat Yard.

Across the Lagoon is Compass Point Marina, home of Caribbean Yacht Charters; St. Thomas Yacht Sales and Crewed Charters; and assorted boutiques.

The marina has dockage for transient vessels, and offers limited provisions, outboard repairs (J.E. Marine Supply), and shops including Caribbean Inflatables, Chris Sawyer's Diving Center, and Coki of St. Thomas, a canvas goods shop.

On the north side of the bay is a small marine complex offering dry stack storage, water, fuel, ice and a small supply store. Next to that is Saga Haven Marina home of Trawler in Paradise offering trawler charters, and VIP Yacht Charters and now CYOA Yacht Charters. This is a convenient location with a market, a secure parking garage, and shops. Several restaurants are nearby. Raffles features a live pianist nightly. The Windjammer serves lunch and dinner. On the water at Scott Beach is For the Birds, which opens at 4 p.m. for dinner and drinks.

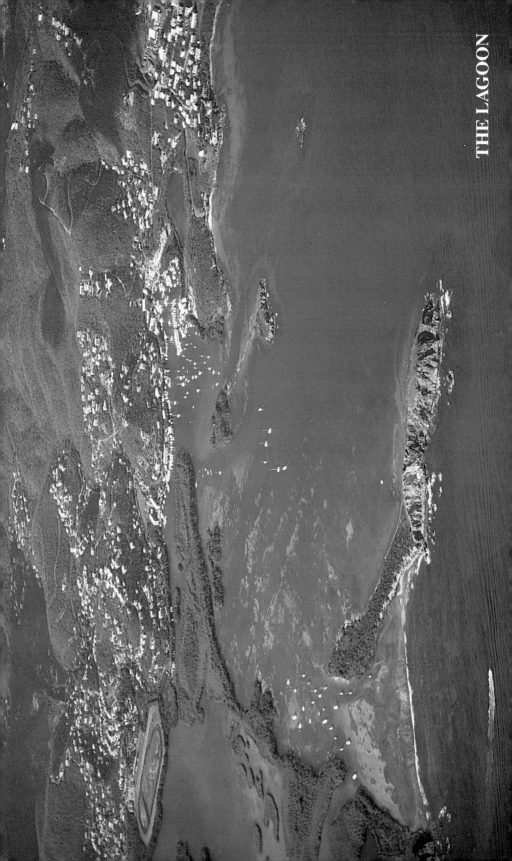

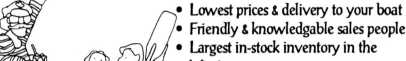
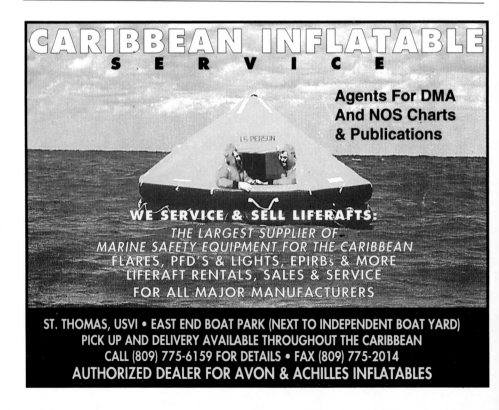
174

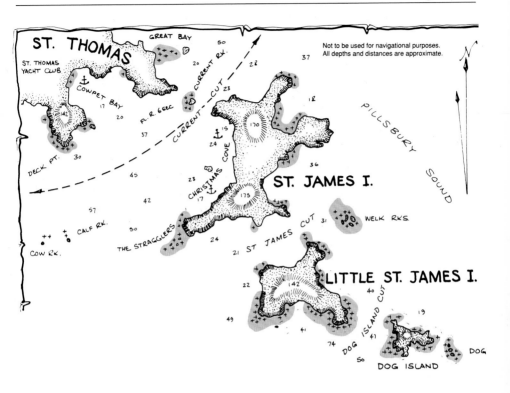

A well protected, all weather anchorage, Christmas Cove is a first and last night stop for many of the charter boats operating out of St. Thomas.

Navigation

Making your approach to Christmas Cove, you will notice it is divided by Fish Cay. There is a reef extending from the cay northeast to the shoreline of St. James.

Current Cut

Approaching Christmas Cove and the south shore of St. James from the north, you will have to negotiate Current Cut. Current Rock sits astride the channel and is marked with a light. The easternmost channel is recommended, although the other can carry 8 feet.

As the name implies, there can be a strong current of up to 4 knots running in either direction depending upon the tide. If approaching from the west, start your en-

gine in advance, as the island of Great St. James tends to blanket the wind. The Cow and Calf, a group of rocks awash to the southwest of Current Cut, are easy to see.

Anchoring

Anchor on either side of Fish Cay in 15 feet of water. Do not anchor too far out as the wind tends to become erratic. Do not pass between Fish Cay and the shore. If anchoring to the north of Current Cut, ensure that you are anchored close enough to the shore in order to be out of the current flow.

Ashore

There is good snorkeling toward the southern tip of the island. When the weather is calm, take the dinghy and explore the waters and reefs around the south end of St. James Island.

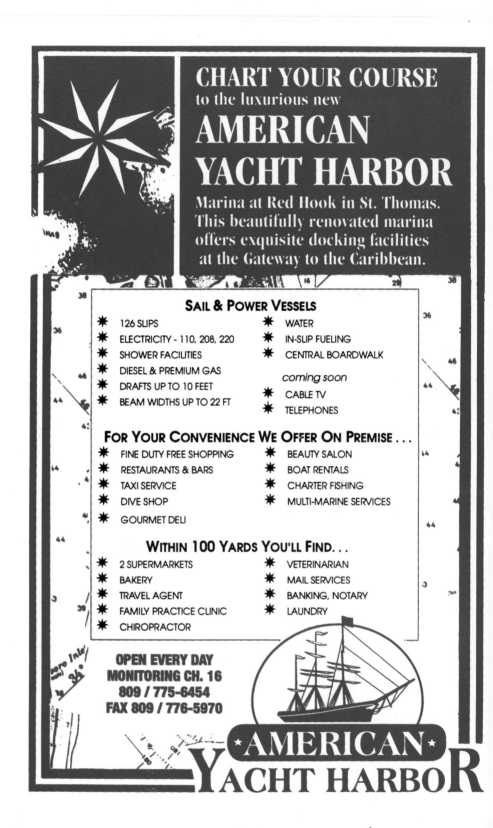

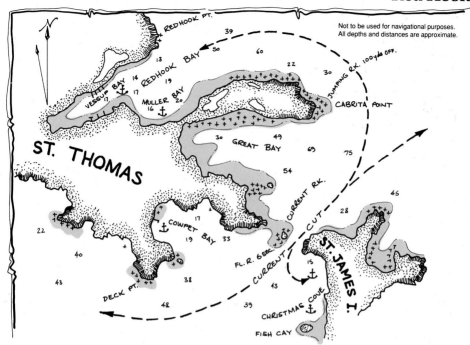

Not to be used for navigational purposes.
All depths and distances are approximate.

Just to the north of Cabrita Point on the eastern end of St. Thomas, Red Hook is a busy harbour with ferries departing for Cruz Bay, St. John on the hour. American Yacht Harbour, on the north side of the bay, provides yachtsmen with all services.

Because of its exposure to the east, Red Hook is often a choppy anchorage.

Navigation

Once around Cabrita Point, favour the northern side of the bay where the water is deepest. Keep an eye out for ferry traffic and stay out of its way.

Anchoring

As there are numerous private moorings and a considerable amount of ferry, and other traffic, it is recommended Muller Bay on the southern side of Red Hook be used for anchoring. Stay clear of the channel and ferry dock and don't go too deep into the bay, as it shoals off rapidly past the last set of docks.

There is a marked channel into Vessup Bay. Care should be taken when laying an anchor not to foul a vacant mooring.

Ashore

American Yacht Harbour includes all the basic yacht services including dockage, ice, water, fuel, etc. Call them on VHF 16. Across the road is a shopping center with an apothecary, restaurant, snack bar and other services.

On the southern side of the harbour is the Vessup Point Marina. The marina, home to Latitude 18's charter fleet, has nine feet of water and more, with water, electricity, ice and a bar and restaurant.

Red Hook is a busy center for bareboat charters, crewed boat charters, fishing charters and many other marine-oriented businesses. For more information and directions, check ashore with the marinas. There is a wonderful new market across the street from American Yacht Harbor that will have everything and more than you will need. It is immaculate and well stocked with mouthwatering goodies. They cater to the crewed and bareboat crowd as well as the locals. Next to American Yacht Harbor is a new, beautiful shopping center with restaurants, shops, boutiques, hair salon, yacht chandlery and more.

Jim Scheiner

Red Hook

The ferry to St. John leaves from Red Hook every hour and the ferries from the British Virgin Islands stop here as well. Rental cars as well as taxis are readily available. The Piccola Marina Cafe is a great place to have lunch or a drink while watching the activity and waiting for a ferry.

A quick trip around the point from Red Hook is Coral World Undersea Observatory. It is housed in a geodesic-domed observatory offshore and enables you, through three stories of windows, to observe the sea, the creatures and coral as though you were part of it.

Sapphire Beach Resort and Marina

Around the corner to the north of Red Hook is the Sapphire Beach Resort Marina. The entrance is marked with an unlit pair of green and red buoys.

The resort offers 67 slips for lease or for sale, with full marina facilities including water, electricity, TV cable, telephones, ice, a fuel dock and commissary.

Sapphire Resort has an exquisite beach that should not be missed. Call the dockmaster on VHF 16. This is a very convenient spot to access St. John and the BVI.

178

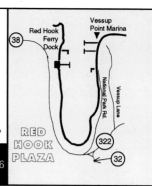
When you're cruising the Islands you should support the local Search and Rescue Units. They could save your Life.

When you are out in the Islands, the Coast Guard is far away. The local volunteer rescue unit is Virgin Islands Search and Rescue (VISAR). They need your money to be ready to help you.

SEARCH (Search and Rescue Charitable Foundation), a U.S. tax-exempt foundation, is devoted to improving and expanding all the volunteer search and rescue units in the Caribbean and the Bahamas.

SEARCH

Send your TAX-DEDUCTIBLE donation today to:

SEARCH
901 S.E. 17th St. • Suite 205 • Fort Lauderdale, FL 33316
Telephone: (809) 362-1574 • Fax: (809) 323-7918

- -

[ ]   I wish to make a tax-deductible donation to SEARCH of $50/$100/more ($..........) My check is enclosed . Please send my contributor's certificate and recognition decal to my address below.

[ ]   Please send me more information.

Name _____ Date _____

Address _____

City _____ State _____ Zip _____

Yacht's name/Aircraft Type & Reg No. _____

Please make checks payable to SEARCH and mail this form with your generous donation.

YOUR MONEY SAVES LIVES - MAYBE YOURS.

179

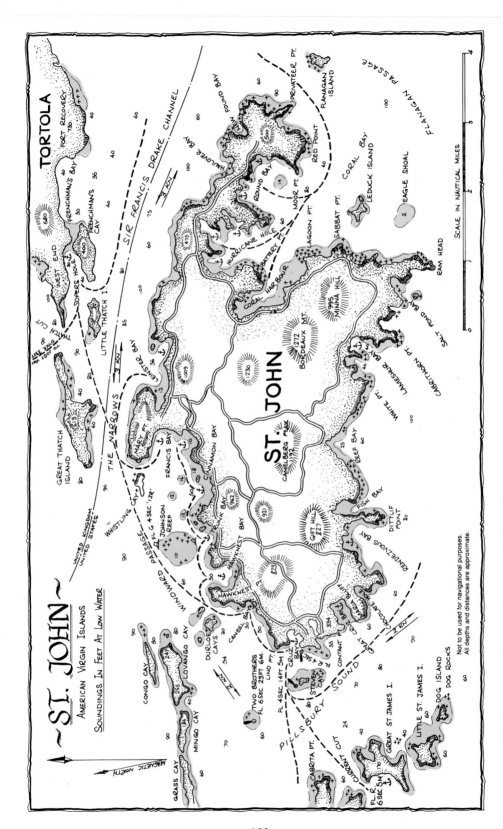

ST. JOHN

U.S. Virgin Islands
Panorama

Cruz Bay, a port of entry, is the main town on St. John and, without doubt, the best place to clear customs. Serviced by ferries to St. Thomas on an hourly basis, many charters elect to leave their vessels in Cruz Bay and take the ferry to Red Hook.

Cruz Bay offers the yachtsman all of the basic services, including banks, post office, grocery markets, etc. Often crowded, the anchorage, though protected, is not necessarily a good overnight stop, as the movement of the ferries tends to make it uncomfortable.

Navigation

Approaching Cruz Bay from the southwest or Great St. James, it is not recommended to go between Stephen Cay and St. John, as there are numerous coral heads. Leave Stephen Cay to starboard.

Two Brothers Rocks are always visible in the middle of Pillsbury Sound, and have good water all around.

Entering Cruz Bay, there is a reef extending out from Gallows Point, marked by a red nun or diamond. Stay well to the north of it, as it is in very shallow water.

A black buoy to the south of Lind Point marks the port side of the channel.

There are two marked channels within the harbour, one servicing the ferry dock to starboard and one servicing the National Parks dock and customs to port.

Anchorage

Shoal water extends from the red marker on the end of the reef about 50 to 60 feet toward the ferry dock, so be careful when anchoring. Be sure to avoid obstructing both channels or you will incur the wrath of

the ferry boat captains. Do not tie up to the dock as it is reserved for commercial traffic. A public dinghy dock has been built on both sides at the base of the pier. Tie up on the west side of the dock using a short scope so that the dinghy doesn't get caught under the dock.

All moorings in Cruz Bay, Great Cruz Bay and Coral Bay are private and subject to stiff fines for unauthorized use.

Ashore

The Customs House is on your right in the northern section of the bay known as the Creek. Vessels clearing into the USVI may tie up to the dock at customs. The depth is 9 feet. There is a dinghy dock pier off the ferry dock for those anchored out in the Bay who are coming ashore to clear customs. If coming ashore this way, turn left along the waterfront to the customs building. Caneel Bay Shipyards, across from customs, is a full-service facility offering repair services for fiberglass, sails, refrigeration, woodwork and storage, as well as ice, fuel and water.

Several shops and offices are located within the waterfront area. Jeep rentals are available and a tour of the island is highly recommended.

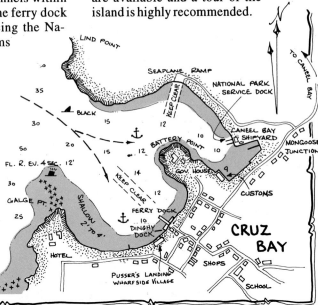

Not to be used for navigational purposes.
All depths and distances are approximate.

Mongoose Junction

Fine Shopping in a Caribbean Setting

STUDIO SHOPS • FINE BOUTIQUES • GALLERIES • JEWELRY SHOPS
RESTAURANTS • WATERSPORTS • SALON • REALTORS • ARTISANS AT WORK

Dozens of unique duty free shops and excellent restaurants in a beautiful Caribbean setting with charming stone buildings and shady courtyards. Exclusive jewelry, many locally made works of art, pottery, resort wear, perfume, fabrics and much more. Come and shop, relax and dine at Mongoose Junction where friendly and courteous merchants offer their specialties.

Cruz Bay, St. John, U.S. Virgin Islands

ACROSS FROM THE NATIONAL PARK VISITORS' CENTER
Phone: (809) 693-7012 • Fax (809) 693-7011
Dial ISLAND FAX (404) 399-3077 • Select Code #1131...For More Information.

Scheduled taxi-buses leave from Cruz Bay to many of St. John's exquisite beaches. Every Monday an historic bus tour leaves from the National Park dock at 9 a.m. It covers a large part of the park and ends three hours later at Cinnamon Bay.

St. John is an artistic community boasting painters, musicians, song writers and writers. For information, contact the Tourism Office near the Post Office, which is open on weekdays only.

The National Parks Service

One of the first stops you should make is to visit the National Park Service Visitor's Center next to Caneel Bay Shipyard. There are many new rules and regulations that you should be familiar with before spending time sailing and boating in the park. Besides the boating regulations you should find out about the fishing and diving regulations.

Almost two thirds of the island of St. John is protected as a National Park. Park rangers also schedule hikes and tours throughout the park lands, identifying the flora and fauna. Annaberg Plantation can be toured on your own with the assistance of a pamphlet.

Any beach in the U.S.V.I. can be used by anyone according to U.S.V.I. law. However, you cannot gain access to that beach by crossing private property, or go beyond the beach onto private property. Some beaches are therefore only accessible by sea.

Mongoose Junction

Just past the Park Service center is a charming shopping arcade built of natural stone, known as Mongoose Junction. Visitors should stop by and browse in the quaint, interesting shops. You will find it hard not to part with some money here!

Mongoose Junction is the home of St. John Water Sports, a charter company of both crewed and bareboats. The Mongoose Junction restaurant is open for breakfast, lunch and dinner, in an informal open air setting.

183

Wharfside Village

Adjacent to the ferry dock is a wonderful collection of shops and restaurants overlooking the action in Cruz Bay. From clothing to shoes to jewelry, it's a great place to poke around if you've got some time and a bit of pocket money to spend.

Pusser's St. John offers a picturesque view of the anchorage from their terrace restaurant, or upstairs in the Crow's Nest — a good place for a frosty beer or a Pusser's Painkiller. You can dinghy up to shore from the anchorage; Pusser's is now three floors of fun.

The TV Sports Bar serves fresh shellfish and chowders daily, as well as the current sporting events on 2 colour TVs.

Pusser's Company Store in the Village features the company's own line of sports and travel clothing, sport watches and chronometers, ship models, antiques of the sea, handmade luggage, unusual giftware and nautical accessories.

Traveling north from Cruz Bay, you will pass several beautiful white beaches, but they represent marginal anchorages because of the surge.

Caneel Bay is the home of the resort of the same name, which is built on the site of an 18th-century sugar plantation. The property extends to the east side of the bay, to Turtle Bay, including the Durloe Cays.

Visiting yachtsmen are welcome in the bay, but are requested to keep noise to an acceptable level and to refrain from hanging laundry on the lifelines.

Anchoring

There is a ferry channel marked that services the small jetty in the middle of the bay. Stay well clear when anchoring. Stay outside of the line of buoys off the beach that designates the swimming area. There is an excellent holding in 15-30 feet of water on a sandy bottom.

Ashore

During the day visitors may go ashore, and are welcome to visit the gift shop and the Plantation Bar. Outside guests may make reservations for lunch and dinner at the Sugar Mill restaurant. There may be times when the hotel must request that outside guests return at another time if the hotel management feels their visitor capacity has been reached. Uniformed hosts and hostesses are stationed throughout the complex to give directions and answer questions.

Eastbound

If you are sailing east, care should be taken negotiating the channel between the Durloe Cays and St. John. The wind can change around the headland and strong currents can create a choppy sea. On occasion, it is prudent to start the motor while negotiating this passage.

Hawknest Bay

The majority of this bay has been designated a swimming and snorkeling area by the National Park Service. There is a small anchorage to the northeast of the bay that is away from the posted area. On the hillside overlooking Hawknest Bay is a large, white statue of Christ with outstretched arms, built as a monument to world peace.

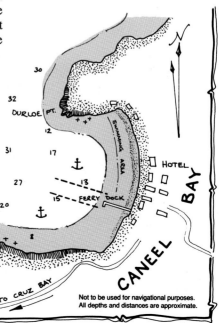

Not to be used for navigational purposes.
All depths and distances are approximate.

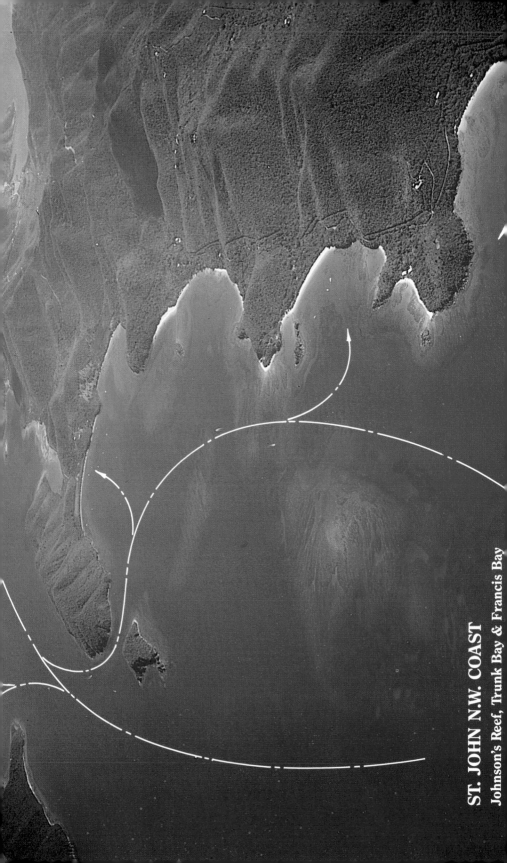

ST. JOHN N.W. COAST

Johnson's Reef, Trunk Bay & Francis Bay

One of the more spectacular beaches in the Virgin Islands, Trunk Bay is the site of an underwater snorkel trail for beginners. During the winter months or when a ground sea is running, it is not recommended as an overnight anchorage because of the bad swell.

Johnson's Reef

A large reef 1/2 mile to the north of Trunk Bay, Johnson's Reef, although well marked, continues to claim its share of wrecks due to negligence. The reef is marked at the northern end by a green buoy (1 JR.). At the southern extremity is a red cone or "nun" buoy (2). The reef extends a considerable distance to the east and west of the buoys, and care should be taken to give it a wide berth.

Navigation

The approach to Trunk Bay is straightforward with the exception of Johnson's Reef, as previously noted. If approaching from the west, there is a small cay off the headland to watch for.

When leaving for the east, you can proceed between Trunk Cay and the red buoy marking the southern tip of Johnson's Reef, taking care to stay at least 200 yards off the shoreline.

When a ground sea is running, there will be considerable surface action and it is recommended to go around the outside, once again giving the reef a good offing.

Anchoring

There will be a line of marker buoys off the beach, which indicates the swimming area. Dinghies going ashore must use the channel marked with red and black buoys toward the western end of the beach.

During ground seas, the surf on the beach can make the landing of dinghies a difficult, if not dangerous, task.

Ashore

The National Park Service maintains an underwater snorkel trail that extends around Trunk Cay. Picnic grounds and facilities are also maintained by the Park Service, and snacks and cold drinks are available.

Cinnamon Bay

The site of the National Park campground, Cinnamon Bay provides a good daytime anchorage. Being exposed, it can be uncomfortable during ground seas. Stay outside the buoys when anchoring.

Maho Bay

Like Cinnamon, Maho Bay is another nice day anchorage in calm weather; the shoreline, however, is private, and you are likely to receive a rather hostile reception if you turn up ashore!

Not to be used for navigational purposes.
All depths and distances are approximate.

Francis Bay

Located on the northern shore of St. John, Francis Bay is the large bay extending to the southeast of Whistling Cay.

Navigation

If you are making your approach from the west, you will be rounding Johnson's Reef. Favour the northern end leaving the large green buoy to starboard. There is also a channel between Trunk Cay, and the red "nun" buoy (leave to port).

If you are approaching from the north, there is plenty of water through the Fungi Passage that lies between Mary Point on St. John and Whistling Cay. A small shoal area extends south from Whistling Cay, where the decaying ruins of an old customs house can still be seen.

Anchoring

Favour the eastern side of the bay and anchor in 20-30 feet of water. When the wind is light, do not anchor close inshore because of the bugs. A small sandbar lies in the northeastern corner. Stay outside the buoys designating the swimming area.

Ashore

For those who feel like taking a healthy walk, the National Park Service maintains a trail that extends from the picnic site to an abandoned plantation house. From there you can follow the road to the Annaberg Ruins.

The Park Service also maintains garbage cans ashore for refuse disposal.

Departing

If you are heading east, you will find yourself in the narrows with the wind and current against you. Many of the local skippers prefer to lay a tack toward Jost Van Dyke. Then tacking back through the cut between Great Thatch and Tortola, rather than fighting the narrows with its strong adverse currents.

Leinster Bay

Located on the north coast of St. John, Leinster Bay lies directly to the south of the westernmost tip of Little Thatch. The anchorage is well protected and quite comfortable.

Navigation

Leaving Waterlemon Cay to port, work yourself up into the eastern end of the bay, known as Waterlemon Bay. There is a channel between Waterlemon Cay and St. John that can carry 6 feet, but it is difficult to negotiate.

Anchoring

Anchor in the southeastern corner of the bay in 20-30 feet of water. The holding is good, but expect to be backwinded when there is no ground sea. There is a delightful anchorage in the lee of Waterlemon Cay.

Ashore

Aside from snorkeling around the cay, there are one or two interesting walks ashore. In the southwest corner of the bay, there is a trail that leads to the Annaberg Sugar Mills, the ruins of which have been restored by the Park Service.

If leaving your dinghy, please make sure that it is well secured. If the nature of the sea is such as to make it difficult, land it on the sandy beach back up in the bay and walk along the beach to the foot of the trail.

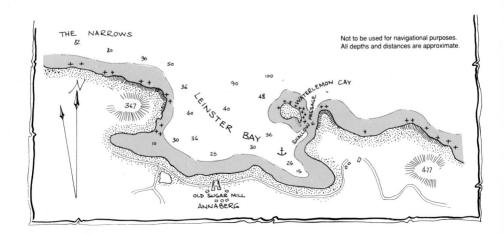

Coral Bay and Hurricane Hole

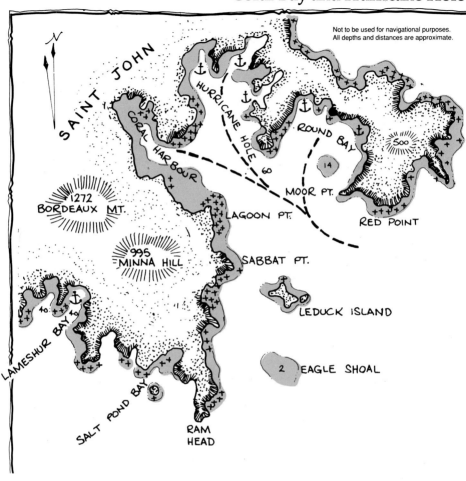

Not to be used for navigational purposes.
All depths and distances are approximate.

Comprised of a series of bays, coves, and fingers of land, Coral Bay and Hurricane Hole are located on the southeast corner of St. John. Hurricane Hole is the name given to the northern and eastern portion of the bay, where it is possible to tie up to the mangroves to gain protection from storms. During the rainy months, the area can be very buggy.

During slave days, when the sugar mills were at their peak, Coral Harbour was the main anchorage on St. John. There are some interesting ruins still in existence.

Navigation

If you are approaching from the east, the route is straightforward. Leave Flanagan's Island to port. Make your entry midway between Red Point on St. John and Leduck Island. It is wise to give all headlands in this area a wide berth as most have rocks extending out from them.

If you are approaching from the south or west, then care must be exercised to avoid Eagle Shoal, which is very difficult to see. When rounding Ram's Head, it is possible to hug the shoreline, passing midway between Sabbat Point and Leduck Island, but the safer route is to stay south of a line drawn between Ram's Head and Water Point on the northern tip of Norman Island until Leduck Island bears northwest. Then enter midway between Leduck Island and Red Point.

190

Anchoring

Round Bay

Once around Moor Point, Round Bay will open up to starboard. There is a reef extending out from the shoreline (see sketch chart). Anchor to the right of the reef in 15–25 feet of water. The holding is good, but occasionally, a swell works its way around the point. If this happens, it is recommended to set a stern anchor.

Hurricane Hole

There are five separate anchorages comprising Hurricane Hole; the holding is good in all of them. The water for the most part is deep, too. But beware of bugs when the wind is light or after a rain.

Coral Harbour

The entrance is straightforward. Stay mid-channel until the stone house on the eastern side of the bay bears northeast. You should then be able to anchor in 15–20 feet of water. Keep the channel clear for fishing boats, and do not pick up the private moorings you will see here.

Ashore

There is no customs service at Coral Bay. There are a number of buildings left over from slavery days, including the Moravian Mission and the ruins of an old sugar mill and a fort. Coral Bay has become the place to eat in St. John. Miss Lucy's, Shipwreck, Seabreeze, Don Carlos, Sputniks, Vie's, Mac's Pizza and Skinny Legs offer a wide variety of dining choices. Nearby Chateau Bordeau is one of the most upscale (and expensive) restaurants on the island. Coral Bay Marine monitors VHF 16 and provides engine repairs and Coral Bay Watersports is a dive company renting dive equipment.

Coral Harbour is home to some wonderfully eccentric and dedicated cruising sorts. It is considered more of a haven from the tourists, rather than a tourist destination.

South Coast Bays of St. Johns

Beyond the point of Ram's Head, there are a number of bays rarely visited by the cruising yachtsman. We have listed below several of these anchorages, along with any pertinent information.

Salt Pond Bay

Salt Pond Bay is an excellent anchorage. It is easy to enter, although there are rocks awash at the entrance. You can pass on either side of them; however, there is more room if you leave them to starboard.

When approaching and leaving, Booby Rock is easy to see (35 feet) with good water all around. Anchoring is forbidden, but the Park Service has provided moorings. The snorkeling around this anchorage is excellent.

A word of caution is that this bay has been subject to some petty thievery. Sunbathers, rental cars and boats all seem to be fair game.

Great Lameshur Bay

Another well-protected anchorage, Great Lameshur Bay is easy to gain access to. Once inside, pick up a Park Service mooring. Anchoring is restricted.

Little Lameshur Bay

To the west of Great Lameshur, Little Lameshur offers good protection except when the wind is in the south. This is another bay with restricted anchoring. Pick up a mooring and head for the water. Snorkeling here is excellent.

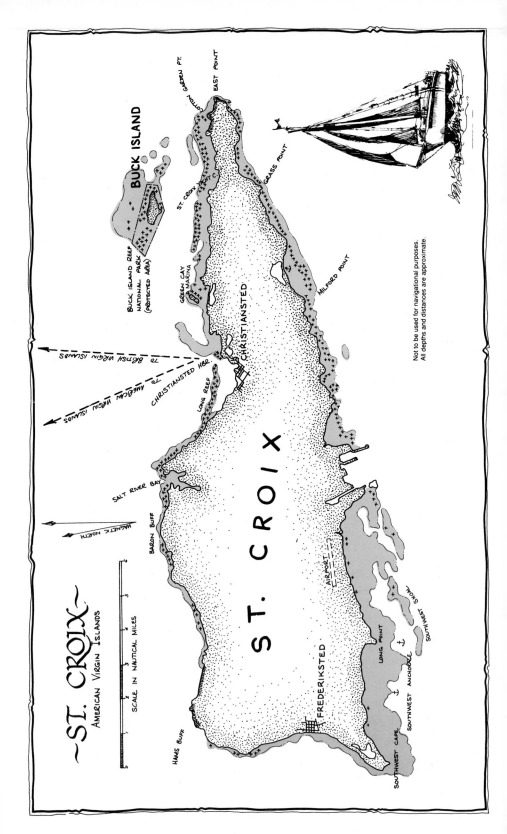

~ST. CROIX~
AMERICAN VIRGIN ISLANDS

SCALE IN NAUTICAL MILES

BUCK ISLAND

BUCK ISLAND REEF
NATIONAL PARK
(PROTECTED AREA)

EAST POINT
GARDEN PT.
NELLY
ST. CROIX YACHT C.
CASS POINT
GREEN CAY
MARINA
CHRISTIANSTED
MILFORD POINT

To BRITISH VIRGIN ISLANDS
To AMERICAN VIRGIN ISLANDS
CHRISTIANSTED HBR.
CHRISTIANSTED
LONG REEF

SALT RIVER BAY

BARON BLUFF

MAGNETIC NORTH

S T.   C R O I X

AIRPORT

FREDERIKSTED

HAMS BLUFF

LONG POINT

SOUTHWEST SHOAL
SOUTHWEST ANCHORAGE
SOUTHWEST CAPE

Not to be used for navigational purposes.
All depths and distances are approximate.

Lying 35 miles south of the other Virgins, St. Croix is the largest island in the group, approximately 26 miles wide. The island has retained more of its Danish character than the other U.S. islands, and many of the original "great" houses have been restored as have some of the historic sights.

In order to preserve such dignity, portions of Christiansted have become national trust in order to preserve the original building facades characteristic of the early Danish architectural style.

When planning your trip to St. Croix, allow yourself a minimum of three days: one day to sail there, one day to sightsee, and one day to sail back. Try to depart from either the eastern end of St. John or Norman Island in the BVI for a better point of sail, either a close or beam reach.

It is imperative that the entrance into Christiansted Harbour be made only in daylight and therefore, in order to allow for delays, it is prudent to depart at first light and no later than 8 a.m.

Navigation

When the weather is extremely clear, it is possible to see St. Croix from either St. Thomas or Tortola. But during hazy periods, you won't be able to see the hills until you are two hours out.

When laying off a course, it is wise to allow for a 1/2-knot westerly current. Therefore, as a rule of thumb, lay your course for the eastern end of the island in order to be set down onto Christiansted.

As you start to approach Christiansted, keep to the eastern side and correct your course accordingly. The saddle formed by Lang Peak and Recovery Hill makes an easy landmark. Head for a point midway between them until you pick up the radio tower (WSTX 070 KHz) on Fort Louise Augusta.

You will pass the sea buoy #1 to port and then line up the radio tower between the channel markers. This should be approximately 170 degrees M.

Long Reef, which extends across the harbour entrance, will be seen breaking to starboard. On your port hand is Scotch Bank and, although the charts indicate that parts of it are covered with adequate water depth, it is wise to stay clear, as it breaks in a ground sea.

Although the entrance to Christiansted Harbour is well buoyed, it should be noted that Round Reef, which lies to the west of Ft. Louise Augusta, represents a major navigational hazard. You may go to either side of it.

The schooner channel can be negotiated by leaving the red and black channel dividing marker to starboard, then leaving Round Reef to starboard, passing midway between the reef and Ft. Louise Augusta, and then directly to the anchorage. This channel is for yachts carrying less than 10-foot draft.

Taking the deeper channel entails leaving the fixed red and black marker to port and passing to the west of Round Reef, following the channel markers.

Anchoring

Most yachts use the anchorage in the lee of Protestant Cay. Head for the fort, which lies to the east of the cay, round the cay to the south and anchor off the southwest end in approximately 10 feet of water.

Do not anchor too far to the west as the water shoals off, and do not be tempted to utilize a mooring buoy that is currently vacant. The moorings are all private and, unless you know what is on the other end, prudence should dictate your using your own ground tackle.

It is a good policy to set two anchors to restrict swinging room as this anchorage is both crowded and prone to a current at certain times, which affects different boats in various ways.

Vessels of over 50 feet should anchor off the St. Croix Marina or may tie up dockside if so desired.

Ashore

Customs and Immigration

Vessels sailing from the BVI must clear customs and immigration, located to the south of St. Croix Marina (or call them at 773-1011 for instructions).

Skippers should bring their identification and ship's papers ashore. If any crew member is not a U.S. citizen, it is wise to take that member and his or her passport with you to immigration (phone 778-1419).

St. Croix Marina is a full-service marina offering fuel, dockage, showers, laundry, restaurant and bar, and ice. The boatyard offers long and short-term storage, fiberglass repair, a chandlery, 60-ton travel lift and many other facilities, and is managed by Larry and Ginny Angus.

Silver Bay dock is located in downtown Christiansted and has transient space available with electric and water for boats to 70 feet. Additionally there is parking at the dock. The maximum draft is 9 feet. The dock is located next to the Caravelle Hotel and dockage can be obtained on site or by calling 778-9650.

The town of Christiansted is an easy walk from St. Croix Marina. This island is also one in which you are allowed a generous $1200 duty exemption on imports.

Christiansted is a charming town with many of the old buildings still intact. The shops are tucked inside many of these carefully rebuilt edifices, along with quaint restaurants in breezy courtyards.

The National Park Service maintains five historic sites within walking distance of the waterfront. Fort Christiansvaern offers a self-guided tour following numbered rooms and reading the history in a well-written pamphlet by the Park Service. This fort was begun in 1734, and while it never engaged in battle, the view from the battlements affords a great panorama of the harbour. Don't miss seeing the dungeons! The fort is open daily and park rangers are on duty from 8 a.m. to 5 p.m.

The Scalehouse, location of the Visitor's Bureau, has been restored to its original mid-1800 condition. It was used originally

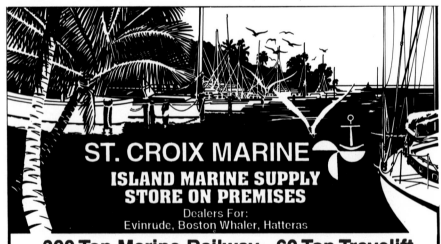

to check merchandise, with a scale built into the floor. This is a good place to get general information and directions for the island of St. Croix.

The West India and Guinea Company Warehouse hold the Post Office opposite the Steeple Building. U.S. Customs is on the second floor. Built in the mid 1700s, the building also houses public restrooms.

The Danish Customs House houses the National Park Service's offices. The building has been recently renovated and is open weekdays from 10 a.m. to noon.

The Government House was once the capital of the Danish West Indies. It is now used by various government departments. Parts of the complex date back to the mid 1700s. An interesting staircase leads to the ballroom on the second floor.

Cramer Park is a cove on the East End of the island, overlooking Buck Island. The park has a beautiful beach, picnic area, bar and restaurant.

The easternmost point of the island is also the easternmost part of the U.S.

Altoona Lagoon is a park and beach near the Fort Louise Augusta radio tower, right in Christiansted Harbor.

Don't miss the St. George Village Botanical Gardens, a restoration of an old sugar plantation. The gardens have plants and flowers indigenous to St. Croix.

Near the airport, on the southwestern part of the island is the Cruzan Rum Distillery. You can visit the distillery and watch the workers making the rum. A tour is available, along with a tasting bar concocting a rum drink every day.

Heading toward Frederiksted is the rain forest, with a 150-foot dam. Mahogany Road is lined with mahogany trees, yellow cedar and Tibet trees. The St. Croix Leap, also located in the rain forest, is a group of woodcarvers and sculptors. You can order items to be shipped to you on completion.

Whim Greathouse, near Frederiksted, is not to be missed. It is a restored greathouse from the late 1700s which houses a museum and gift shop. It is open daily from 10 a.m. to 5 p.m. There is a small charge for admission.

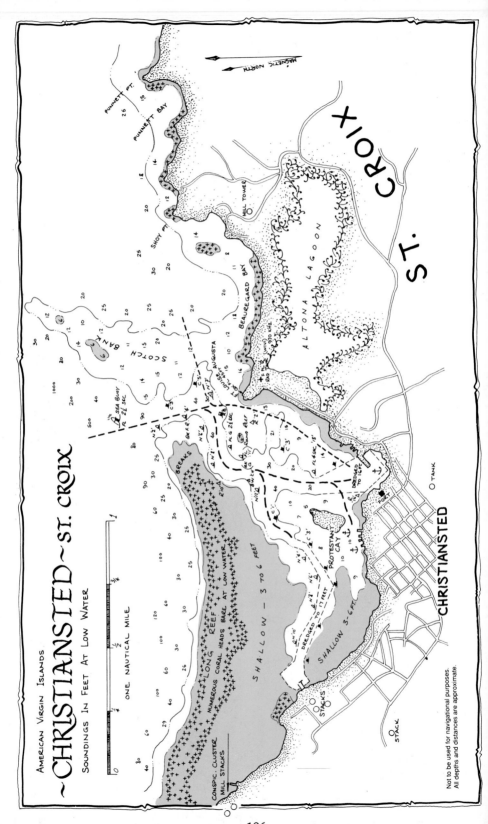

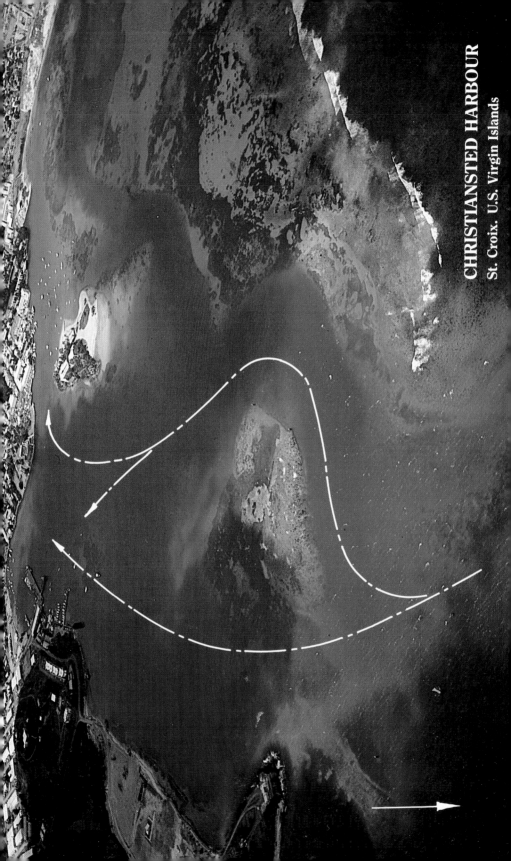

Lying some 4¹/₂ miles northeast of Christiansted Harbour, Buck Island is a national park and its surrounding coral reef is marked with underwater signs.

Numerous day-sailing boats make the trip from Christiansted and Green Cay Marina daily, and anyone wishing to go along should contact the appropriate vessel at dockside. Although not recommended as an overnight anchorage, Buck Island provides an excellent day's diversion of sailing and snorkeling.

Navigation

Leave Christiansted Harbor the way you came in until you reach the sea buoy "C" 1. Proceed northeast toward Virgin Gorda for 2 miles along Scotch Bank, and then head for the prominent point on the south end of the island.

An alternate route is to proceed out of the harbour to buoy "C" 7 (see chart) off Fort Louise Augusta. Do not go further inshore, owing to two shoal areas that have taken their toll in the past. Leaving Green Cay to starboard, stand out for the white beach on the western end of Buck Island.

There are two white buoys that mark the western extremities of the reef.

Anchoring

The best anchorage is directly off the white, sandy beach at the western end of Buck Island in approximately 15 feet of water on the sandy bottom.

Boats drawing less than 5 feet may use another anchorage inside the reef. Proceed eastward along the island, keeping the white buoy to port, until you see a large brown sign, placed by the Park Service.

You will also see red and green buoys that mark the entrance through the reef. Follow the passage to the eastern end of the island and pick up one of the National Park Service moorings.

If you have to anchor, please keep well clear of the reef and set your anchor only in sandy areas.

Ashore

The Park Service maintains picnic chairs and tables, as well as barbecue grills on the beach at the western end. A picnic pavilion is located east of the small pier on the south shore for your convenience.

There is a marked underwater trail here, which has been designated as a National Park. The snorkel trail starts at the southeast corner of the island, and those wishing to explore it should dinghy through the passage described above and moor at the start of the trail. Snorkeling here is spectacular, but do not touch the coral.

For those wishing to get some exercise, an overland hiking trail will provide an interesting walk among prickly pears, cactus and wildflowers.

Green Cay Marina

Navigation

Green Cay Marina is a full-service, well-protected marina on St. Croix's northern coast. Located east of Christiansted, it should be approached from the western side of Buck Island, from which you will see Green Cay.

Leave Green Cay to port and head for the rock jetty. You can see yellow buildings with white roofs as a landmark from three miles offshore. The marina monitors VHF 16. If you call ahead, the dockmaster will meet you at the fuel dock and lead you to a slip. The marina carries 8 to 10 feet of water and is very well protected.

Ashore

The marina is very well kept and has all of the amenities including showers, laundry, water, electricity, fuel, and ice. There is also a restaurant and a new 46 room hotel.

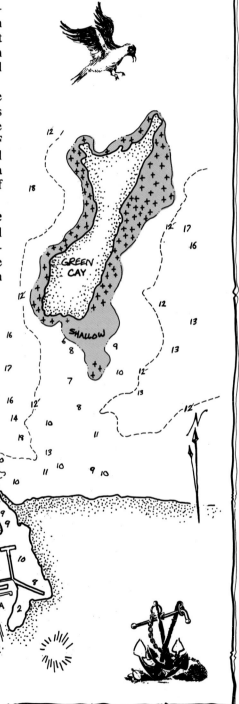

Not to be used for navigational purposes.
All depths and distances are approximate.

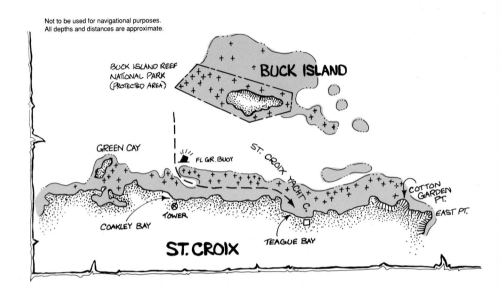

Not to be used for navigational purposes.
All depths and distances are approximate.

BUCK ISLAND REEF
NATIONAL PARK
(PROTECTED AREA)

BUCK ISLAND

GREEN CAY

FL GR. BUOY

ST. CROIX YACHT C.

COTTON GARDEN PT.

EAST PT.

COAKLEY BAY

TOWER

TEAGUE BAY

ST. CROIX

Navigation

South of Buck Island, protected by a reef, is Teague Bay. There are two entrances to the bay, the first being the Coakley Bay Cut, marked by a lighted green U.S. Coast Guard marker. Leave the marker to port, go well into the bay towards the windmill, then head east, favouring the shore side. This entrance is good for 12-foot depths.

The second entrance, the Cotton Valley Cut, is good for 7-foot depths. It is unlit and marked by privately maintained buoys of red and black. Head in between the buoys, watching for patch reefs east/southeast of the cut. Once inside, head east towards the Yacht Club.

Anchoring

There is good holding in sand, but take care to avoid fouling the private moorings which you will see here. Do not get too close to shore, as it shoals to 5 feet.

Ashore

The St. Croix Yacht Club extends a friendly welcome to visiting yachts. There is a small dinghy dock to the east, where you can tie up and go ashore. The restaurant and Bar are open from 11:30 a.m. to 2 p.m. The Club is open Wednesday through Sunday and holidays year-round. Duggans Reef nearby can be reached by dinghy for dinner. Showers are available, ice may be purchased, and garbage may be left. However, no fuel, laundry, or provisions are available. Reciprocal use is offered to yachtsmen of recognized yacht clubs and other yachtsmen may request a guest pass. The Yacht Club stands by on VHF 16.

Salt River

Columbus anchored off of Salt River and sent a party ashore in search of water. An unfriendly reception by the local Indians sent him sailing off. Salt River has been given National Park status, to further insure its future will remain protected and much as it was when Columbus first saw it.

Navigation

This is a tricky anchorage to get to, but one which provides a very safe anchorage once you are in. Local knowledge is a big help for picking your way in. If you are approaching from the east avoid the White Horse Reef off of the Salt River Point; it

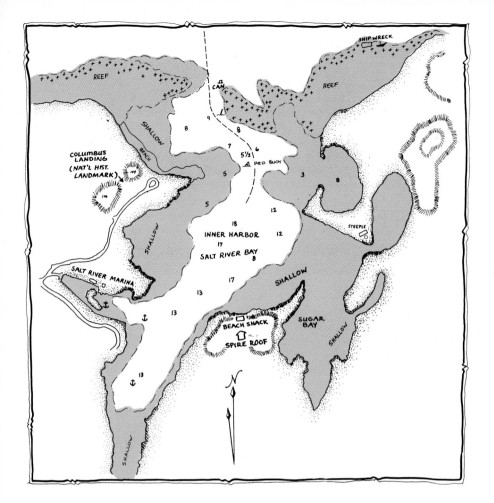

usually breaks even during calm weather. Find the break in the reef. Once inside White Horse Reef, turn to port, paralleling the inside of the reef and head towards the steeple. Align Can 1 with the beach shack and spire roof and turn south. This can is privately maintained and, with no official support, can not be guaranteed that it will always be there. It is strongly advised that you call Salt River Marina for advice, and feel your way carefully with a depth finder.

In the west section of the bay is Salt River Marina, which provides all services to dockside customers; fuel requires 24 hours' notice. The Marina boasts a fine island setting, restaurant, marine supply store and dive shop—Salt River Canyon is rated as one of the 10 best dive locations in the Caribbean. The marina office and restaurant are open 7 days a week.. They monitor VHF 16 during daylight hours. Because of limited space available, advance notice is recommended when possible.

You should be able to take 6 feet into the harbour. This is a well-protected and interesting anchorage, although not convenient to any shore-based amenities; taxis are easy to access and rides to town can be arranged.

Frederiksted

This is a harbour used by large ships. It is seldom used by yachts as an anchorage, as the water is extremely deep.

The town does have some interesting old buildings, and is worth a visit if you are touring the island.

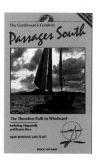

WEST INDIAN GRUB & GROG

Few recipes have actually survived from the days of the Arawaks, although we know they hunted agouti and iguana, made cassava bread and seasoned their foods with salt and pepper. Arawak hunters reputedly caught wild duck and fowl by covering their heads with gourds (cutting tiny eye slits) and standing neck-deep in the swamps or lagoons until an unwary bird passed near enough to grab it by the legs and drown it!

The Caribs' favourite recipes are unlikely to prove popular today, but the pirates provided us with a still-popular cooking technique: The word *boucan* means to cure meat by smoking strips over a slow fire, which is what the early Brethren did with the wild pigs and cattle which escaped or were "liberated" from the farms of Spanish settlers. Hence these men came to be called *boucaniers*. Eventually they returned to the sea as *buccaneers*, where, of course, they drank rum, still the basis for many West Indian drinks. Made by the fermentation of molasses or cane juice, rum was defined in 1909 as "the spirit of sugar" and was originally called *kill-devil* or *rumbullion*.

Generally, West Indian foods represent the cosmopolitan visitors who have passed through the islands over the centuries—South Americans, East Indians, Chinese, Europeans and Africans—so there is no single "West Indian" style of cooking. What has evolved, however, is a fascinating hodgepodge of customs and cuisines reflecting their diverse origins.

On the following pages are a sampling of favourite recipes originated by Caribbean chefs in popular island restaurants with more traditional ingredients.

Illustration by Sally Erdle

CONCH FRITTERS

Mariner Inn, Tortola
Serves: 4-6

1 lb. conch meat, cleaned & ground
1 tbsp. chopped onion
1 tbsp. chopped sweet pepper
1/4 stick minced celery
2 cloves garlic, minced
3 eggs, beaten
1/2 cup flour (more or less) to bind
1 tbsp. baking powder
1 tsp. chopped parsley
2 tbsps. cooking oil
salt & pepper to taste
hot oil for deep frying

Combine all ingredients except oil for frying and stir to form a thick batter. Allow to stand for 30 minutes before frying. Heat frying oil to 360-375°, drop batter by spoonfuls, and fry for about 4 minutes.

Serve with
COCKTAIL SAUCE:
3/4 cup chili sauce
2 tbsps. horseradish
1/2 tsp. Tabasco sauce
juice of one lemon
Note: Any type of fish will do in place of the conch

CURRIED SHRIMP AND SCALLOPS

Chez Michelle, Virgin Gorda
Serves: 4

3 tbsps. vegetable oil
16 large shrimp, peeled & deveined
16 small-to-medium scallops
1/2 small red bell pepper, finely diced
1/2 small green bell pepper, finely diced
2 tbsps. minced shallot or onion
2 tsps. minced garlic
1 tbsp. Madras curry powder
cayenne pepper/hot sauce to taste
1/2 cup heavy cream
1 tbsp. demi glace (optional)*
3 tbsps. butter, cut into 4 pieces

Heat 2 teaspoons oil in large skillet over moderately high heat. Quickly brown shrimp & scallops, about 15 seconds on each side, and remove from pan. Heat remaining oil, add peppers and shallots, reduce heat to medium and cook until tender (about 2 minutes), stirring frequently. Add garlic and curry powder and cook 1 minute, stirring constantly. Add cream, demi glace (optional) and cayenne or hot sauce. Stir well to blend, bring to boil and add seafood and salt to taste. Simmer a minute or two until seafood is just firm to touch, and remove to warm serving plate with a slotted spoon. Raise heat and boil sauce for several seconds, stirring constantly, until thickened. Remove from heat, stir in butter and pour over seafood.

*Note: Demi glace is concentrated veal stock, available in specialty food stores.

CARIBBEAN SEAFOOD CHOWDER

Chenay Bay Beach Resort, St. Croix
Serves: 5

1 bunch fresh cilantro, chopped
1 bunch fresh parsley, chopped
1 large chef potato, peeled & diced
1 green pepper, diced
2 red peppers, diced
1/2 tsp. minced Haitian hot pepper
1 large onion, diced
2 cloves garlic, minced
pinch of thyme
chicken base to taste
1 lb. conch meat, minced
1/2 lb. mahi mahi, chunked
1/2 lb. tuna, chunked
1/2 lb. wahoo, chunked
1 qt. heavy cream
1 cup sherry

Put all herbs and vegetables in a large pot with enough water to cover and boil for 15 minutes. Add chicken base, seafood, cream and sherry, and simmer all together for 20 minutes. Add salt and pepper to taste and serve hot.

Note: Minced clams for conch and mild, firm white fish for mahi mahi or wahoo; canned, drained tuna for fresh tuna; Scotch bonnet peppers for Haitian red pepper. Chenay Bay uses Dry Sack brand sherry.

GROUPER WEST INDIAN

Mariner Inn, Tortola • Serves: 1

6-oz. grouper fillet
1/4 cup flour
salt & pepper to taste
2 oz. cooking oil
1/4 onion, sliced
1/4 sweet pepper, chopped
1 oz. margarine
1/4 tomato, sliced
1 clove garlic, minced
1 oz. vinegar
hot pepper sauce to taste
lemon and parsley to garnish

Season fish with salt and pepper and dredge in flour. Heat oil in pan and saute fish, presentation side first (the side from the backbone). Turn and cook a few minutes on the other side, then remove to plate. Saute onion, pepper and tomato in margarine for 4 minutes. Add remaining ingredients except garnish and simmer 5 minutes. Pour over fish and serve.

Note: Try this dish served with vegetables and boiled potatoes or boiled green bananas.

CHENAY BAY'S CURRY GOAT

Chenay Bay Beach Resort, St. Croix
Serves: 10

5 lbs. goat meat with bone
3 onions, chopped
2 red peppers, chopped
1 stalk celery, chopped
1 bunch thyme, crumbled
West Indian hot sauce to taste
Jamaican curry powder to taste
salt to taste
cornstarch to thicken

Put goat in large pot, cover with water and boil 3 hours or until tender. Remove from heat and refrigerate until cool and fat rises to top. Skim fat from top of pot, add thyme and vegetables, return to stove and simmer until vegetables are done. Add curry, hot sauce and salt to taste. Whisk cornstarch into cold water and add to pot a little at a time to reach desired thickness. Serve with hot rice, white or seasoned to taste.

LUCY'S CHICKEN CURRY

Biras Creek, Virgin Gorda
Serves: 10

5 lbs. chicken legs
5 lbs. onions, chopped
oil or fat for frying onions
5 cloves garlic, crushed
1 fresh ginger root, crushed
2 28-oz. cans tomatoes
4 cloves
4 heaping tbsps. good Indian curry powder
dash cinnamon
1 tsp. chili powder
coconut cream to taste (optional)

Fry onions gently until well reduced. Add garlic, ginger and whole tomatoes, drained. Mix curry powder and chili powder with reserved tomato juice and add tomatoes and onions. Add cloves, cinnamon and chicken, cover lightly with foil and bake at 325° for about one hour or until chicken is done. Add coconut cream, if desired, about 15 minutes before taking from oven.

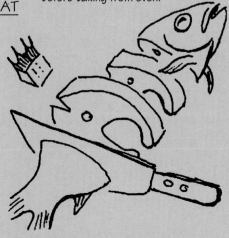

SPICE RICE

Sunny Caribbee Spice Co., Tortola
Serves: 4

1 chicken bouillion cube
1/2 tsp. herb pepper blend <u>or</u>
1/4 tsp. black pepper plus
1/4 tsp. minced garlic
1/2 tsp. seasoned sea salt <u>or</u>
1/4 tsp. sea salt plus
1/4 tsp. minced onion
1/2 tsp. Sunny Caribbee hot curry
1/4 green or red pepper, minced
dash of cayenne pepper (optional)
1 cup rice

Combine chicken bouillion, spices and peppers with 2 cups water in heavy saucepan and bring to boil. Add rice, reduce heat to simmer, cover tightly and cook until water is absorbed and rice is tender, adding more water if necessary or if softer rice is desired.

Note: Adding a tablespoon or more of butter to water before adding the rice will help to keep the rice grains from sticking together.

CARIBBEAN BARBECUE SAUCE

Sunny Caribbee Spice Co., Tortola
Makes: 1 cup

1 cup catsup
2-6 tsps. West Indian hot sauce
2 tbsps. vegetable oil
salt & pepper to taste
2 tbsps. minced garlic
2 tbsps. minced onion

Combine all ingredients except hot sauce in glass container and mix well. Add 2 teaspoons hot sauce, mix well and taste. Add hot sauce as desired. Refrigerate overnight and stir well before using. A tasty marinade or basting sauce.

Note: If you've just bought your first bottle of West Indian hot sauce, use it with caution at first! Island spices and condiments are often more pungent than similar products sold widely in Europe or the States, and can deliver quite a kick to the uninitiated palate.

PASSIONFRUIT CAKES

The Landing (Pusser's), Tortola
Serves: 10

2/3 cup heavy cream
1 cup passionfruit puree
4 tsps. cornstarch
7 eggs, separated
3-4 leaves gelatin
cold water
2/3 cup sugar

Put gelatin leaves in cold water and let stand to soften. Combine cream and passionfruit puree in double boiler and bring to a boil. Add cornstarch and egg yolks, cook until thickened, stir in gelatin and remove from heat. Beat egg whites until stiff. Cook sugar to 110°, fold slowly into egg whites to make meringue, then fold into cream mixture. Pour into flan rings, dust with powdered sugar and bake for 5-8 minutes in 350° oven, then broil quickly, just until glazed. Remove from molds, dust again with powdered sugar and place on a bed of fresh passionfruit to serve.

CHOCOLATE MOUSSE CHALWELL

Roger & Jana Downing, Tortola
Serves: 8

12 ozs. dark chocolate chips
1 1/4 cups heavy cream
4 large eggs
4 tbsps. Grand Marnier

Soften chocolate chips in double boiler or place in microwave-safe bowl and microwave until soft enough to spread. Place cream and eggs in blender or food processor and blend for a minute or two.

Gradually add softened chocolate, the Grand Marnier and blend several minutes until mixture is dark and velvety. Pour into glass dishes, cover with plastic wrap and refrigerate before serving.

True "grog" had its beginning in the Royal Navy in the 18th century—specifically on August 21, 1740. It is the most traditional of all sea drinks.

Prior to 1740, Pusser's Rum was issued to the men "neat"—that is, without water. But Admiral Vernon, the hero of Porto Bello and Commander-in-Chief West Indies was to change all this by the issuance of his infamous *Order to Captains No. 349,* given on board his flagship *HMS Burford* on August 21, 1740.

His order refers to the

"...unanimous opinion of both Captains and Surgeons that the pernicious custom of the seamen drinking their allowance of rum in drams, and often at once, is attended with many fatal effects to their morals as well as their health besides the ill consequences of stupefying their rational qualities. ...You are hereby required and directed ... that the respective daily allowance ... be every day mixed with the proportion of a quart of water to a half pint of rum, to be mixed in a scuttled butt kept for that purpose, and to be done upon the deck, and in the presence of the Lieutenant of the Watch, who is to take particular care to see

that the men are not defrauded in having their full allowance of rum."

The tars had already nicknamed Vernon "Old Grog" from the grosgrain cloak he often wore when on the quarterdeck. The watered rum gave great offense to the men, and soon they began referring to it contemptuously as "grog" from the name they'd already provided Vernon.

Vernon's order provided that every man's half-pint Pusser's Rum allowance be diluted with one quart water. This was later changed to two parts water and one rum. In 1756, the daily ration was increased to one pint per man! Just before the end in 1970, it was reduced to one-eighth pint.

On board another ship of Vernon's squadron, the *HMS Berwick*, and just after the issuance of Vernon's order, one of the men wrote this poem that became famous throughout England:

"A mighty bowl on deck he drew
And filled it to the brink.
Such drank the Burford*'s gallant crew*
And such the Gods shall drink.
The sacred robe which Vernon wore
Was drenched within the same,
And hence its virtues guard our shore
And Grog derives its name."

LIMEY

Tall glass or old-fashioned glass filled with
  ice cubes
2 ozs. Pusser's Rum
Soda water

Squeeze the juice from one half lime. Add
sugar to taste (optional, but not traditional).
Top off with soda water, stir, and float the
expended lime peel on top.

ROYAL NAVY FOG CUTTER

Ice cubes to fill shaker
2 ozs. Pusser's Rum
$\frac{1}{2}$ ounce gin
$\frac{1}{4}$ cup lemon juice
2 tbsps. orange juice
1 tbsp. orgeat syrup
1 tsp. dry sherry
Fruit slices for garnish

Shake first 6 ingredients well, and strain
into tall glass filled with ice cubes. Float
sherry on top, garnish and serve with a straw.

THE BIG DIPPER

Ice cubes to fill shaker
1 oz. Pusser's Rum
1 oz. brandy
1 tbsp. lime juice
$\frac{1}{2}$ tsp. sugar
dash of Cointreau
Club soda

Shake well rum, brandy, lime juice, sugar
and Cointreau. Strain into an old-fashioned
glass with several ice cubes, fill with club soda
and stir slightly. This is a popular drink on
Atlantic crossings just before star time.

EMPIRE TOP

2 parts Pusser's Rum
1 part French Vermouth
1 part Grand Marnier
1 dash Angostura bitters
Crushed ice

Shake all the ingredients well and serve.

DIFFERENT DRUMMER

3 cups orange juice
$\frac{3}{4}$ cup coffee liqueur
6 orange or lemon slices (garnish)
$\frac{3}{4}$ cup Jamaican or dark rum
2 dozen ice cubes

Combine ingredients and shake well. Garnish with orange or lemon slices and serve
immediately. Serves 6.

PLANTER'S PUNCH

1 cup cracked ice
3 ozs. Pusser's Rum
1 oz. lime juice
1 oz. sugar syrup
3-5 dashes Angostura bitters
soda water

Shake all ingredients together well and
pour unstrained into tall glass with several
ice cubes. Top off with soda water, stir,
garnish with lime slice and serve with a straw.

THE DEEP SIX

Tall glass filled with crushed ice
2 ozs. Pusser's Rum
1 tbsp. lime juice
$\frac{1}{2}$ ounce sugar syrup
Champagne

Combine rum, lime juice and sugar, and stir
well. Fill glass with champagne and stir gently. Garnish with a slice of lime. This is an
unusual drink—smooth, flavorful & powerful.

FORCE 12

Ice cubes to fill shaker
$\frac{1}{4}$ cup Pusser's Rum
1 oz. vodka
1 tbsp. lime juice
1 tbsp. grenadine
$\frac{1}{4}$ cup pineapple juice

Shake well and pour into tall glass. Garnish with fruit slices. This drink is a good test
for sea legs.

---

*"The Origin of Grog" and the above recipes are provided courtesy of
Pusser's Ltd., Road Town, Tortola, B.V.I.*

Fabulous Island Fruits & Vegetables

Illustrations by Joan Potter

A *collection of some of the most delicious tropical produce to be found in the Virgin Islands.*

Sugar Apple

A favourite throughout the islands, the sugar apple looks like it wears a coat of armour! Actually when ripe, it breaks open easily and the delicious, custard-like interior can be scooped out by the spoonful or by eating it by the mouthful, taking care to spit out the shiny seeds inside. It is well worth the effort, as the inside is sweet, with a wonderful sort of soft texture.

Guava

This colourful fruit is used for making jams, jellies, and is scrumptious in pies and tarts. The guava is a small, usually round fruit that grows on a tree. The skin is green to yellow-green, and pulp inside is pink or peach to an almost red colour, with lines of seeds. Guava ice cream is a delicacy not to be missed.

Passion Fruit

Despite the connotation of the name, this fruit may be rather baffling to the first time taster. It is actually quite unattractive with a tough, wrinkly, brownish skin and is about the size of a lemon. The interior has a yellow green jellyish pulp with edible brown seeds. When the seeds are removed, the passion fruit essence is used to flavour exotic drinks, ices, tarts and pies, becoming an interesting, perfumey addition to many recipes.

Genip

Looking like a bunch of green grapes, these small, round fruits are a bit more challenging to eat! First the somewhat tough skin encasing the pulp must be pulled off (usually with your teeth). Once the skin is gone, the inside is yours to tug the sweet, sometimes tart pulp from the rather large pit. Although not easy fruits to eat, genips can keep you busy for quite awhile!

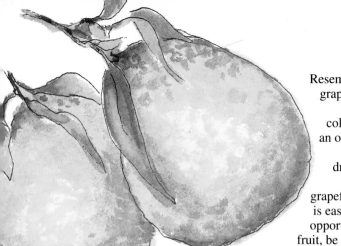

Ugli Fruit

Resembling an ugly version of a grapefruit the ugli fruit is light green to a yellowy orange colour, and can be the size of an orange to the size of a large grapefruit. Succulent and dripping with juice it is best eaten the same way as a grapefruit or an orange (the skin is easily peeled). If you have an opportunity to try this wondrous fruit, be sure to enjoy its blessings.

Tamarind

Growing from large, lovely shade trees are the pods of the tamarind tree. Used in many sauces such as Worcestershire, chutney, and piccalilli, tamarind is also used for sweet candies, and jams. One has to develop a taste for this often tart fruit, but, once acquired, it is hard to stop the attachment. To eat you must first crack open the pod, remove the threads and then consume the sticky paste attached to the large seeds.

Papaya

Growing from a tall, slender umbrella-shaped tree, the fabulous "paw-paw" varies from an eggplant shape to an oval or round shape. The colours vary from a green to orange or yellow, but the fruits must be tested by squeezing to ascertain whether it is ripe or not. The texture of the lovely orange, melon like interior of the fruit is almost as heavenly as the taste, especially when sprinkled with a bit of fresh lime. Green papaya still hard to the squeeze, is used as a cooked vegetable in many delectable recipes.

Sapodilla

About the size of a medium apple, the sapodilla should be eaten only when very ripe and almost mushy like a plum. The skin is a pale tan or beige colour with shiny black seeds inside that should not be eaten. This fruit is used in making many dessert dishes, and is delicious when eaten with other fruits in a fruit salad.

Soursop

A very unlikely looking delicacy this fruit is large (often weighing several pounds), with a green, spiny exterior. The shape is like that of a large pine cone irregularly formed. Only very few are eaten fresh, as most are used in flavouring other dishes with its sweet fragrance, like soursop ice cream, or in tropical fruit drinks with a healthy measure of rum!

Mango

The mango grows from a large, leafy tree that during mango season becomes heavily laden with its scented fruit. Mangos come in many varieties, but are usually best eaten at the beach, where one can jump into the sea to clean off the delicious stickiness. Grafted mangos are less fibrous, and when peeled are a delight. One may see children and adults sucking on mangos to extract the juicy, orange flesh from the fibers and bulky seed in the middle.

Breadfruit

The breadfruit tree is a
common sight on many
Caribbean islands. Mature
fruits have dimpled green
skins and grow to 6 inches or
larger in clusters on magnificent
trees of up to 60 feet in height
with huge, long-fingered leaves.
Inside, the soft, fleshy fruits are
yellowish-brown to white in color and
rich in carbohydrates and vitamins A, B and C.
Breadfruit can be cooked as a starchy vegetable
side dish or in breadfruit breads, puddings and
pies. Try it baked with salt, pepper and butter.

Dasheen

This versatile plant grows to a height of four to six feet. The large, handsome, arrow-shaped leaves, sometimes called elephant ears, are similar to spinach. The young, tender leaves are used in callaloo soup, while the tubers, shown here, are generally stubby and similar in size to potatoes. Also called *cocoyam, taro, eddo* and *kalo*, the dasheen tubers are usually boiled, roasted or baked and eaten like potatoes.

Christophene

The pear-shaped christophene originated in Mexico where it is known as *chayote*, and is a member of the gourd family. It can be eaten raw or cooked and is crisp, juicy and nutty flavored, with a taste like fresh, young squash. Large christophenes may be stuffed with a mixture of bread crumbs, meat, cheese, onions, herbs and seasonings and broiled or baked.

Aubergine

This egg-shaped member of the potato family is a common plant throughout the Caribbean, as it relies on the warm climate and plentiful rain supply to support its growth. The large, glossy fruits are known by various other names, including *Chinese eggplant, Jew's apple, egg fruit, melongene, garden egg* and *mad apple*. The skin colors range from dark purple to mottled purple-and-white. Served as a vegetable, the ripe aubergines may be cubed and boiled or cut into strips or slices, battered and fried. Comprised of over 90 percent water, aubergines are low in both calories and nutritional value.

MEDICAL INFORMATION

British VI: Ambulance/Fire/Police 999
USVI: Ambulance 922 / Fire 921 / Police 915

The sailing area comprising the Virgin Islands stretches from St. Thomas in the U.S. Virgin Islands to Anegada in the British Virgin Islands. Therefore, it is reassuring to know that good medical help is never far away.

Both St. Thomas and Tortola have well-equipped hospitals should a serious injury occur, but the majority of minor boating mishaps require only the attention of a physician; hospitalization is seldom required. Accidents do happen, however, and when they do, it is good to know what facilities are available and where they are located.

When you are cruising or vacationing in the Virgin Islands, the last thing which you anticipate is sickness or injury. These notes are based on years of experience in practice in these Islands treating the visitor who unexpectedly becomes sick. They are not intended to replace any good first aid book issued by the Red Cross or St. John's Ambulance Brigade.

If you have a medical condition that requires ongoing medication, check with your physician before leaving home to ensure that you have enough medication to last during your vacation. *Please* carry the medication with you in your hand luggage, as checked baggage can be temporarily mislaid during flight changes and may not arrive until the next day. While most commonly used medications are available at Peebles Hospital (494-3497), pharmacies, or any of the six health centers in the islands, there may be a delay before these can be dispensed and valuable time may be lost.

Peebles Hospital in Roadtown, Tortola, is a small, modern 60-bed hospital with an operating room, x-ray department, pharmacy and laboratory, and can handle most routine emergencies. The hospital is staffed with a general surgeon, gynecologist, internist, anaesthetist and two general physicians. These physicians, as well as several others, are in private practice. There is also a private clinic specializing in plastic and reconstructive surgery. In the event of a more serious illness or accident requiring more specialized care, the hospital is only 15 minutes by air from St. Thomas, USVI, and 35 minutes by air from Puerto Rico; air evacuation can be arranged if necessary.

Should you require emergency medical treatment, a doctor is on call at Peebles Hospital 24 hours a day; there is also a resident doctor in Virgin Gorda.

Radio Tortola can patch a ship's radio through the telephone system to any of these physicians in an emergency; sometimes advice on the radio may suffice without the necessity of returning to home port.

The water around the islands gives you some of the best sailing, swimming, snorkeling, and scuba diving in the world. Enjoy it—but cultivate a deep respect for it.

Sunburn

Probably the commonest ailment. This area is classified as subtropical, and the sun can be very harmful if taken in large doses at the beginning of vacation. On a boat there is a lot of reflected sunlight from the surface of the water.

Wear a long-sleeved shirt and light, long pants part of the day for the first few days. Socks will protect the tops of your feet and wearing a T-shirt while swimming will protect your back. Use plenty of sunscreen lotion—the higher the SPF factor, the better the protection.

If, in spite of these precautions, you suffer a severe burn, cover up and use an anti-allergic cream such as Benadryl or Phenergan. Solarcaine or other burn lotion, liberally applied, and a couple of aspirin or acetaminophen every four hours or so will diminish the pain.

If the burn develops blisters, leave them intact as long as possible to protect the sensitive tissues beneath. Once the blisters have burst, apply an antibiotic ointment to prevent infection.

Eye
Conjunctivitis

Wind, dust, overchlorinated water in pools, aerosol sprays, etc., can cause mild to moderate discomfort. Symptoms include constant watering of the eye(s) with redness due to vascular congestion. Wash the eyes with clear water and use decongestant eye drops every four hours. Wear sunglasses as a preventative measure.

Foreign Body In The Eye

When examining the eye for a foreign body, a good source of light is necessary. Lay the patient on his back and have an assistant hold a flashlight from the side of the eye. Check the lower lid first by pulling the lid down with the thumb. The upper eyelid can be examined by having the patient look down towards his feet. Hold the upper eyelashes with the thumb and forefinger and roll the lid back over the shaft of a Q-tip. Gently remove the foreign body with a *moist* Q-tip and instill eye drops afterwards. Do not use a dry Q-tip as it can damage the surface of the eye.

Bowel Upset
Constipation

Constipation is rarely a problem in the tropics but may be worrisome during the first few days while acclimatizing to a new diet and the crowded quarters on a boat. Eat plenty of fruit and drink fruit juices, prune juice, and plenty of other fluids. If these remedies are unsuccessful, try some Milk of Magnesia or a mild laxative of your choice. If the condition persists, call a physician.

Diarrhea

Diarrhea is a common ailment on a tropical vacation, probably due to a change in diet and the availability of many exotic fruits. If you suspect the drinking water, boil it before drinking. If the diarrhea lasts more than a day, rehydrate using a glucose/salt solution like Gatorade or a solution of 1 pint water with 1/4 teaspoon salt and 1 tablespoon sugar, and stick to clear liquids only for 24-36 hours. If the diarrhea is accompanied by fever, contact a physician, who will probably prescribe an intestinal antibiotic.

Hemorrhoids

A frequent complication of the above conditions. Treat with long soaks in warm water and use glycerine suppositories twice a day and after each bowel movement. Suppositories should be kept refrigerated.

Burns

Minor burns can be treated with a simple antibiotic ointment and covered with vaseline gauze and then gauze dressings held in place by a bandage. If blisters appear, leave them intact as long as possible; puncturing them may lead to infection. If the burn appears to have penetrated through the skin layer, consult a physician.

Fish Hooks

The best way to remove a fish hook is to cut the shaft of the book with wire cutters and pull the hook, point first, through the skin with a pair of pliers. Treat afterwards as a puncture wound with antibiotic ointment and gauze dressing.

Fractures

The immediate first aid treatment is to immobilize the limb and use an analgesic or painkiller to relieve pain. Splints can be improvised from everyday items such as pillows, magazines, broom handles, or paddles, padded and tied firmly around the limb. In suspected fractures of the neck or back, lay the patient flat and prevent any movement, rolling or otherwise, by the use of pillows or other supports. Seek medical attention as soon as possible.

Headaches

May be due to too much to drink the night before, eyestrain (wear sunglasses), sinusitis from swimming and diving (take aspirin, acetaminophen or sinus tablets every four hours), or from too much direct sun (wear a hat). Bed rest and icepacks will relieve the ache. If the symptoms do not resolve in 24 hours, seek the advice of a physician.

Sprains

The early application of icepacks to the affected area during the first 8 hours will greatly reduce the amount of swelling. Elevate the limb on a pillow and apply an ace bandage from the affected area to above it.

Stings from Sea Urchins, Jellyfish or other Aquatic Creatures

First and foremost, watch where you are going. A weedy or stony approach to a beach means you may find sea urchins—don't step on them.

If you do get stung, do not attempt to dig the stinger out, as this can cause a secondary infection. Dab tincture of iodine on the stingers, and take antihistamines to reduce the reaction.

There are no lethal creatures in these waters, but there are a few with self-protection devices that can give you a nasty painful sting.

Cystitis & Urinary Tract Infections

Urinary infections are most frequently caused by sitting around in wet bathing suits. Drink plenty of fluids—cranberry juice is a favourite home remedy. A doctor will likely prescribe a urinary tract antibiotic, such as Septrin (2 tabs. 2x/day) or Gantrisin (2 tabs. 4x/day).

Insect Bites

For bites of mosquitoes, sandflies, no-see-ums or blister bugs, apply an anti-allergic cream, such as Phenergan or Benadryl, to the area.

For prevention, there are a wide variety of insect repellent sprays, lotions and creams which are very effective when applied to exposed skin, especially in the late afternoons or early evenings, when the cooler temperatures lure these insects from their hiding places.

Allergic Dermatitis

The leaves of several tropical plants such as manchioneel or oleander, especially after rain, can produce a severe skin reaction. Apply antihistamine cream and take Phenergan or Benadryl 25 mg., 4 times a day.

The manchioneel tree produces a fruit resembling a small green apple, which is highly poisonous. *Do not eat it.*

Earache

Ear discomfort is frequently due to wax buildup after swimming, snorkeling and diving. The mixture of salt water and wax can create swelling which may cause temporary deafness.

If you are subject to wax formation in the ear canal, visit your physician and have him or her syringe your ears before vacation. Frequently a few drops of warm olive oil in the ear will soften the wax and alleviate the symptoms.

Earache associated with a runny discharge may denote an infection in the canal and will usually respond to antibiotic ear drops with hydrocortisone used 4 times a day. There are numerous preparations on the market containing isopropyl alcohol and boric acid crystals, which are helpful for drying the ear canals after swimming.

Suggestions for a Marine Medical Kit

If you will be cruising out of sight of land for any length of time, a first aid kit is essential. The following items will meet most of your medical requirements:

- Ace bandages
- Antacid tablets
- Antibiotics (ampicillin, erythromycin, tetracycline, etc.)
- Antibiotic ear drops
- Antibiotic eye drops & ointment
- Antihistamines (Benadryl 25 mg., Phenergan 25 mg., etc.)
- Anti-seasickness medication (Dramamine, patches, etc.)
- Antiseptic powder or cream
- Aspirin, acetaminophen (Tylenol, etc.), ibuprofen (Nuprin, Advil, etc.)
- Assorted dressings: Rolled gauze, gauze squares, bandage strips, roll bandages, cotton, adhesive tape, triangular bandage, butterfly strips, safety pins, etc.
- Azo gantrisin or Septrin
- Insect repellant sprays
- Laxatives (Milk of Magnesia, etc.)
- Lomotil tablets 2.5 mg.
- Oil of cloves
- Paregoric
- Rubbing alcohol
- Solarcaine
- Sunburn relief cream
- Sunscreen lotions
- Thermometer

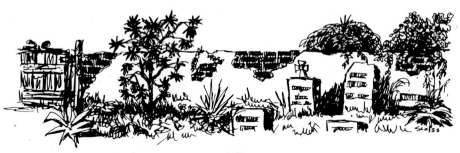

Jim Scheiner

The Virgin Islands offer the world's best long-distance windsurfing and consistent summer trades with stronger winter winds.

All the features that make the Virgin Islands so alluring to yachtsmen make them equally alluring to windsurfers. The gentle trade winds, year-round sun and warm waters make the Virgins a mecca for all levels of windsurfing.

Best of all, while sailors have known about these islands for many years now, the area remains relatively unexploited by "boardheads."

Consistent summer trades and potentially strong winter winds allow all levels of windsurfers to enjoy some of the world's best boardsailing. Blessed with an ideal climate, the Virgins are arguably one of the best locations for learning the sport, and are endowed with excellent sailing schools catering to the windsurfer. Beginning and intermediate windsurfers will benefit from the many sheltered sounds and bays with clear, shallow, reef-protected waters and steady winds.

Advanced sailors can enjoy the world's best long-distance sailing between the multitude of islands and cays comprising this rich cruising ground. Island-to-island sailing is a favourite form of windsurfing.

Safety should always be your first priority. Confidence in your equipment is another must.

If you are learning or still honing your skills as a windsurfer, be careful of off-shore winds. It is often helpful to have a partner following in the dinghy.

More advanced sailors should always windsurf with a buddy, particularly when travelling by board between islands. Long-distance sailing—certainly the most challenging aspect of windsurfing in the Virgins—demands certain minimum safety measures, including informing someone of your destination and your estimated time of arrival.

The Virgin Islands are a collection of unique windsurfing locations. In North Sound at the top of Virgin Gorda, the windsurfing is outstanding. Off the Bitter End Yacht Club in adjoining EustatiaSound, the flat water shredding is about as good as can be found anywhere. The water is a translucent 10-20 feet deep, with a long barrier reef which demarcates the relatively placid Sound from the pumping blue ocean. The wind blows from the east, hugging the steep hill that the resort clings to, before emptying into North Sound.

Beginning and intermediate level sailors alike can take advantage of the shallow waters off Bitter End to hone their jibing and waterstarting techniques. More advanced sailors can explore the sound or sail across the channel to private Necker Island. It's a good idea to bring a mask for jumping overboard and checking out whatever catches your fancy.

The Bitter End has a large Mistral fleet including 1993 Energy and Explosion boards, as well as all new 1993 Gaastra sails. The resort is host to a series of windsurfing clinics each November/December, when professional racer Andy Morrell from Tortola spends a month at the resort for "Fast Tacks," a unique sailing and watersports extravaganza. Morrell teaches the basics, hosts "Wind Safari" long-distance sailing and holds clinics on speed sailing, racing tactics, etc.

Trellis Bay, beside the airport, is known for its good wind in the channel between Beef Island and Marina Cay. When the current is running counter to the wind, this channel is a chop jumper's heaven—and possibly the most challenging place to windsurf in all the Virgin Islands. Protected Trellis Bay is ideal for learning. Lessons and rentals can be easily arranged through Jeremy at Boardsailing BVI.

Windsurfing Tortola, at Nanny Cay below Road Town, is where most Tortolans gather for their wind fixes. Nanny Cay juts out into the Sir Francis Drake Channel, making it an ideal staging point for windsurfing ventures to Norman or PeterIslands, or just up and down the coast. Situated perpendicular to the predominantly easterly winds and protected by a shallow reef from the channel's rougher waters in a several-acre lagoon, Windsurfing Tortola boasts an idyllic location for beginners. The facility offers guaranteed success lessons and hourly, daily or weekly rentals of all new equipment.

Jost Van Dyke offers great windsurfing possibilities. To windsurf here, however, you must bring your own gear by boat, as there are no rental facilities. Intermediate or advanced sailors will enjoy the area around Green and Sandy Cays (the latter, with its more sheltered waters, appealing to the less experienced). Beginners may appreciate either Great Harbour or White Bay, though when the wind is north of east,it can be a bit puffy.

In the USVI, there is good windsurfing off St. John's north shore. In Leinster Bay you can enjoy flat water sailing closer to shore. If you prefer, there is good jumping out in the channel towards Tortola, or above Johnson's Reef out of Trunk Bay. The area around Johnson's Reef can be particularly challenging in the winter months.

Further west, towards St. Thomas, the hot spot is Bluebeard's Beach, around the corner from Redhook. Despite the relative congestion from the new hotel, this is still a pleasant place to drop the hook and enjoy the wide open bay with its clean wind and flat water. This is the favourite gathering and sailing spot for local windsurfers.

On the whole, windsurfing in the Virgin Islands is a light to moderate wind affair. The trade winds blow 12-18 knots on average from May to September. In the winter

Whether a beginner, an intermediate or an expert, there are locations and sea conditions to match all skill levels of windsurfing in the Virgin Islands.

and spring, occasional light spells can give way to passing fronts that provide winds in the 15-20-plus knot range.

The equipment of choice is big, floaty slalom boards. Local sailors rely on boards in the 9'2" to 9'6" range, and sails from 6 to 7.5 square meters. For long-distance sailing, course boards with centerboards are best relied upon to get through the occasional holes behind islands.

If you bring your own gear, remember to pack it well for airline travel, and keep it under wraps on the boat, because decks and hull fittings are not kind to fragile epoxy boards. Also, whenever possible, carry your sail to shore where rigging is easier without stanchions and sheets in the way.

The Virgin Islands provide a unique and relatively undiscovered windsurfing vacation. In most places you can enjoy incredible conditions with a stunning backdrop and in the company of only a few others. Plus, windsurfing among the islands perfectly accentuates the sailing vacation—the two were really made for each other.

ANDY MORRELL, *a professional windsurfer, lives in Tortola, BVI, and is the 1992 U.S. National Champion and 1991 Caribbean Champion. He is also a travel writer and watersports event organizer.*

221

FOR THE BIRDS

From the Pelican, whose death-defying dives delight observers, to the charming yellow and black Bananaquit, who gracefully flits from flower to flower, birds are an integral part of the B.V.I.'s landscape. In all, there are 154 species of birds present in the British Virgin Islands, and imagining the islands without them would be like imagining them without blue seas and palm trees.

Some of the B.V.I.'s birds are visitors from afar. Each year these migratory birds make the trek from points north to enjoy the Territory's mild winters, often joining a smaller population of the same species that live here year-round. Perhaps 90 percent of the birds that inhabit the B.V.I. are also found in North America and just a handful or so are native solely to the Caribbean.

Of these natives, one of the most common is the Zenaida (*Zenaida aurita*) for whom these islands are named. Tortola is the Spanish word for pigeon or dove, and it is believed that when Columbus sailed past the Virgin Islands on his second voyage to the New World, he named the chain's main island after this abundant bird. Locally called the Mountain Dove, the Zenaida frequents open areas, particularly coastal ones, but is also seen on the hillsides. About 10 to 11 inches long, with a round tail and a white band on its wing tips, the Zenaida can also be recognized by its cooing sound, similar to that of the Mourning Dove.

Commonly seen like the Zenaida, is the Ground Dove (*Columbina passerina*). Smaller (about 6 to 7 inches) than the Zenaida, and with purple-gray feathers, the Ground Dove is often spotted hopping along unpaved roads as it feeds, flying close to the ground and only for short bursts. The Ground Dove prefers arid scrub lands, and nests in low bushes or trees or directly on the ground.

One of the islands' most distinguished residents is the American Kestrel (*Falco sparperius*) which is often found floating effortlessly astride the many updrafts and air currents prevalent in the B.V.I.'s steep valleys. Also called the Killy-Killy, the American Kestrel has the typical hooked beak of a hawk, is small in size (9 to 12 inches) and has a red tail with a broad black terminal band and a mottled facial pattern. The male has blue wings.

With its dark black feathers, long tail and dark, parrot-like bill, the Smooth-billed Ani (*Crotophaga ani*) is easy to spot. Known locally as the Black Witch, the bird is a member of the Cuckoo family, has a loud squawk-like whistle and lives in small flocks. The females have the impractical habit of laying their eggs in layers in communal nests, so that only the eggs in the top-most layer hatch.

The Green-throated Carib (*Sericotes holosericeus*), one of the B.V.I.'s most delightful residents, can often be seen darting at lightening speed in and out of flowering shrubs. The iridescent green hummingbird has a sapphire blue mark on the breast and is considered large for the species (4½ to 5 inches). It is known locally as the Doctor Bird.

Bold and aggressive, the Pearly-eyed Thrasher (*Margarops fuscatus*) is not beyond helping himself to a picnic lunch left unattended. But if you're lucky, the raspy call of the Threshy, as he is called here, may warn you that he is on the way. A fairly large bird (around 11 to 12 inches), he

The British Virgin Islands provide a well-suited habitat for 154 species of birds. Photographer Dougal Thornton has captured many of these on film including the three pictured; a Great Heron in flight, a Little Blue Heron perched on a piling and an American Kestrel.

has a white iris, brown upper body, white tail tips and a white belly dappled with brown.

One of the area's prettiest land birds is the Bananaquit (*Coerba flaveola*) which can often be seen partaking of the nectar of the islands' prolific tropical blooms. A small bird, about 4 to 5 inches tall, the Bananaquit has a dark back, white stripe above the eye, a gray throat and yellow breast, belly and rear. In order to attract this pretty little creature, many island residents place a bird feeder filled with sugar water near the house.

As you travel in the B.V.I., you will almost certainly notice the Gray Kingbird (*Tyrannus dominicensis*), one of the islands' most abundant residents. It is often seen perched on telephone wires. It is about 9 to 9½ inches long, gray on top, pale gray-white on the abdomen and breast and has a distinct black mark extending under the eye to the ear. It also has a yellow and orange-red mark at the top of its head which is difficult to see. Locally, the bird is called the Chichery.

Among the British Virgin Island's most dramatic birds are the sea birds, and perhaps the most spectacular of these is the aptly named Magnificent Frigatebird (*Fregata magnificens*). With its eight-foot wing span, the Frigatebird is considered one of the bird world's most accomplished flyers. Although they can perch on branches and cliff edges, their legs are too small to walk and as a result they have honed their skill in flying, spending days in the air and often sleeping in-flight. Male Frigatebirds are all black with glossy green and purple feathers on the back, and an inflatable red throat-pouch which he blows up with air like a balloon to attract females during mating season. The females are black with a white breast, while juveniles have a white head and breast.

An avid fisherman, the Brown Pelican (*Pelecanus occidentalis*) is often seen swooping into the sea from great heights in order to scoop up a large bill full of fish. This large bird (42 to 54 inches) is common along beach and shore areas, and is often seen perching on a bowsprit or bollard in marinas. Clumsy on land, it is graceful in the air, flapping its wings for a burst and then gliding. Unlike other seabirds, the pelican's neck is drawn back onto the shoulders and is not extended in flight.

Another common seabird is the Brown Booby (*Sula leucogaster*), distinctive with its sleek brown head and upper body, long pointed beak and white belly and abdomen. Approximately 28 to 30 inches long, the bird is often seen resting on buoys or rocky cliffs. It nests on the ground.

Like most of the B.V.I.'s seabirds, the Royal Tern (*Sterna maxima*) is more commonly seen in the summer when it comes to shore to breed, and least commonly seen in the winter when it spends its time at sea. White to mottled white, the Tern has dark wing tips and an entirely black head in summer, while in the winter its forehead is white. The Royal Tern ranges from 18 to 21 inches in length.

The Cattle Egret (*Bubulcus ibis*) is almost always seen in the islands' many cattle pastures, often sitting on the back of a contented cow as it feeds off insects. The Cattle Egret is 19 to 25 inches, has a thick yellowish bill and unlike the other aquatic egrets, it is rarely seen near water, except to drink

As it flies, neck extended forward and legs tucked below its sleek white body, or as it stands in shallow water, the Great Egret (*Casmerodius albus*) is the picture of elegance. It is much larger (35 to 42 inches) than the Cattle Egret and has a yellow bill and black legs. While this lovely aquatic bird is occasionally seen in the Virgin Islands, it is not common.

At 42 to 52 inches in length, the Great Blue Heron (*Ardea herodias*) is the largest heron in the B.V.I. It is blue-gray in color and is often seen wading in shallow mangrove areas or in quiet lagoons in hope of dinner. It is rarely seen in the summer when it breeds in remote areas.

Reprinted with permission by THE NATIONAL PARKS TRUST. The National Parks Trust is working to conserve the natural and cultural heritage of the British Virgin Islands.

FISHING IN THE VIRGIN WATERS

Jim Scheiner

The Virgin Islands are known for outstanding sportfishing, especially for blue marlin.

The vast numbers of sailors who cruise the Virgin Islands waters each year attest to the fact that there is a seldom quelled sense of adventure lurking in all of us; but few who come to these islands in search of excitement ever really delve below the sparkling surface of the turquoise and indigo waters to meet the equally cosmopolitan inhabitants below.

The colourful underwater residents come in every size, shape and character from mean-toothed barracuda to genially smiling grouper, and the annual pelagic visitors are just as varied; sleek, powerful marlin, graceful sailfish and vivid, rainbow-hued dolphin.

The range of gamefishing is therefore broad enough to please every type of angler, whether their inclination is towards a peaceful, reflective stroll along a quiet beach to cast for bonefish or the lusty adventure, so glamourized by Hemingway, tossing about on the high seas to battle with solitary billfish or giant tuna.

Fishing can be a very enjoyable supplement to a sailing vacation and one of the beauties of the sport is that a lucky novice has as much chance as an expert of landing a good sized fish. As the saying goes, "gamefishing is the only sport in which a complete novice has a realistic chance at a world record."

The modes of fishing in the Virgin Islands can vary from jetty fishing (guaranteed to keep the kids occupied for hours to the dedicated pursuit of the Atlantic blue marlin, requiring boat, tackle and a skilled crew. Generally, however, the fishing available can be categorized into three main areas: shoreline angling, inshore fishing and blue water trolling.

Jim Scheiner

Your fishing options are limitless in the Virgin Islands, ranging from bluewater offshore angling to flats fishing for bonefish.

SHORE FISHING

Shore Fishing and the variety of sport this provides is probably the least documented and the least utilized of all the types of fishing in the Virgin Islands, and yet for zealots of this king of sport, the area really has it all. The quarry includes bonefish, tarpon and permit, fish that in other parts of the world have as many ardent followers as the blue marlin, yet the potential in these waters is largely untapped and relies mainly on the reports of a few who, without the availability of a guide, still manage to locate enough of these wary demons of the shallows to return year after year.

Fresh water casting gear, fly rod or spinning tackle can be put to good use along the shoreline. In the lagoons and shallow banks a variety of smaller fish can be found, and the meandering channels that wind sluggishly through walls of mangroves are a have for jacks, parrot fish, schools of snap-pers, lady fish and the occasional barracuda or grouper.

Live shrimp are excellent bail for fishing off these banks, but good results can also be obtained with strips of fish, flies, small spoons, feathers or spinners.

Off rocky ledges snapper can be enticed with feathers or bucktailed jigs, and with spinning tackle and light test line the battle must be won quickly before the fish dives for cover to cut the line on a sharp-edged cranny.

Off the beach, the shallows are sometimes frequented by jacks, mackerel and runners for which ordinary fresh water casting tackle with surface lures and six to eight pound test line is ideal.

The same type of tackle can be used to hunt bonefish, permit and tarpon in the surf or on banks and flats where the angler can wade out into the warm shallows to peer eagerly into the weed for the flash of silver.

Bonefish

The bonefish can be found in shallow flats or off quiet beaches, feeding like a grey ghost along the bottom. A narrow, streamlined fish with a pointed snout, it ranges from 3-16 pounds, with an average size of about 5 pounds. It is a fussy eater with a highly suspicious nature, fickle and difficult to persuade; however, it can be tempted with conch, crab or shrimp and artificial lures such as streamer flies. Small feathers or bucktails can be successfully used with spinning tackle, but accurate casting and skillful working of the lure helps considerably. Because of its nervous

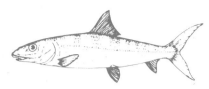

disposition better results can be achieved by stealthy wading rather than poling out into the shallows in a dinghy.

The scientific name for bonefish, Abula vulpa means white fox, an accurate name for this wily, fast-moving fish which, when hooked, produces an astonishing turn of speed, zig-zagging with sizzling fury in one of the most exciting battles to be found in angling.

Tarpon

These bulky, energetic fish, largest member of the herring family, can be found in a variety of feeding grounds including harbours, reefs, shallow flats and creeks. They are a good-sized fish ranging from 20 to 280 pounds, but are more commonly found at less than 80 pounds. They tend to snooze through the day in holes and deep creeks and feed at night, when they can be heard splashing an leaping in pursuit of their prey—small fish, crabs and grass shrimps. Fly rod plugs and spinning gear

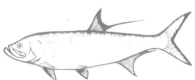

are sure to produce some good sport with these hefty adversaries who are very willing to plunge after a variety of baits, tackle and fishing modes. The larger specimens require a considerable weightier test line, yet still give excellent sport. Local fishermen should be consulted for advice on the best areas and tackle for tarpon.

Permit

Largest of the pompanos, the permit ranges in size between 5 and 50 pounds, though is more common between 12 and 25 pounds. It is a flat-sided fish with an angry frown which warns that, for its size, it possesses surprising strength. It can be found bottom feeding, looking for crabs, sea urchins, clams, starfish and shrimp in the surf, the creek estuaries or on the reefs. Permit are fast feeders, flitting from one spot to another with flashing birdlike movements, always alert and on the go.

Permit can be taken on artificial lures, live bait or, if conditions are right, a skillfully used fly. Besides frequenting the shallows they like to feed in waves crashing over a reef or in curling breakers on sandy beaches.

INSHORE FISHING

Inshore fishing covers a multitude of species and equally diverse methods of capture. By far the most popular method is

trolling around shallow reefs and headlands with the principal quarry being the kingfish or mackerel. At a slower speed, trolling with a 59-pound test line and strip bait, whole baits or spoons, large grouper of up to 75 pounds or snapper between 10 and 20 pounds can be caught.

Most practical for the yachtsman is bottom or still fishing which can be done more easily from a sailboat. This can produce fine catches of snapper and grouper, hogfish, grunts, hinds and many other bottom dwellers. For the still fishing enthusiast one just needs to anchor over any of the deeper reef areas—say 16 to 20 fathoms—

and drop over a handline or two, or maybe a leadhead jig and the fish will do the rest. In calm weather drifting rather than anchoring will always produce better results. Strips of cut fish are commonly used as bait, but small live bait is by far the best and easily obtained by swiping the results of the kids' jetty fishing.

Chumming conch or tiny bits of any fish will often get the action going as the smaller fish will start to feed, stimulating the larger ones into striking at the bait.

Amberjack

The amberjack is a long fish with heavy shoulders and tapered body. Like the bonefish it has crushers instead of teeth. When hungry or excited it displays feeding stripes —a black band across each side of the head. They range in size from 20 to 150 pounds, more usually between 30 and 40.

Known for its dogged stubbornness and line-cutting tactics, amberjack provides first class sport on any tackle. Live bait is best, although the amberjack can readily be persuaded to gulp a properly worked bucktail or feather jig, and can also be tempted

towards the surface with popping plugs or spinning lures. These fearless fish are often found around wrecks, travelling in small groups or schools at a fair depth. When hooked they rush for the bottom, but if one can be brought up, often the rest of the school will follow, allowing other anglers an excellent chance for a good battle.

Barracuda

This sleek, wolfish, sharp-toothed fish is one of the most easily captured in the area. Found everywhere from deep ocean to shallow flats, the barracuda is a voracious and impulsive feeder, happy to pounce on practically any bait offered. The usual specimen is about 12 pounds, but often goes over 50 and occasionally up to 80 pounds.

Barracuda are most often caught when anglers troll the reefs and "drop offs" for

other gamefish. Despite the ease with which it can be caught, "cuda" is not a popular prey in the Virgin Islands, where it not only is considered inedible but also has a stench which can make the entire boat smell like a garbage tip. Nevertheless, if an angler is prepared to throw it back promptly, barracuda gives some good sport on light tackle.

Kingfish

The kingfish is actually a member of the mackerel family and a fine food fish, sought by commercial fishermen as well as sportsmen. Ranging from 4 to 80 pounds it is more often found between 7 and 20. Like the amberjack, the kingfish prefers the depths but will race upward in pursuit of a trolled lure often clearing the surface of the water in its enthusiasm. When drifting or still fishing,

plug casting gear or spinning tackle can tempt the kingfish, as can a carefully worked feather or bucktail jig. Having a similar shape to the speedy wahoo, kingfish can be tremendous sport on light tackle.

BLUE WATER TROLLING

Made famous the world over by the likes of Hemingway and Zane Grey, and more recently in the Virgin Islands by a string of world records, blue water trolling is by far the most popular method of angling in the area and also the most advanced as far as providing services for the would-be angler. The technique is to trail behind the boat a variety of baits and artificial lures at speeds usually ranging from four to eight knots and occasionally faster, working a pattern back and forth across the edge of the continental shelf.

This edge, or "drop-off" as it is usually known, plunges from an average depth of 25 fathoms to in excess of 300 fathoms, and in places is within two miles of the Virgin Islands group. Ocean currents striking thisformidable cliff create a huge upswelling of microscopic food from the depths and, in turn, a food chain of small fish and larger predators. It is for thesepredators that the offshore angler is looking and the results of his search depend on such things as weather, moon and tide

and of course, most importantly, the skill of the captain and crew. To go after the bigger pelagic (ocean roaming) species it is necessary to use a fishing boat, equipment and skilled crew. These can be chartered with ease throughout the Virgin Islands.

The various types of pelagic fish one normally encounters here include blue marlin, white marlin, sailfish, dolphin fish or dorado, wahoo, tuna and bonito.

Blue Marlin

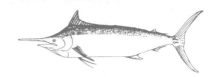

Found in the Virgin Islands from July to September, the Atlantic blue marlin, grandaddy of the fleet, probably the most difficult of the pelagic fish to locate, to tempt into striking, to hook successfully and then to land. A marlin can get really mad at a bait, so mad that it keeps coming back over and over again to "kill" it or swallow it, smashing at it with its powerful bill. Anyone observing this fury will surely be hooked themselves. The challenge of this extraordinary fish matches its size which ranges from 90 to over 1,000 pounds. Up to 500 pounds is most common.

To tempt these solitary billfish that roam where there is plenty of space in the deep, a whole 2-5 pound mackerel, bonefish or mullet is used as bait. These, or large artificial lures, are trolled from outriggers to skip enticingly across the surface of the waves. Often a "teaser" is dragged behind the boat to create additional commotion.

Some anglers use light tackle—30 to 50- lb. test line—or a medium 80-lb., but the majority prefer a heavier 130-lb. line. A hooked marlin is perhaps the most exciting fish in the world, leaping out of the water in enormous bounds, "tailwalking" on the surface, shimmering with rushes of bright colour in its fury. A "green" fish (one brought in so quickly that it isn't even tired) has been known to wreck a boat without much difficulty and the fight can be long and arduous, sometimes lasting for several exhausting hours that require grim determination and constancy from the angler.

However, the satisfaction of catching and tagging one of these monsters is well worth all the tossing around on high swells, the empty hours of no fish and the hard physical work involved.

Sailfish

Easily recognised and distinguished from other billfish by the enormous dorsal fin, the sailfish ranges from 20–140 pounds in size. It first arrives in the Virgin Islands in December, peaks in January and early February and generally leaves by March.

Its habits are somewhat different from the other pelagic fish in that it prefers to feed in shallow waters of 20 fathoms or so. Small ballyhoo or strips of fish trolled at 5–7 knots are a very effective enticement and, for the expert, a live bait worked in the right manner can produce good results.

With an average weight in these waters of

30–40 pounds, sailfish are not normally eaten and are usually released.

Like the blue marlin, when the sailfish becomes excited, as when going for the trolled bait, it frequently "lights up," as waves and waves of irridescent blue ripple up and down its body. When hooked, the sailfish puts on a magnificent acrobatic display, its slender body leaping out of the water with extraordinary grace and beauty.

White Marlin

The smaller cousin of the big blue, the white marlin ranges between 40 and 60 pounds. The methods of capture are the same as for the bigger marlin, although, of course, the tackle is lighter (20-50 pound test), and the bait smaller.

Like sailfish, white marlin readily strike a

variety of artificial lures or even a simple yellow-feathered lure trolled in the wake.

Dolphin

Although also named dolphin, this fish bears no resemblance to the porpoise. The dolphin start to arrive in numbers in late March, and depart in late May, though they are caught occasionally year-round. For the light tackle enthusiast few fish can give such a good account of themselves leaping and somersaulting repeatedly into the air, their brilliant blue and golden bodies flashing in the sunlight. They also jump in long leaps to catch their prey which, due to their sharp eyes, they can spot from quite a distance.

Dolphin are always greedily on the move and will savage almost any offering trolled at a good clip. They range in size from 5–85

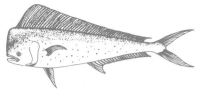

pounds, most commonly from 10–20. On 8 or 12-lb. test line and spinning tackle the dolphin can give a spectacular battle, the aerial display being followed by a dogged broadside fight. It is quite common to have every rod on the boat bending when these fish are around, for they like to school, particularly around floating flotsam or driftwood. Dolphin also provide some of the best table fare in the islands.

Tuna

There are several types of tuna around the Virgin Islands, the black fin being the most common. Usually weighing from 5–15 pounds, they tend to school in large numbers. Their compact bodies are powerful and speedy, always providing some hard action, with the angler only too aware that, if it is not boated quickly, the tuna will fall prey to a marauding shark; and sharks just love tuna!

Growing considerably larger than the blackfin tuna, the Allison or yellowfin tuna reaches weights in excess of 300 pounds, and, pound for pound, can match any other fish in the sea for brute strength and pigheadedness. Around the Virgin Islands the Allison is seldom found over 100 pounds and more usually around 40 pounds. They can be

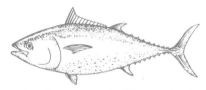

caught all year round, although the larger specimens seem to show up around June. The Allison will feed on almost any trolled offering, from the favourite ballyhoo through a whole range of strip baits and artificial plastics and feathers.

Tuna are steady, stubborn opponents which, once hooked, will usually sound several hundred feet and there engage the angler in a tiring and dogged fight. On the right test, the tuna will provide some of the best sport in gamefishing.

Bonito

The usual size of the oceanic bonito is between 10 and 20 pounds, though they range between 3 and 40 pounds. The smaller fish are popular as live bait for marlin, but the bonito can be a worthwhile catch in itself, the large schools often providing plenty of action for a boatful of fishermen.

Like the blackfin tuna, the bonito feeds on bait fish, which can be found in clusters of thousands. The feeding frenzy leaves scraps floating in the churning water which are promptly dived on by quarreling seabirds. It

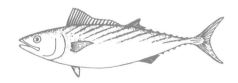

is these birds, hovering over the feeding schools, which will give away the presence of tuna or bonito. If the boat can get there before the birds finish feeding, feathers, or lures trolled rapidly around the roiling mass will almost certainly be snatched.

Wahoo

One of the most elegant fish to be found in the islands, the wahoo is sleek and torpedo-shaped, its upper body tiger-striped in shades of blue, its pointed mouth lined with razor-sharp teeth. This long, lean body slashing through the water has the appearance of a marine projectile. It ranges in size between 10 and 150 pounds, but is more often found between 30 and 50.

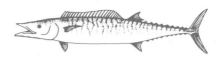

The wahoo is world famous for its immensely powerful strike and fantastic speed. Light tackle, 12 to 30 pound test, will guarantee the best sport, but 50 to 80 pound test is often used as 60 or 80-pound wahoo are not unusual.

They can usually be found singly or in small groups, prowling along the edge of a drop off, and will readily attack any trolled offering be it real or artificial. Wahoo have also been known to go after the teaser itself. Although present all year round they do predominate from late October through December.

For the competitive angler, the various gamefishing clubs of the Virgin Islands and Puerto Rico offer numerous tournaments throughout the year. The majority of these are run during July, August and September, when the blue marlin season is at its peak. International angling teams come from as far away as South Africa and numerous boats come from the United States to compete.

To find out the dates of all of the various fishing tournaments, contact:

BVI:
BVI Yacht and Anglers Club
Road Town, Tortola
809-494-3286

USVI:
Virgin Islands Fishing Club
St. Thomas, USVI 00801
or inquire at
American Yacht Harbor
Red Hook.

232

REAL ESTATE IN THE VIRGIN ISLANDS

Jim Scheiner

Waterfront property, like in other parts of the world, is at a premium in the Virgin Islands. Condos and homes dot the hillside facing Leverick Bay.

REAL ESTATE IN THE BRITISH VIRGIN ISLANDS

For many a property investor in the BVI the love affair begins on the first day of the first charter when, upon clearing the harbour, the decision to go to port is as difficult as the decision to go to starboard, because in every direction there is Virginal splendour to be explored.

For some, a whirlwind romance ensues, with the decision to purchase property transpiring within a week or two; for others it is a long and pleasurable engagement, the visitor returning year after year, each time promising himself that next year he will purchase property.

Why this enduring love affair with the BVI for so many people?

Certainly there are a number of obvious reasons, such as a perfect climate, miles and miles of pristine sailing waters and an underwater habitat to rival that of almost any resort area. Add to these an extremely stable and self-determining government, numerous tax advantages and proximity to both the USVI and Puerto Rico. The U.S. dollar economy is the biggest selling point in the British Virgin Islands.

The reasons go beyond the obvious, however—they also include a proud and friendly people and an environment that, as one of nature's finest achievements, is jealously guarded against outside intrusion or influence unless these are for the common good

of the people of the BVI.

Around us is the land and the sea, and the use or abuse to which we subject these elements has a far-reaching and permanent effect on the environment. It doesn't take long for the potential investor, looking for his home in the sun, to realize that it is the local government's program of directed and controlled development that has maintained the relaxing and unhurried atmosphere that prevails in the BVI.

Having made the decision to buy, the question of just where to purchase property is relatively simple, as properties are available the whole length and breadth of the BVI on over a dozen different islands. Making contact with a local real estate agent at this point will considerably cut the search time needed and will also provide the investor with up-to-date information on the laws and Government requirements pertaining to property purchase. Though many of the local agents market the same properties, by "shopping around" one may find a property that no one else has.

In short, the purchase of property in the BVI revolves around a "Non-Belonger's Land Holding License" which is issued by the Government after consideration of certain factors, including how much property is involved. The purchaser, if a non-belonger, is required to develop the property within three years.

Apart from a careful scrutiny of potential buyers, the Government's main concern is the sale of previously undeveloped land; its chief concerns are how many acres are involved, what does the intended development consist of, and how much money will be spent in the Territory on the project.

The licensing procedure is relatively straightforward with a developed property such as an existing residence. With larger projects that will bring money into the territory, the government is amenable to expediant approval.

Throughout the BVI there is a wide range of existing houses and condominiums for sale. Prices range from $200,000 and well up. For those intent on building there is a limitless variety of sites to choose from, either on the waterfront or on one of the many hillsides that make up the islands. Most investors opt for the hillsides, to take advantage of the spectacular views and also benefit from year-round trade winds — a definite advantage in the summer.

Building a house in the BVI is not the trial it used to be. With increased shipping from both England and the U.S. mainland, together with the advent of container service in recent years, the variety of building materials, fixtures and fittings now available has eased the burden on local architects and contractors, who can now purchase locally everything that is required for the average residence. Building is still expensive, however, with concrete blocks being the only material locally produced.

Although far less demanding than Stateside or British authorities, the local Building Department and Planning Authority do have guidelines and regulations which must be followed. It is recommended that a local architect be consulted during the planning stages, preferably before the land is purchased. Generally, the guidelines control building setbacks, sewage disposal, cistern requirements and hurricane proof construction, together with special applications such as for jetties and land reclamation.

Most of the banks in the BVI are active in the home mortgage market, although their individual policies do vary from time to time, often in relation to the prime lending rate. Represented in the BVI are Barclays Bank International, Chase Manhattan Bank, Bank of Nova Scotia and the Banco Popular of the BVI. At time of writing, one could still obtain 50 % on land and 75% on development of property. Interest rates vary, but the average is 2.5% over the New York prime lending rate at the time of the loan agreement.

The investor, having built or purchased a home in the BVI, may not intend to live there year-round, and often leaves the house in the hands of a local real estate agent for the purpose of rental. There are two rental options; the short-term vacation market and the long-term residential market; the decision to opt for either one usually depends on the location of the house.

Houses located near a good swimming beach and furnished to a high standard make ideal vacation homes and can rent for more per week than the long-term rentals do per month. On the other hand, long-term rental can be 52 weeks a year, whereas 20 weeks is considered average in the rental market. This, together with weighing the long-term tenancy against the wear and tear of vacation rentals and the advertising, cleaning, and maintenance costs involved, would seem to indicate that, in the long run, the options even out.

In any case, the investor's main concern is normally capital appreciation, and in that department the BVI has always been and should continue to be a good investment.

The British Virgin Islands may not be for everyone and the area is certainly an expensive place to live; but the people of the BVI do live well and enjoy not only the magnificent environment but also many other advantages.

The BVI is a close-knit, friendly society, and there is no lack of facilities. Considering the combined activities of the Sports Club with its squash and tennis division, the Yacht Club with its sailing, angling and rugby division, both Lions and Rotary clubs, soccer, baseball, golf and cricket clubs, plus a ladies' club, botanic society and drama group, the only problem can be having enough time left to relax and take a vacation!

There's always something happening in the BVI, but it's also a perfect place to relax and do absolutely nothing—so if the pressures of the big smoke have been getting you down, the BVI just may be for you.

REAL ESTATE IN THE U.S. VIRGIN ISLANDS

When the United States bought St. Thomas, St. Croix and St. John from Denmark in 1917, it cost them less than $300 an acre. Inflation has taken its toll since then, and today the average price for a home in the Virgin Islands is over $150,000. By modern real estate standards, however, buying property here is still an excellent investment.

With some of the finest weather and scenery to be found under the protection of the U.S. flag, the USVI has a great deal to offer the prospective buyer. Stunning views are complemented by beautiful beaches, fascinating historical buildings, good restaurants and a leisurely approach to life.

Because the tourist industry is so vital to the island economy, there are plenty of facilities for sports, entertainment and the arts. Both St. Thomas and St. Croix have top quality golf courses, and sailing is, of course, an integral part of the lifestyle throughout the Virgins.

The U.S. Virgin Islands differ enormously in their character. St. Thomas is the busiest of the three; it contains the headquarters of most of the major businesses in the USVI, most of the government agencies and most of the people.

Charlotte Amalie is the commercial heart of the U.S. Virgins; the town bustles with tourists and traffic, and the harbour teems with yachts, cruise ships and visiting naval vessels. In consequence, St. Thomas offers the broadest range of facilities and events

and the choice of shops, restaurants, hotels and entertainment is pleasingly varied.

St. Croix is somewhat quieter. Set apart from the rest of the Virgin Islands it is, in fact, the largest of the group and was once the main agricultural producer. The miles of gently rolling hills are liberally dotted with ancient sugar mills and gracious colonial homesteads like Whim Great House and Sprat Hall.

The historic buildings of Christiansted and Frederiksted still look out over a slower pace of life, and the attractions of this island have persuaded many talented artists and musicians to make it their home.

St. John, the quietest of them all, once belonged to Lawrence Rockefeller, who donated it to the United States under the proviso that most of it be designated as a National Park. Consequently the island is very unspoiled and, with its uncluttered beaches and untouched hills, it truly lives up to its name as a Virgin Island. In terms of property investment, this pristine quality means that the available real estate is often the most expensive, the most highly restricted and the most exclusive in the U.S. Virgins—and often the most spectacular, too.

Visitors considering the purchase of property in the USVI must first choose which island most suits their taste, then examine the alternative types of property. Whether to buy land and build, whether to renovate an old building or invest in a new, whether a self-contained residence or a

condominium is best, are some initial questions. The choices are considerable and an experienced realtor can give invaluable advice at this stage.

In some ways an undeveloped homesite may be the easiest way to start. There is no time limit for how long land can be held before development must begin, and so the new owner can take his time in deciding on the kind of home he wants and financing.

Depending on the view and the location, a half-acre homesite can vary in price to over $800,000 for waterfront property. In general, building costs run to roughly over $150 per square foot. There are plenty of competent architects and, though slower than on the mainland U.S., construction has become a good deal easier over the last few years.

Buying a finished home, of course, saves time. Condominiums are a popular choice; they can generate a healthy income if rented as vacation units and usually have excellent amenities, such as swimming pools, beaches, tennis courts, golf courses, restaurants, etc.

Most condominiums offer an on-site management team whose function is to advertise the apartments as resort hotel rooms, book reservations on a rotating or pool basis, provide maid service, do the accounting and disburse income to the owners. Management fees vary from 35%

to 60% of the gross income, however, and there is generally a monthly maintenance charge, depending on the size of the unit. Typically this covers upkeep of the exterior of the building and the grounds, pool service, cleaning, gardening and insurance.

The major advantage of having a condominium is the relatively worry-free ownership. There is always adequate security, and all the details of rental and maintenance are taken care of by the management.

An alternative to purchasing a condominium outright is time-sharing, which provides a refinement of the traditional condominium ownership. Instead of holding the unit year-round, the buyer can own it for as little as two months per year.

Perhaps better suited to those who want to spend a greater proportion of their time in the islands, an individual residence offers more privacy and space. Most sites are at least half an acre and keen gardeners can take advantage of the profusion of fast-growing tropical plants to create colourful and imaginative surroundings.

Single-family homes are as varied in type as they are in price, which ranges from about $225,000 to $1.5 million. Maintenance on a home is generally less expensive than on a condominium and mortgage interest, maintenance and property taxes

are all tax-deductible items.

The government maintains an efficient system of surveys and titles, and title insurance can also be arranged though local attorneys.

Anyone can buy real estate in the USVI. There are no restrictions on nationality or on speculation purely for investment purposes. Land can be held for any length of time and no development plan is required by the government.

Land use, however, is another matter. It is dictated by zoning laws, deed restrictions and building permit requirements, including approval by the Coastal Zone Management Committee. The ease with which this approval is obtained is largely dependent on the location of the property and the type of development proposed.

The Coastal Zone Management is the organization responsible for keeping the USVI looking good enough to be described as the "American paradise." They have a scale of restrictions designed to preserve the beauty of the island by limiting such things as density, height of building, type of construction and so on. The severity of the limits varies according to the area.

For example, the majority of St. John's land belongs to the National Park Service. The remaining land available for development is R1 density, which mean no more than two dwelling units per quarter acre. These are mostly concentrated around Cruz Bay and Coral Bay areas.

Other restrictions may include details like clothesline placement and other visuafeatures. Fortunately, St. John has excellent architects and builders, making

building a home remarkably hassle-free.

St. Thomas and St. Croix have more medium and high density residences available, as well as extensive business and commercial areas. The choices for potential real estate buyers are wide. Many begin by trying out something from the range of rental and leasing arrangements which, like cohabitation before marriage, allow the participants to try the lifestyle before making a heavier commitment.

The advantages of VI living are less tangible—the islands are obviously sunny, pretty and cosmopolitan, but for many people the fascination runs deeper. They find themselves returning again and again, spending longer periods of time and scraping their savings together to buy a foothold. Down here, the islanders call it "getting sand in your shoes," and a sailing vacation is often just the beginning.

People go on to buy real estate in the Virgin Islands because they want to make an investment and because they like the lifestyle and the environment. From an investment point of view, the chances of a worthwhile return are good.

So if you get home and unpack to find half the beach in your docksiders, it could be that your next visit to the Virgin Islands will include "just checking it out" at the nearest real estate office.

ISSUE II • VOL. I
ISSN: 1074-908X

CRUISING GUIDE'S QUARTERLY

Caribbean JOURNAL

A Quarterly Journal Covering The Eastern Caribbean From The Bahamas South To Venezuela
A Supplement To Cruising Guide Publication's Caribbean Cruising Guides

Summer Temperatures Soar While Caribbean Sailing Charter Rates Plunge

The Pages of Cruising Guide Publications' *Caribbean Journal* Are Your Window to Adventure.

You are invited to join sailors throughout the islands for Caribbean cruising adventures. The quarterly *Caribbean Journal* is a publication designed to keep you abreast of happenings and news that will be important to your next vacation, charter or voyage.

You will learn about new marinas, boatyards, charter operations, resorts and restaurants that cater to the cruising sailor. Navigational updates, including sketch charts, anchorage information, cultural events, travel tips, diving and snorkeling, cooking recipes, features on people and places, and a host of other topics will be covered in coming issues.

The *Caribbean Journal* is published in full-color and is packed with news, features and photos. It is the ideal companion update to our Caribbean Cruising Guides.

Join us in our cruising adventures by subscribing at a special introductory rate of $14.95 annually. Call **(800)330-9542** to subscribe.

Caribbean Journal is published by:
Cruising Guide Publications, P.O. Box 1017, Dunedin, FL 34697-1017, Phone: (813) 733-5322, Fax: (813) 734-8179

VIRGIN ISLANDS DIRECTORY

This directory is arranged in two sections: BVI and USVI. The two largest British Virgin Islands are listed first, followed by the other, smaller islands, in alphabetical order, followed by the U.S. Virgin Islands in alphabetical order. F = Fax; VHF = VHF Radio Channel

To call from outside the VI, dial 1-809 plus 7 digits. Within the BVI, dial only the last 5 digits.

BRITISH VIRGIN ISLANDS GENERAL INFORMATION

AIRLINES

Air Ambulance Network, 305-447-0458.
Air Anguilla Inc., 495-1616.
American Eagle, 495-2559.
British Airways, 494-2215.
Eastern Caribbean Airways, 495-2396.
Fly BVI, 495-1747.
Four-Star Air Cargo, 495-2256.
Gorda Aero, 495-2271, 495-2261.
Liat, 495-1187.
Sunair Express, 495-2480.
W.R.A. Air Service, 496-5682

FERRIES

Beef Island to Virgin Gorda Service, 495-5240, 495-5235.
Inter-Island Boat Services, 495-4166.
Native Son, Inc., 495-4617.
North Sound Express, 495-2271.
Peter Island Boat, 494-2561.
Smith's Ferry Services, 494-4430, 494-2355, 495-4495.
Speedy's Fantasy/Speedy's Delight, 495-5240, 495-5235.

MISCELLANEOUS

Ambulance/Fire/Police, 999.
Bluewater Books & Charts, (305) 763-6533.
BVI Customs & Immigration, 494-3701.
BVI Dept. Conservation & Fisheries, 494-3429.
BVI Port & Marine, 494-3435.
BVI Post Office, 494-3701.
BVI Tourist Board, 494-3134.
Cable & Wireless (WI) Ltd., 494-4444.
Tortola Radio Marine Operator, 494-4116, 115,
Virgin Islands Search & Rescue (VISAR), 494-6613, 494-4357, VHF 16.

TORTOLA

AUTO/BICYCLE/MOPED RENTALS

Airways Car Rental, 494-4502; airport 495-2161.
Alphonso Car Rental, 494-3137, 494-4886.
Anytime Car Rental, 494-2875.
Avis Rent-a-Car, 494-3322, 494-2193.
Budget Rent-a-Car, 494-2639.
Del's Scooter Rentals, 495-9356.
Denully's, 494-6819.
Hertz Rent-a-Car, 495-4405.
Honda Scooter Rentals, 495-5212.
International Car Rental, 494-2516, 494-2517.
Island Suzuki, 494-3666.
National Car Rental, 494-3197.
Rancal Rent-a-Car, 494-4535.

BANKS

Banco Popular, 494-2117.
Bank of Nova Scotia, 494-2526.
Barclays, 494-2171.
Chase Manhattan, 494-2662.
Development Bank of the VI, 494-3737.
DISA Bank BVI Ltd., 494-6036.

CHANDLERIES

Cay Marine Chandlery, 494-2992.
Golden Hind, 494-2756.
Island Marine Supply, 494-2251; F: 494-2290.
Nanny Cay Chandlery, 494-0329.
Richardson's Rigging, 494-5169, 494-2739.

CHARTERS

BVI Bareboats, 494-4289.
Catamaran Charters, (305) 462-6706.
Dream Weaver Charters, 494-4000.
Ed Hamilton & Co., (207) 549-7855.
Marine Enterprises Ltd., 494-2786.
Misty Isle, 495-5643.
The Moorings, 494-2331; F: 494-2226.

North Sound Express, 495-2271.
North South, 800-387-4964.
Sail Caribe, 1-800-785-7245.
Seabreeze Yacht Charters, 495-1560,
  800-388-6224.
Smith's Ferry Services, 494-2355, 495-4495.
Stardust Charters, 1-800-634-8822.
Sun Yacht Charters, 800-772-3500.
Sunsail, 495-4740, F: 495-4301.
Swift Yacht Charters, 1-800-866-8340.
Tom Collins Yachts Worldwide,
  (800) 637-5407.
Tropic Island Yacht Mgmt., 494-2450;
  (Canada, 416-696-9711).
Virgin Islands Sailing, 494-3658, 494-2774;
  F: 494-6774.
Yacht Connections, 1-800-238-5582.

DIVING, SNORKELING
Baskin In The Sun, 494-2858, 495-4582.
Blue Water Divers, 494-2847.
Caribbean Images Tours Ltd., 495-2563.
Island Diver Ltd., 494-3878, 495-2367.
Island Hopper, 495-4870.
Underwater Safaris, 494-3235; (800) 537-7032.

ELECTRONICS
Al's Marine Ltd., 494-4529.
Big Leo Electronics Ltd., 494-3983.
BVI Electronics, 494-2723.
Cay Electronics Ltd., 494-2400.
CCT Boatphone, 494-3825, 494-3153,
  494-5783.
Clarence M. Christian Ltd., 494-2492,
  494-5986; F: 494-5807.
Island Care Electronics, 494-6183, 494-3998.

EMERGENCY/MEDICAL
Ambulance/Fire/Police, 999.
K.P. Adamson, dentist, 494-3274.
N. Joyce Brewley, M.D., 494-2196, 494-3882.
BVI Red Cross, 494-6349.
Jana Downing, M.D., 494-4477.
Marvin E. Flax, dentist, 494-3474.
Health Department, 494-3701.
Medicure Health Center, 494-6189, 494-6469.
Q.W. Osborne, M.D., 494-2498.
Peebles Hospital, 494-3497, 494-6836.
J.E. Rhymer, dentist, 494-5303, 495-1261.
D. Orlando Smith, M.D., 494-3330.

Robin E. Tattersall, M.D., 494-2181.
Heskith A. Vanterpool, M.D., 494-2346.
**Virgin Islands Search & Rescue (VISAR),
  494-4357.**

HAUL-OUT
Nanny Cay Marine, 494-2512, 494-4895.
Tortola Yacht Services, 494-2124.
West End Slipway, 495-4353, 495-4678.

LAUNDRY/DRY CLEANERS
A & M Coin Laundry, 494-5656.
Brackwell's Laundromat, 495-2369.
Freeman's Laundromat, 494-2285.
Sylvia's Laundry, 494-2230.
West End Laundromat, 495-4463.

LIQUOR, BEER, WINE
A.H. Riise Ltd., 494-4483.
Ample Hamper, 494-2494.
Bubblin' Barrel, 494-5136.
Esme's Shoppe, 494-3961.
Fort Wines & Spirits, 494-2388.
Rite Way Food Market, 494-2263, 494-2266.
Santo's, 494-3799.
Tico, 494-2211.

LODGING
A & L Inn House, 494-6343.
Beef Island Guest House, 495-2303.
BVI Aquatic Hotel, 495-4541.
Club Mariner, 494-2501.
Fort Burt Hotel, 494-2587.
Fort Recovery, 495-4354, 1-800-367-8455.
Frenchman's Cay Hotel, 495-4844.
Hall Guest House, 494-3946.
Janet Dart Little Mountain Rentals, 495-2538.
Long Bay Beach Resort, 495-4252, 495-4122.
Moorings Mariner Inn, 494-2331, 494-3776,
  494-3876.
Nanny Cay Resort, 494-2512, 494-4895.
Prospect Reef Resort, 494-3311.
Rhymer's Cane Garden Beach Hotel, 495-4639.
Sebastian's On The Beach, 495-4212, 495-4272.
Smuggler's Cove Hotel, 495-4234.
Sugar Mill Hotel, 495-4355.
Treasure Isle Hotel, 494-2501.
Village Cay Marina/Hotel, 494-2771, 495-2849.
Way Side Inn Guest House, 494-3606.
Well Bay Cottages, 494-2186.

MARINAS

Fort Burt Marina, 494-4200.
Inner Harbour Marina, 494-4502, VHF 16.
Leverick Bay Hotel & Marina, 495-5450.
Moorings/Mariner Inn, 494-2331, 494-3776.
Nanny Cay Resort & Marina, 494-2512.
Prospect Reef Resort, 494-3311.
Puerto Del Rey Marina, 809-860-1000
Road Reef Marina, 494-2751.
Soper's Hole Marina, 495-4553.
Sunsail Yachts, 495-4553, 495-4740.
Tortola Yacht Services, 494-2124.
Tropic Island Yacht Mgmt., 494-2450,
494-4150, 495-2655.
Village Cay Resort Marina, 494-2771.

MARINE REPAIR & SUPPLIES

Air Devices, 494-2314.
Al's Marine Ltd., 494-4529.
BVI Diesel Sales & Service, 494-2298.
BVI Marine Management, 494-2938, 494-3382;
F: 494-5006.
BVI Marine Services, 494-2393, 494-3870,
494-0047.
Caribbean Battery, 494-2938.
Clarence Thomas Ltd. Plumbing Supplies,
494-2359.
Golden Hind at Tortola Yacht Services,
494-2756.
High Tech Caribbean Ltd., 494-3811
Island Marine Supply Ltd., 494-2251.
Marine Enterprises, Ltd. 494-2786.
Marine Power Service, 494-2738.
Moor Secure, 494-4488.
Nanny Cay Marine Center, 494-2512.
Napa Auto Parts, 494-2193, 494-2122.
Nautool Machine Ltd., 494-3187.
Parts & Power Ltd., 494-2830.
Richardson's Rigging Services, 494-2739.
T&W Machine Shop, 494-3342.
Tortola Marine Mgmt. Ltd., 494-2751.
Tortola Yacht Services Ltd., 494-2124.
Tradewinds Yachting Services Ltd., 494-3154.
Triton Marine Services, 494-4252.
Wickham's Cay II Rigging, 494-3979.

MISCELLANEOUS

Alcoholics Anonymous, 494-3125.
American Express, 494-2872.

BVI Port Authority, 494-3435.
BVI Tourist Board, 494-3134, 494-3489, 495-
5182.
Conservation & Fisheries, 494-5681, 494-5682.
Customs, 494-3475, 494-3701.
DHL Worldwide Express, 494-4659.
East End Public Library, 495-2472.
Federal Express, 494-2297.
Happy Heart Barber Shop, 494-2260.
Immigration, 494-3701.
Inland Messenger Service, 494-6440.
Miracles Unisex Beauty Salon, 494-3525.
Monelle's Beauty Salon, 494-2546.
Narcotics Anonymous, 494-3125.
National Parks Trust, 494-2069, 494-3904.
New Image Beauty Salon, 495-5135.
Public Library, 494-3701.
Rhymer's Beauty Salon, 495-4847.
Rush-It Inc., 494-4421.
Tortola Humane Society, 494-2284.
Tortola Travel, 494-2215.
Tortola Vision Center, 494-2020.
Veterinarian, C.W. George, 494-4498.
Vision Cinema, 494-4789.
Waves Hair Salon, 495-4208.

PHARMACIES

BVI Drug Center, 494-2702.
Lagoon Plaza Drug & Hardware Stores,
494-2498.
J.R. O'Neal Ltd. Drug Store, 494-2292.
Medicure Ltd., 494-6189; F: 494-6284.
Ruth's Drug Store, 495-1173.
Vanterpool Enterprises Ltd., 494-2702.

PROVISIONS

Ample Hamper, 494-2494, 494-2784.
Bobby's Supermarket, 494-2189.
Bon Appetit Delicatessen, 494-5199.
Brewley's Superette, 494-3839.
C & F Grocery, 494-4356.
Central Bakery, 494-6854.
Dorothy's Superette, 494-3757.
Fine Foods Supermarket, 495-2362.
Franklin's General Market, 494-2670.
Frett Butcher Shop, 495-2253.
Gourmet Chandler, 494-2894.
K-Mark's Supermarket, 494-4649, VHF 16.
Little Circle Provisioners, 494-3779.

M & S Unique Pastry Shop, 494-5424.

Marlene's Delicious Designs Pastry Shop, 494-4634.

Pie In The Sky, 494-2263.

Port Purcell Market, 494-2727, 494-2724.

Rite Way Food Markets, 494-2263.

Santo's, 494-3799.

Sunbeam Grocery, 494-2307.

Sunrise Bakery, 494-2425.

Sunshine Grocery & Restaurant, 494-2520.

TICO, 494-2211.

Tortola Ice, 494-3333.

Trellis Bay Market, 495-1421.

REAL ESTATE

Caribbean Realty, 494-3566; F: 494-5127.

Duffs Valley Real Estate, 494-4510.

Island Real Estate, 494-3186, 494-4386.

Romney Associates, 494-3352; F: 494-5095.

Smiths Gore Overseas Ltd., 494-2446; F: 494-2141.

Trude Real Estate, 494-2500; F: 494-6969.

RESTAURANTS

Airport Restaurant, West Indian, 495-2323.

Apple, West Indian, 495-4437.

Aries Club, West Indian, 494-1324.

Beach Club, West Indian, 494-2272.

Beef Island Guest House, West Indian, 495-2303.

Bing's Drop Inn, international, 495-2627.

The Bistro, international, 494-1132.

Brandywine Bay, international, 495-2301.

Butterfly Bar & Restaurant, West Indian, 494-3606.

BVI Aquatic Hotel, international, West Indian, 495-4541.

Capriccio di Mare, Italian, 494-5369.

Captain's Table, international, 494-3885.

Cell #5 Lounge, continental, 494-4629.

Chopsticks, southeast Asian, 494-3616.

The Cloud Room, international, 494-2821.

Clubhouse Restaurant, 495-4844.

Conch Shell Point, international, 495-2285, VHF 16.

Fish Trap, 494-3626.

Fort Burt Restaurant, Old English, international, 494-2587.

Frenchman's Cay Hotel, international, 495-4844.

Hungry Sailor, 494-3885.

Jolly Roger Inn, international, 495-4559; VHF 16.

The Last Resort, international, 495-2520.

Long Bay Hotel, international, 495-4252.

Maria's, West Indian, 494-2595.

Marina Cay, international, 494-2174; VHF 16.

Marlene's, West Indian/bakery, 494-4634.

Marina Plaza Cafe, international, 494-4895.

Mario's, West Indian, 494-3883.

Midtown, West Indian, 494-2764.

Moorings Mariner Inn, international, 494-2332.

Mrs. Scatliffe's, West Indian, 495-4556.

Myett's Restaurant, 495-9543.

New Happy Lion, West Indian, 494-2574.

Oliver's Restaurant, seafood, 494-2177.

The Palms, West Indian, 494-4876.

Pam's Kitchen, 495-9237.

Paradise Pub, international, 494-2608.

Peg Leg Landing, international, 494-0028.

Pelican Roost, West Indian, 495-1515.

Popeye's Inn, West Indian, 495-1380.

Pusser's Co. Store & Pub, English, 494-2467.

Pusser's Landing, international, 495-4554.

Pusser's Outpost, international, 494-4199.

Quito's Gazebo, West Indian, 495-4837.

Rays of Hope, 494-5223.

Rhymer's Beach Bar, West Indian, 495-4639.

Roti Palace, West Indian, 494-4196.

Scatliffe's Tavern, West Indian, 494-2797.

Scato's Snack Bar, West Indian, 494-2230.

Sea View Hotel, international, 494-2483.

Sebastian's on the Beach, internat'l, 495-4212.

Skyworld, international/gourmet, 494-3567, VHF 16.

Spaghetti Junction, Italian, 494-4880.

Stanley's Welcome Bar, West Indian, 495-4520.

Struggling Man's Place, West Indian, 494-4163.

Sugar Mill Hotel, international, 495-4355.

Tamarind Country Club, barbecue, 495-2477.

Tavern in the Town, English pub, 494-2790.

Treasure Isle, international, 494-2501.

Village Cay, 494-2771.

Virgin Queen, West Indian, European, 494-2310.

The Wharf/Mr. Fish, Caribbean, 494-3626.

William Thornton Restaurant, 494-2564.

SAILING, WATER SPORTS

Boardsailing BVI, 495-2447.
BVI Sailing Adventures, 494-4726.
Camelot Charters, Ltd., 494-3623.
Capricorn Charters, 494-3174.
Club Mariner, 494-2501; F: 494-2507.
Conch Charters, Ltd., 494-4868.
Discovery Yacht Charters, 494-6026.
Encore, 494-3623.
Endless Summer II, 494-4486.
Fontana, 496-0345, 494-0108.
Golden Skye, 496-0236.
Island Hopper, 495-4870.
Jet Sea, 1-800-262-JETC; F: 305-467-6661.
Johnny's Maritime Services, 494-3661.
King Charters Ltd., 494-5820.
Kuralu Charters, 495-4381.
The Last Resort, 495-2520.
Marine Enterprises, 494-2786, 494-6300.
The Moorings Ltd., 494-2331.
North South Yacht Vacations, 494-0096.
Offshore Sail & Motor, 494-4726.
Pagradise Yacht Club, 800-258-8753
Patouche II, 494-6300.
Phantom, 496-0872.
Privilege, 1-800-262-0308: F: 305-462-6104.
Prospect Reef Resort, 494-3311.
Sea Escape Daysails, 496-0044.
Seabreeze, 495-1560.
Shadowfax Day Sails, 494-2175.
Stardust, 1-800-634-8822
Smith's Ferry Services, 494-2355.
Sun Yacht Charters, 1-800-772-3500;
    F: 207-236-3972.
Sunsail, 495-4740.
Tortola Marine Mgt. Ltd., 494-2751.
Trimarine Boat Co. Ltd.., 494-2490.
Tropic Island Yacht Mgt., 494-2450.
Virgin Island Sailing Ltd., 494-2774,
    800-233-7936.
White Squall II, 494-2564.
Yacht Promenade, 494-3853.

SAILMAKERS

Doyle Sailmakers, 494-2569.
E.L.M. Sailmakers Ltd., 494-6455.
Nanny Cay Sailmakers, 494-6455.

SHOPPING, GIFTS

Bolo's Department Store, 494-2867.
Bonker's Gallery Boutique, 494-2535.
Bounty Boatique, 494-3615.
BVI Apparel, 494-5511: F: 494-3867.
Caribbean Handprints, 494-3717.
Carousel Gift Shop, 494-4542.
Castaways Ltd., 494-3346.
Clovers Department Store, 494-3724, 494-4110.
Cockle Shop, 494-2555.
E. A. Creque, footwear, 494-3368.
Crown Jewellers Ltd., 494-3399.
Elm Gift Shop, 494-3247.
Esme's Shoppe, 494-3961.
Family Fashion, 494-4232
Fluke's Designs, 495-1421.
Hodge's Department Store, 494-3943.
Hollywood Discount Store, 494-3554.
Island Treasures, 495-4787.
J & C Department Store, 494-3121.
Jehmary's Gift & Souvenir Centre, 494-4512.
Jennings Fashion Store, 495-2144.
Kayed Fashion Store, 494-3335.
Kids In De Sun, 494-3343.
Learn 'N' Fun Shop, 494-3856.
Malone Sporting Goods, 494-4591.
Naucraft Galleries Ltd., 494-4790.
Ooh La La Gift Shop, 494-2433.
Pace Setter Store, 494-2162.
Pasea Stationery & Book Store, 494-2556.
Past & Presents, 494-2747.
Pusser's Co. Store & Pub, 494-2467.
Pusser's Landing, 495-4554.
Roadtown Wholesale, 494-2263.
Royal Shop, 494-3209.
Samarkand Jewelers, 494-6415.
Sea Urchin Shop, 494-6234, 494-4108.
Shirt Shack, 494-4851.
Smith's Boutique, 495-2204.
Sunny Caribbee Spice Co., 494-2178, 494-
    5481.
Tropical Touch, 495-9358, 494-6982.
Turtle Dove Boutique, 494-3611.
Unique Fashion, 494-6471.
Violet's, 494-6398.
Zenaida, 494-4867.

TAXIS/TRANSPORTATION

BVI Taxi, 494-3942, 494-3456, 494-2322.

Scato's Bus Service, 26 seats, public, 494-2365.
Style's Taxi, 494-2260 (day), 494-3341 (night).
Turtle Dove Taxi, 494-6274, 494-3942.

VIRGIN GORDA

AUTO/BICYCLE/MOPED RENTALS
Andy's Taxi & Jeep Rental, 495-5511.
Honda Scooter Rental, 495-5212.
L & S Jeep Rental, 495-5297.
Mahogany Car Rental, 495-5469, 495-5542.
Potter's Car Rental, 495-5329, 495-5960.
Speedy's Car Rental, 495-5235.

CHANDLERIES
Virgin Gorda Yacht Harbour Ship's Store,
495-5318; F: 495-5685.

CHARTERS
Misty Isle Yacht Charters, 495-5643.
Freedom Yach Charters, 800-999-2909,
401-848-2900

DIVING, SNORKELING
Baskin In The Sun, 495-5239
Dive BVI Ltd., 495-5513, 800-848-7078.
Kilbride's Underwater Tours, 495-9638.
Mahogany Watersports, 495-5469.

LAUNDRY/DRY CLEANERS
Stevens Laundry & Dry Cleaners, 495-5525.

LODGING
Big Yard, 495-5930.
Biras Creek Hotel, 494-3555.
Bitter End Yacht Club Hotel, 494-2745.
Drake's Anchorage, 494-2254, 494-5871.
Fischer's Cove Beach Hotel, 495-5252.
Little Dix Bay Hotel, 495-5555.
Mango Bay Resort, 495-5672.
Necker Island, 494-2757.
Olde Yard Inn, 495-5544.
Paradise Beach Resort, 495-5871.
Virgin Gorda Villa Rentals, 495-5644, 495-5450.

MARINAS
Biras Creek Estate, 494-3555.
Bitter End Yacht Club, 494-2746.
Leverick Bay Resort, 495-5644, VHF 16.
Virgin Gorda Yacht Harbour, 495-5500.

MISCELLANEOUS
American Express, 495-5586.

BVI Tourist Board, 495-5182.
Hair Creation, 495-5670.
New Image Beauty Salon, 495-5135.
Sandra's Exquisite Hair Designs, 495-7222.
Vivian's Beauty Salon, 495-5641.

PHARMACIES
Medicure Ltd., 495-5479.
O'Neal Drugs, 495-5325.

PROVISIONS
Andy's Ice Chateau, 495-5987.
Bitter End, 494-2745; F: 494-4756.
Buck's Food Market, 495-5423, 495-5141.
Leroy B. Frett Butcher Shop, 495-2253.
N & M Bakery, 495-5054.
North Sound Superette, 495-7424.
Pool's Economart / Virgin Gorda Freight &
Trade Co., 495-5465.

REAL ESTATE
Trude Real Estate, 495-5648.

RESTAURANTS
Bath & Turtle, international, 495-5239.
Biras Creek Hotel, international, 494-3555.
Bitter End Yacht Club, international, 494-2746,
VHF 16.
Chez Michelle, international, 495-5510.
Crabhole Bar & Restaurant, West Indian,
495-5307.
Drake's Anchorage, international/French,
494-2254, VHF 16.
Fischer's Cove Beach Hotel, West Indian,
495-5252.
Little Dix Bay Hotel Rockresorts, international/
buffet, 495-5555.
Mad Dog, sandwiches, 495-5830.
Olde Yard Inn, international, 495-5544.
Pelican's Pouch, 495-5477, 495-5599.
Pirate's Pub and Grill, barbecue/West Indian,
495-9537.
Pusser's Leverick Bay, international, English,
495-7369.

SAILING, WATER SPORTS
Bitter End Yacht Club, 494-2746.
Euphoric Cruises, 495-5542.
Leverick Bay Watersports, 495-7376.
Misty Isle Yacht Charters, 495-5643.
Speedy's Fantasy, 495-5240.

SAILMAKERS
Next Wave Sail & Canvas, 495-5623, 495-5662.

SHOPPING, GIFTS
Flamboyance Perfume Shoppe, 495-5946.
Island Woman, 495-5237.
Kaunda's KYSY Tropix, 494-6737.
L & L Marketing, 495-7374.
O'Neal Variety Store, 495-5230.
Roadtown Wholesale of Virgin Gorda,
495-5228, 495-5572.
Virgin Gorda Craft Shop, 495-5137.

ANEGADA
LODGING
Anegada Reef Hotel, 495-8002.
Neptune's Treasure, 495-9439; F: 495-9443.

RESTAURANTS
Anegada Reef Hotel, international, 495-8002,
VHF 16.
Neptune's Treasure, international, 495-9439,
VHF 16 or 68.
Pomato Point Beach Restaurant, international/
West Indian, 495-9466, VHF 16.

SHOPPING
Pat's Pottery (no phone).

COOPER ISLAND
LODGING
Cooper Island Beach Club, 494-3721.

RESTAURANTS
Cooper Island Beach Club, international,
494-3721; Radio 43111, VHF 16.

SHOPPING
Underwater Safaris Gift Shop, 494-3235.

JOST VAN DYKE
PROVISIONS
Harris' Place, 495-9302.
Nature's Basket, (no phone).

RESTAURANTS
Abe's, West Indian, 495-9329, VHF 16.
Ali Baba's, West Indian, 495-9280, VHF 16.
Club Paradise, West Indian, 495-9267.
Foxy's Tamarind, West Indian, 495-9258.
Happy Larry's, West Indian, 495-9259.
Harris' Place, West Indian, 495-9302.

Rudy's Mariners' Rendezvous, West Indian,
495-9282, VHF 16.
Sandcastle White Bay, international, 494-3502,
VHF 16.
Sydney's Peace & Love, 495-9271.

NORMAN ISLAND
RESTAURANTS
The William Thornton, international, 494-2564,
VHF 16.

PETER ISLAND
DIVING
Dive BVI Ltd., 494-2561.

LODGING
Peter Island Hotel and Yacht Harbour,
494-2561, F: 494-2313.

MARINAS
Peter Island Hotel & Yacht Harbour, 492-2561,
VHF 16.

RESTAURANTS
Peter Island Resort, continental, 494-2561.

U.S. VIRGIN ISLANDS GENERAL INFORMATION

*To call from outside the VI, dial 1-809 plus 7
digits. Within the VI, dial only the last 5 digits.*

AIRLINES
Air Anguilla, 776-5789.
American Airlines, 1-800-474-4884.
American Eagle, 1-800-474-4884.
Continental Airlines, 1-800-231-0856.
Delta, 1-800-221-1212.
LIAT, 774-2313.
Sunaire Express, 778-9300.
Virgin Air, 776-2722.

MISCELLANEOUS
Inter-Island Boat Services, 776-6597.
Smith's Ferry, 775-7292.
Transportation Services of St. John, 776-6282.
USVI Customs, 774-6755, 774-1719.
USVI National Parks Service/Visitor
Information Center, 776-6201.
Western Union, 1-800-325-6000.

ST. JOHN

AUTO/BICYCLE/MOPED RENTALS

Avis, 776-6374, 1-800-331-1084
Budget Rent-a-Car, 776-7575.
Cool Breeze Car Rental, 776-6588.
Delbert Hills, 776-6637.
Hertz, 776-6695.
O'Connor Car Rental, 776-6343.
Penn's Jeep Rental, 776-6530.
Spencer's Jeep Rentals, 776-7784.
St. John Car Rental, 776-6103.
Varlack Car Rental, 776-6695.

BANKS

Chase Manhattan Bank, 776-6881.

CHARTERS

Proper Yachts, 776-6256.

DIVING, SNORKELING

Cinnamon Bay Camp Grounds, 776-6330.
Coral Bay Water Sports, 776-6850.
Cruz Bay Watersports, 776-6234.
Low Key Watersports, 776-7048.
Paradise Watersports, 776-7618.
St. John Water Sports, 776-6256.

ELECTRONICS

Third World Electronics, 776-6600.

EMERGENCY/MEDICAL

St. John Clinic, 776-6400, or 922.

HAUL-OUT

Caneel Bay Ship Yard, 774-3771.

LAUNDRY

Paradise Laundromat, 776-8060.

LODGING

Caneel Bay, 776-6111.
Cruz Inn, 776-7688, 776-9762.
Gallows Point Suite Resort, 776-6434.
Hyatt Regency/St. John, 776-7171, *i*
   800-233-1234.
Intimate Inn of St. John, 776-6133.
Raintree Inn, 776-7449.
Serendip Condo Hotel, 776-6646.
Zootenvaal Estate, 776-6321.

MARINE REPAIR & SUPPLIES

Caneel Bay Shipyard, 774-3771.
Coral Bay Marine Service, 776-6859.

Knight D. & Co., 776-7958.

MISCELLANEOUS

Decisions Hair Salon, 776-6962.

PROVISIONS

Convenience Market, 776-6193.
Hercules Pates Delight, 776-6352.
Marcelino's Bakery, 776-6873.
Supermarket & Deli, 774-3193.
Supernatural Foods, 776-7781.

REAL ESTATE

Cruz Bay Realty, 776-7001.
Holiday Homes of St. John Inc., 776-6776.
Islandia Real Estate, 776-6666.

RESTAURANTS, CRUZ BAY

Back Yard, West Indian, 776-8553.
Beni Iguana's, light fare, 779-4068.
Cafe Roma, Italian/pizza, 776-6524.
Fish Trap, seafood, 776-9817.
Fred's, West Indian, 776-6363.
Joe's Diner, international, 776-6888.
Lime Inn, West Indian/international, 776-6425.
Marcelino's Bakery, 776-6873.
Mongoose, international, 776-7586.
Old Gallery, West Indian/internat'l, 776-7544.
Paradiso, Italian, 776-8806.
Pusser's, international, 774-5489.

RESTAURANTS, OUTSIDE CRUZ BAY

Cafe Grand, Caribbean/international, 776-7171.
Chow Bella, Italian/Oriental, 776-7171, x 1764.
Ellington's, Caribbean/American, 776-7166.
Sea Breeze, international, 693-5824
Shipwreck Landing, West Indian, BBQ,
   776-8640.
The Still, continental, 776-6866.
T'ree Lizards, West Indian, BBQ, 776-6330.

SAILING, WATER SPORTS

Big Planet Adventure Outfitters, 776-6638.
Cinnamon Bay Camp Grounds, 776-6330.
Coral Bay Water Sports, 776-6850.
Cruz Bay Watersports, 776-6234.
Low Key Watersports, 776-7048.
Paradise Watersports, 776-7618.
St. John Watersports, 776-6256.

SAILMAKERS

Canvas Factory & Lee Sails, 776-6196.

Virgin Canvas, 776-6223.

SHOPPING, GIFTS

The Athlete's Foot, 779-4222.
Batik Caribe, 776-6465.
Bamboula Collections, 776-7699.
Canvas Factory, 776-6196.
Caravan Gallery, 776-8677.
Caribbean Casting Co., jewelers, 776-7232.
Clothing Studio, 776-6585.
Colombian Emeralds International, 776-6007.
Donald Schnell Pottery Studio, 776-6420.
Fabric Mill, 776-6194.
Guava Gallery, 779-4110
I Catchers Sportswear, 776-7749.
Lee Sails, 776-6196.
Mongoose Junction, 779-4713.
Monkeyfist Studio & Gallery, 776-6636.
Paradise Design, 776-6070.
Pink Papaya, 779-4110
Seasons, 776-6130.
Virgin Canvas & Crafts, 776-6223.
Wicker, Wood & Shells, 776-6909.

ST. THOMAS

AUTO/BICYCLE/MOPED RENTALS

A Better Car Auto Rental, 777-8888.
ABC Auto & Jeep Rentals, 776-1222,
American Yacht Harbor, 775-6454.
Anchorage E-Z Car Rental, 775-6255.
Aristocrat Auto Rental, 776-0026.
Avis, 774-1468, 774-4616.
Budget Rent-a-Car, 776-5774, 800-626-4516.
Caribbean Jeep & Auto Rental, 776-5337.
Cowpet Auto Rental, 775-7376.
Dependable Car Rental, 774-2253,
    800-522-3076.
Discount Car Rental, 776-4858.
Hertz Rent-a-Car, 774-1879.
J & C Car Rental, 776-5440.
National Auto Rental, 776-3616.
Paradise Car Rental, 775-7282, 776-5335.
Sea Breeze Car Rental, 774-7200.
Sun Island Car Rentals, 774-3333.
Trade Winds Car Rentals, 775-6262.
Tri-Island Car Rental, 776-2520, 776-2879.
VI Auto Rental & Leasing, 776-3616.

BANKS

Banco Popular de Puerto Rico, 776-7800.
Bank of Nova Scotia, 774-0037.
Barclays Bank, 776-5080.
Chase Manhattan Bank, 775-8838.
Citibank, 774-4800.
First Federal Savings, 774-2022.
First Virgin Islands Federal Savings, 776-9494.

CHARTERS

CSC, 1-800-824-1331, 774-1748
CYC, 1-800-225-2520.
CYOA, 1-800-944-2962.
Ed Hamilton & Co., 1-800-621-7855.
Island Yachts, 775-6666.
Journeys By Sea, 775-3660; F: 775-0613.
Ocean Incentives, 775-6406.
Regency Yacht Vacations, 776-5950;
    F: 776-7631.
St. Thomas Yacht Sales/Charters, 774-3215,
    1-800-433-2654.
The Brokerage, 775-6072, 1-800-949-6080.
Trawlers in Paradise, 775-9002,
    1-800-458-0675.
VIP Power Yacht Charters, 776-1510,
    800-524-2015.

DIVING, SNORKELING

Aqua Action, 775-6285.
Caribbean Divers, 775-6384.
Coki Beach Dive Club, 775-4220.
Chris Sawyer Dive Center, 775-7320.
Dive In, 775-6100.
Joe Vogel Diving, 775-7610.
Mask & Fin, 774-7177, 779-2877.
Sea Horse, 774-2001.
St. Thomas Diving Club, 776-2381.
Underwater Safaris, 774-1350.
Virgin Islands Diving School, 774-8687.

ELECTRONICS

Ace Electronics, 776-1128, 776-1116.
Boolchand's Electronics, 776-0302, 776-0794.
Cellular One, 777-7777.
Electronics Unlimited, 777-7000.
Geary Electronic Services, 776-1444.
Thomas Electronics and Communications,
    775-4510.
Topp Electronics, 775-7069.
Virgin Islands Telecom, 774-8999.

Vitel Cellular, 776-8588, 777-8899.
Vitelcom, 776-9900.

EMERGENCY/MEDICAL
Ambulance/Fire/Police, 911.
Doctors-On-Duty, 776-7966.
Thomas E. Drakes, dentist, 776-8018.
Francis J. Farrell, M.D., allergist, 776-0506.
Island Eye Care, 776-2600, 776-2015.
Richard A. Lloyd, dentist, 774-8155.
Optical Shoppe, 776-2642.
Pearle Vision Express, 774-2020.
St. Thomas Hospital, 776-8311.
Stuart M. Wechter, dentist, 774-1429.

HAUL-OUT
Haulover Marine, 776-2078.
Independent Boat Yard, 776-0466.

LAUNDRY/DRY CLEANING
Island Laundry & Dry Cleaning, 774-4567, 774-2076.
One-Hour Martinizing, 774-5452.
One-Stop Laundry, 776-1111.
Rodgers Laundromat, 776-9697.
Solberg Supermart & Laundromat, 776-5121.
Supercat Laundromat, 774-6056.
Washboard Laundry, 774-8276.

LIQUORS
Al Cohen's Discount Liquors, 774-3690.
Plaza Cellars Fine Wines, 774-2960.
A.H. Riise Gifts & Liquors, 776-2303.
Universal Liquor & Gifts, 776-3287.

LODGING
Blackbeard's Castle, 776-1234.
Bluebeard's Castle Hotel, 774-1600.
Bunker's Hill Hotel, 774-8056.
Carib Beach Hotel, 774-2525.
Danish Chalet Inn, 774-5764.
Emerald Beach Resort, 777-8800.
Heritage Manor Guest House, 774-3003.
Island Beachcomber Hotel, 774-5250.
Island View Guest House, 774-4270.
Mafolie Hotel, 774-2790.
Maison Greaux Guest House, 774-0063.
Midtown Guest House, 776-9157.
Ramsey's Guest House, 774-6521.
Sapphire Beach Resort, 775-6100.

Scott Hotel, 774-6830.
Secret Harbour Beach Resort, 775-6550, 800-524-2250.
Soto Town Guest House, 774-1124, 776-1107.
Stouffer Grand Beach Resort, 775-1510, 800-768-3571.

MAIL DROP
Nisky Mail Boxes, 774-7055, F: 777-8910.
The Post at Compass Point, 775-7229.
Red Hook Mail Services, 775-5262.

MARINAS
American Yacht Harbor, 775-6454.
Avery's Boathouse/Marine, 776-0113.
Compass Point Marina, 775-6144.
Crown Bay Marina, 774-2255, VHF 16.
Fish Hawk Marina, 775-9058.
Haulover Marine Yachting Center, 776-2078.
Independent Boat Yard, 776-0466.
Lattitude 18, 775-9964.
La Vida Marina, 775-6901.
Lighthouse Marine, 774-4379.
Saga Haven Marina, 775-9671.
Sapphire Beach Marina, 775-6100.
Wesk Marine Inc., 776-8077.
Yachthaven Marina, 774-6050.

MARINE REPAIR & SUPPLIES
Avery's Marine, 776-0113.
Banks Sails Caribbean, 774-8354.
Caribbean Auto & Marine, 775-3900.
Caribbean Battery, 776-3780.
Caribbean Inflatable Service, 775-6159; F: 775-2014.
Crown Bay Maritime Center, 774-8780.
Diesel Distributors, 775-9080, 775-6998.
Island Marine Supply, 776-0753, 776-0088, 775-6621, 775-6789.
Island Rigging and Hydraulics, 774-6833.
J.E. Marine Services, 775-6372.
Knot-Hole Inc., 775-9255.
Lighthouse Marine, 774-4379.
Monty's, 774-4538.
Offshore Marine, 776-1416, 776-5432.
Proper Pitch, 774-9965.
Reefco Marine Refrigeration, 776-0038.
Ruan's Marine Service, 775-6346.
Tropical Marine, 775-6595.
Virgin Islands Canvas, 774-3229.

Yachtworks, 779-2628.

MISCELLANEOUS
Alcoholics Anonymous, 776-5283.
Animal Hospital/St. Thomas, 775-3240, 774-6861.
Atlantis Submarines, 776-5650, VHF 18.
Breaklight Business Services, 776-2121.
Bruno's Le Salon, 774-2086.
CG's Barber & Beauty Salon, 774-1337.
Colon Barber & Beauty Salon, 776-0110.
Ed's Barber Shop, 774-4515.
Frank's Lock & Key Service, 774-1094.
Genesis Hair Care Center, 776-7687.
Helen's Beauty Salon, 774-0977.
Jan Michael's Hair Studio, 776-1151.
Lock-It Please, locksmiths, 776-5290.
Moore Veterinary Clinic, 775-6623,
Nisky Business Center, 776-1448.
Priscilla Unisex Beauty, 776-4644.
Pure Tropical Water (bottled), 776-4245.
Rush-It, Inc. Courier, 776-9414.
UPS, 776-1700.
Vitel Cellular, 776-8588.
Western Union, 800-325-6000.

PHARMACIES
Cathedral Pharmacy, 776-4080.
Doctors' Drug Prescription Center, 776-4801.
Drug Farm Pharmacy, 776-7098, 776-1880.
Family Health Center, 776-3805.
Frenchman's Reef Drug Store, 776-8559.
Frenchtown Drug Center, 774-1466.
Havensight Pharmacy, 776-1235.
Nisky Pharmacy, 776-4759.
Virgin Islands Apothecary, 774-1341.

PROVISIONS
A & F Bakery, 776-5145.
Bachman's Bakery, 774-4143.
Crown Bay Bakery, 774-5102.
Daylight Bakery, 776-1414, 774-6328.
The Deli, 775-2944.
Joe's Convenience Market, 776-1809.
Long Path Superette, 774-1090.
Natural Food Grocery & Deli, 774-2800.
Nordside Grocery, 774-4852.
Ocean Treasure Seafood, 776-2027.
Pueblo International, 777-8195, F: 776-0607.

Red Ball Grocery, 774-1682.
Shop Rite Grocery, 774-2645.
Solberg Supermart, 776-5121.
Super Foods, 774-4200.
Supermarket & Deli, 774-3193.
The Fruit Bowl, 774-8565.
Tri-Mart Convenience Center, 774-4666.
Twin City Grocery, 774-4330.
Upper Crust Bakery, 776-0144.

REAL ESTATE
April Newland/Terry Moran R.E., 774-8888.
Crown Real Estate, 776-3416.
Danish Hill Real Estate, 774-1778.
Sun Real Estate, 774-0027.
Rudy Thompson, 774-1111.

RESTAURANTS, DOWNTOWN
Akasha Cafe, West Indian/vegetarian, 776-5675.
Bumpa's, Sandwiches, 776-5674.
Cafe Amici, international, 774-3719.
Coconuts, sandwiches, 774-0099.
DannyLi Cafeteria, West Indian/Spanish, 777-8099.
Diamond Barrell, West Indian, 774-5071.
Drake's Inn, international/American, 774-9075.
Eat Street, deli, 774-1637.
Fiddle Leaf, Caribbean/internat'l, 775-2810.
Gladys' Cafe, West Indian, 774-6604.
Green House, international, 774-7998.
Little Bo Peep, West Indian/American, 774-1959.
Panchita's, American/Mexican, 776-8425.
Parkside, French Creole/American, 774-1405.
Peking House, Chinese/Japanese, 776-3256.
Sinbad's Garden, Middle Eastern/American, 774-2434.
Ventura's, West Indian, 774-4747.
Virgilio's, Italian, 776-4920.
Wet Willy's, West Indian, 774-8769.
Zorba's, Greek/American, 776-0444.

RESTAURANTS, ABOVE TOWN
Blackbeard's Castle, American, 776-1234.
Bluebeard's Terrace, American/French, 774-1600.
Entre Nous, European/gourmet, 776-4050.
The Frigate at Mafolie, American, 774-2790.

The Mark St. Thomas, American/continental, 774-5511.

Sib's, Caribbean/BBQ, 774-8967.

RESTAURANTS, EAST ST. THOMAS

Bavarian, German/continental, 775-3615.

Little Bo Peep, West Indian, 774-1959.

Moghul, Indian/Chinese, 776-3939.

Ocean City, Chinese, 776-3566.

Penelope's Place, American/continental, 774-7779.

Top of the Reef, gourmet, 776-8500.

Virgin's Oar House, American, 774-8747.

RESTAURANTS, WEST ST. THOMAS

Andiamo's, Italian/American, 776-4655.

Arians, West Indian/American, 776-1401.

Barnacle Bill's, pizza/American, 774-7444.

Cafe Normandie, French, 774-1622.

Chart House, American, 774-4262.

Danny's Fisherman's Wharf, international, 774-6669.

Epernay, light/international, 774-5348.

Eunice's at Crown Bay, West Indian/American, 774-4776.

Hook, Line & Sinker, American, 776-9708.

JP's Steakhouse at The Mill, American, 776-3004.

Kum Wah, Chinese, 774-5575.

L'Escargot, international, 774-6565.

Percy's Bus Stop, West Indian, 774-5993.

Petite Pump Room, West Indian/American, 776-2976.

Pinocchio's, West Indian/American, 776-9459.

Prego's Ristorante, West Indian/Italian, 775-0777.

Sugar Reef Cafe, continental, 776-4466.

Victor's New Hideout, West Indian, 776-9379.

RESTAURANTS, NORTH SIDE

Berry's Farm, international/BBQ, 774-3020.

Bryan's, international, 774-3522.

Ferrari's, Italian/pizza, 774-6800.

Magen's Bay Cafe & Pizzeria, light fare, 775-4669.

Northside Hideaway, international, 774-8955.

RESTAURANTS, EAST END

Agave Terrace, continental, 775-4142.

Akasha Sweet Life, vegetarian/macrobiotic, 775-2650.

Baci's, Italian, 775-2822.

BayWinds, Caribbean/American, 775-1510.

Bottoms Up, light fare, 775-4817.

David's, international, 775-6870.

El Papagayo, Mexican/American, 775-1550.

Eunice's Terrace, West Indian/American, 775-3975.

Fabian's Landing, American, 775-9742.

For the Birds, Tex-Mex/BBQ, 775-6431.

The Frigate East, international, 775-6124.

Horsefeathers, Mexican/internat'l, 775-6436.

Iggie's, West Indian/continental, 776-4770.

Palm Court, American/continental/gourmet, 775-1000.

Piccola Marina Cafe, pasta/continental, 775-6350.

Raffles, international, 775-6004.

Romano's, Italian/continental, 775-0045.

Sea Shells, West Indian/continental/Oriental, 775-1800.

Seagrape, American/Caribbean, 775-9750.

Three Virgins, American/international, 775-6434.

Tropical Terrace, Caribbean, 775-1555.

Windjammer, German/continental, 775-6194.

SAILING, WATER SPORTS

Atlantis Submarines, 776-5650, VHF 18.

Caribbean Boardsailing, 776-3486.

Charter Fishing Fleet, 775-3690.

East Wind Windsurfing, 775-5066.

Nauti Nymph Waterskiing, 775-5066.

Ocean Incentives, 775-6406.

See & Ski, 775-6265.

St. Thomas Sport Fishing Center, 775-7990.

West Indies Windsurfing, 775-6530.

SAILMAKERS

Banks Sails Caribbean Inc., 774-8354.

Dittrich Manfred Canvas Works, 774-4335.

West Ray Corporation, 774-8354.

SHOPPING, GIFTS

Alstein Dress Shop, 774-1949.

Amsterdam Sauer Jewelry, 774-2222, 776-3828.

Better Man, Apparel, 776-3400.

Blue Diamond, 776-4340.

Bobby's Jewelers, 776-1748.

Boolchands, 776-0794.

Caribbean Sportswear, 776-4322.
Cardow Jewelers, 776-1140, 774-5905.
Cartier Les Must, jewelers, 774-1590.
Coin D'Oro Jewelers, 774-0555.
Colombian Emeralds, 774-3400.
Cosmopolitan, apparel, 776-2040.
Crystal Shoppe, 774-0708..
Dockside Bookshop, 774-4937.
The English Shop, 776-3776.
Gem Palace, 774-6181.
Jonna White Art Gallery, 774-3098.
Julie's, toys, 774-3703.
Kassandra Boutique, 776-0572.
Land of Oz, toys, 776-7888.
Leather Shop, 776-0290, 776-0040.
Little Switzerland, 776-2010.
Mai-Tai Toys, 776-0809.
Mama's, 774-3350.
Mango Tango, 776-1110.
Name Dropper, 774-0577.
Ninfa's Gift Shop, 774-0460.
Nita's Jewelry & Gift Shop, 776-3042.
Pearl Factory, 776-9101.
Phil's Paradise, 774-5549.
Poinciana Tree, apparel, 776-4282.
Poor Richard's Tropical Boutique, 776-1344.
Red Fort Antiques, 777-8222, 774-0300.
A.H. Riise, 776-2303.
Scandinavian Center, 776-5030, 776-0656.
Silk & Lace Lingerie, 774-1060.
Soft Touch Boutique, 776-1760.
Sona International, 774-4202, 774-5204.
H. Stern Jewellers, 776-1939.
Straw Factory, 774-4849.
Tillett Gardens Art & Craft Gallery, 775-1929.
Trident Jewelers, 776-7152.
Tropicana Perfume Shoppes, 774-0010.
Vanita's Jewelry & Gift Shop, 776-1662.

TAXIS/TRANSPORTATION
Dohm's Water Taxi, 775-6501.
East End Taxi, 775-6974.
Independent Taxi, 776-1669, 776-1006.
Islander Taxi, 774-4077.
Reliable Taxi, 776-8584.
VI Taxi, 774-4550.
Wheatley Taxi, 775-1959.

ST. CROIX

AUTO/BICYCLE/MOPED RENTALS
Berton Car Rental, 773-1516.
Budget Rent-A-Car, 778-9636.
Caribbean Jeep & Car Rental, 773-4399, 778-1000, 1-800-548-4452.
Centerline Car Rental, 778-0450.
Charlie's Car Rental, 778-8200.
Go Around Rent-A-Car, 778-8881.
Green Cay Jeep & Car Rental, 773-7227.
Hertz Rent-A-Car, 778-1402.
Midwest Auto Rental, 772-0438.
Olympic Rent-A-Car, 773-2208, 772-1617.
Thrifty Car Rental, 773-7200.
Travellers Car Wash & Car Rental, 773-2249, 778-6849.

BANKS
Banco Popular de Puerto Rico, 778-5955, 773-0077.
Bank of Nova Scotia, 773-1013, 778-5350.
Barclay's Bank, 773-8500.
Chase Manhattan Bank, 773-1222, 773-1200.
Banco Popular - St. Thomas, 773-0440, 772-0050.
First Federal Savings Bank, 773-0504.

DIVING, SNORKELING
Anchor Dive Center, 778-1522.
Blue Dolphin Divers, 773-8634.
Cane Bay Dive Shop, 773-9913.
Cruzan Divers, 772-3701.
Dive Experience, 773-3307.
Dive St. Croix, 773-3434.

ELECTRONICS
Glentronics, 778-6505.
Radio Shack, 778-5667.
Roberts Electronics, 778-6640.
S & T Electronics, 778-5222.
St. Croix Communication Center, 772-5800.
Westronix, 778-5663.

EMERGENCY/MEDICAL
Frank T. Bishop, M.D., 778-0069.
Rodney A. Fabio, Jr., dentist, 778-6900.
Donna M. Green Christian, M.D., 773-2030.
Daniel T. Kenses, dentist, 773-6604.
Arakere Prasad, M.D., 778-7788, 773-8173.

LAUNDRY/DRY CLEANING

Classic Cleaners Wash Club, 773-6979.
CT Laundromat, 772-1770.
Fast Dry Cleaners, 773-1101.
Johannes Laundry, 778-7602.
Neighborhood Laundry, 778-6138.
Tony's Laundromat, 772-4580.
Town Laundromat, 772-2066.
Tropical Cleaners & Launderers, 773-3635.
Wash-It Laundry, 778-0545.
WFB Laundromat, 773-9788.

LIQUOR, BEER, WINE

City Liquor & Grocery, 772-0125.
Cruzan Rum Distillery, 772-0280,
   1-800-225-3699.
Grog & Spirits, Inc., 778-8400.
Jaime's Liquor Center, 773-7760, 773-0070.
People's Drugstore, 778-5537, 778-7355.
Ship's Galley, 778-8966.
Tradewinds Liquor, 772-0718.

LODGING

Ackie's Guest House, 773-3759.
Anchor Inn Hotel, 773-4000.
Breakfast Club, 773-7383.
Buccaneer Hotel, 773-2100.
Caravelle Hotel, 773-0687, 773-1556.
Caribbean Country Club Guest House,
   772-0277.
Chenay Bay Beach Resort, 773-2918.
Club St. Croix, 773-4800.
Cormorant Beach Club, 778-8920.
Frederiksted Hotel, 772-0500.
Hill View Guest House, 773-1375.
Hilty House, 773-2594.
Hotel Colibri, 773-6610.
King Christian Hotel, 773-2285.
King's Alley Hotel, 773-0103.
Prince Street Inn, 772-9550.
St. Croix by the Sea Hotel, 778-8600.

MAIL DROP

St. Croix Communication Center, 772-5800.

MARINAS

Green Cay Marina, 773-1453.
Salt River Marina, 778-0706.
St. Croix Marine, 773-0289.

MARINE REPAIR & SUPPLIES

Island Marine Supply, 775-6621.
Mike Mechanic, 773-3686.
Paint Locker, 773-0105.
Sailboat Supply Co., 773-3666.
St. Croix Marine, 773-0289.

MISCELLANEOUS

Ada's Creative Touch Beauty Salon, 778-8467.
Beautiful Hair, 773-7212.
Blue Mountain Mineral Water, 778-6177.
Caledonia Springs, bottled water, 778-1281.
Class Plus Unisex Beauty Salon, 773-7228.
Crago Animal Clinic, 773-5610, 773-1256.
Dee Dee's Hair Care Center, 778-4991.
Gem's Beauty Salon, 778-7808.
Monique Beauty Studio, 778-5889.
Personally Yours Hair Care Center, 778-6771.
Security Unlimited, locksmiths, 773-5000.
St. Croix Animal Hospital, 773-7109.
Veterinarian, Karen Clarke Ashby, 773-7109.

PROVISIONS

Centerline Bakery, 772-1541.
Central Meat Market, 772-0362.
Edcel Bakery, 778-3434.
Estate Mountain Grocery, 772-4660.
Gallows Bay Food, 773-4200, 773-6640.
Good Samaritan, 778-7581.
Hendrick's Meat Market, 773-2935.
Mencho's Bakery, 773-2920.
Pueblo Supermarket, 778-1272, 773-0118.
Sam's Supermarket, 773-8291.
Ship's Galley, 778-8966.
Smokey's Shop-Mart, 772-4820.
Solitude Country Store, 773-9354.
Stop & Save Food Market, 773-7050.
Top Food Supermarket, 778-9755.
Town Super Market, 772-3232.

REAL ESTATE

Anchor Realty, 773-1212.
Byrne-Brown Realty Assocs., 773-3401.
Farchette & Hanley, 773-4665.
Landmark Realty, 773-6688.
Pivar Real Estate, 778-8595, 800-537-6242.

RESTAURANTS

Blue Moon, continental, 772-2222.

Motown Bar & Restaurant, West Indian, 772-9882.

P & M Bar & Restaurant, West Indian, 772-0171.

Sica's Health Food Store & Deli, 772-9500.

Sprat Hall Plantation, international/gourmet, 772-0305.

Vel's, Latin/West Indian, 772-2160.

Villa Morales, Spanish, 772-0556.

SAILMAKERS

Canvas Loft, 773-3044.

Wesco Awning & Marine Canvas, 778-9446.

SHOPPING, GIFTS

Avant-Garde, 778-6122.

Ay Ay Gold, 773-8305.

Carl-Michael Boutique, 772-4249.

Cinderella Dress Shop, 772-0160.

CMS Variety, 772-0939.

Colombian Emeralds International, 773-1928.

Design Works, 773-5355.

Eagles Fashion, 778-2447.

Eileen's Fashion Boutique, 778-5944.

The Elegant Woman, 773-7194.

Enchantment, 773-2070.

Evangeline's Creative Boutique, 778-8666.

Faces, 772-1124.

First World Kulture & Bookstore, 778-8308.

Foot Locker, 778-3585.

The Gold Shop, 773-0365.

Holyland Store, 772-0482.

Java Wraps, 773-3770, 773-7529, 778-8147..

Jezebel's Secrets, 772-4333.

Kinney Shoes, 778-5287.

La Femme Amore, 772-2019.

La Parfumerie, 778-7799.

La Vancia's Gift Shop, 772-9202.

Land of Oz, 773-4610.

Me Dundo's Place, 772-0774.

Royal English Shop, 772-2040.

Shoe Palace, 778-5752.

Simply Cotton, 773-6860.

Sylvia's Dress Shop, 772-4380.

Violette's Boutique, 773-2148.

TAXIS

Antilles Taxi Service, 773-5020.

Bright Star Taxi, 773-3873.

Caribbean Taxi Service, 773-9799.

Cruzan Taxi, 773-6388.

Frederiksted Taxi, 772-4775.

Gold Dust Taxi, 773-0228.

St. Croix Taxi, 778-1088.

St. Croix Taxicab Assoc., 778-6887.

ABOUT THE AUTHORS

Nancy and Simon Scott are well qualified to write a guide book on the Virgin Islands, as they met while cruising in these fabulous islands in 1974. Managing a major bareboat charter company for the next eight years in the Virgins enabled them to see things through the eyes of both the cruising yachtsman and the charterer.

Now living in Florida, Simon continues his work in the bareboat charter field as CEO for an international charter company, while Nancy manages the offices of Cruising Guide Publications. Several trips a year, sailing with their two daughters keeps the Scotts informed and involved in the happenings above and below the sparkling blue waters of the Virgin Islands.

The editors would like to thank the following individuals for their assistance in compiling the information for this guide; Capt. Baboucar Sallah, Joy Seal, Paul Thomas, Cordelia Robb, Milt Baker, Capt. Fatty Goodlander, Jim and Odile Scheiner, Lowell Wheatley, Sue Robinson, Simon P. Welch and Barney Crook. Additional thanks are extended to Cruising Guide Publications ad sales representatives Dougal Thornton and Don Wilson.

Sail with a sense of déjà vu ... and save!

Just fill out the questionnaire on the next page and mail it in with your order to receive a discount on the purchase of VIRGIN ANCHORAGES.

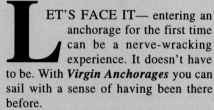

LET'S FACE IT— entering an anchorage for the first time can be a nerve-wracking experience. It doesn't have to be. With *Virgin Anchorages* you can sail with a sense of having been there before.

This companion cruising tool to the *Cruising Guide to the Virgin Islands* features spectacular aerial views of the most popular island anchorages.

Valuable navigational information is superimposed to clearly delineate safe passages. Reefs, landmarks, and channels are revealed with crystal clarity.

Now you can receive your copy for only $15.50 plus shipping (see order form for details) just by filling out the questionnaire on the next page and sending it in with your order!

QUESTIONNAIRE

All you have to do to receive your copy of VIRGIN ANCHORAGES for $15.50... discounted from the regular price (plus shipping and handling) — is take a few minutes to fill out this official questionaire (no photocopies accepted), and mail it in **with the order form on the next page.** It's that easy! Your answers will help Cruising Guide Publications improve our editorial and advertising content throughout our publications. Thank you for your time.

Publication: **Cruising Guide to the Virgin Islands (1995-1996)**

State _____ Age _____ Sex _____

Occupation _____ Marital Status _____

Annual Household Income: ☐ under $50,000 ☐ $50,000-$100,000 ☐ over $100,000

Do you own a boat? _____

If you chartered a yacht, how many people were in your charter party? _____

If you cruised the Islands, how did you cruise? ☐ On my own boat
☐ Bareboat Charter ☐ Bareboat Charter w/Hired Captain ☐ Crewed Charter

How long was your cruise? _____

How often do you cruise? ☐ Less than once a year ☐ Once a year ☐ More than once a year

How did you book your charter? ☐ Through a charter broker ☐ Directly

What activities did you participate in during your cruise? ☐ Fishing ☐ Diving ☐ Snorkeling
☐ Windsurfing ☐ Underwater Photography ☐ Other _____

What activities did you participate in ashore? ☐ Dining ☐ Shopping ☐ Tennis ☐ Golf
☐ Tours/Sightseeing ☐ Entertainment ☐ Other _____

Did you travel between islands by: ☐ Ferry ☐ Plane

Hotel or rental property use: ☐ Before cruise # of nights _____
☐ After cruise, # of nights _____ ☐ Did not stay at a hotel

Did you rent a car? ☐ No ☐ Yes (# of days _____)

How many times did your party eat in a restaurant? _____

What type of items did you and your party purchase during your cruise?
☐ Perfume ☐ Clothing ☐ Jewelry ☐ Alcoholic Beverages ☐ Real Estate ☐ Souvenirs
☐ Art ☐ Tobacco ☐ Dive Equipment ☐ Other_____

Did you visit an advertiser *as a result of seeing their ad in this guide?* ☐ No ☐ Yes

What was most useful to you in this guide? _____

What would you like to see more of? _____
_____

What was the most memorable place you visited? _____
_____

COMMENTS: _____
_____

Thank You

CRUISING GUIDE PUBLICATIONS

ORDER FORM

To order, please fill out coupon on back and send check or money order to:
Cruising Guide Publications, P.O. Box 1017, Dunedin, Florida 34697-1017.
For credit card orders only, call 1-800-330-9542.

NEW ❑ $17.95   CRUISING GUIDE TO THE VIRGIN ISLANDS *(New Aerial Photos)*
(7th Edition) by Simon and Nancy Scott.

❑ $24.95   VIRGIN ANCHORAGES *(Aerial photos of the Virgin Islands' anchorages)*

❑ $19.95   CRUISING GUIDE TO THE LEEWARD ISLANDS
(3rd Edition) by Chris Doyle.

NEW ❑ $19.95   SAILOR GUIDE TO THE WINDWARD ISLANDS
(7th Edition) by Chris Doyle. *(New color sketch charts & GPS coordinates.)*

NEW ❑ $19.95   CRUISING GUIDE TO TRINIDAD & TOBAGO, VENEZUELA &
BONAIRE (1st Edition) by Chris Doyle. *(Color photos and sketch charts)*

NEW ❑ $24.95   CRUISING GUIDE TO CUBA
(1st Edition) by Simon Charles. *(First time published sketch charts)*

❑ $24.95   GENTLEMAN'S GUIDE TO PASSAGES SOUTH
"Thornless Path to Windward," by Bruce Van Sant with GPS coordinates.

❑ $18.95   CRUISING GUIDE TO THE FLORIDA KEYS with Florida West Coast
Supplement by Capt. Frank Papy.

❑ $29.95   CRUISING GUIDE TO TAHITI AND THE FRENCH
SOCIETY ISLANDS by Marcia Davock.

❑ $12.00   CRUISING MANUAL TO THE KINGDOM OF TONGA IN THE VAVA'U
GROUP (Chart included) The Moorings.

❑ $22.50   AT ANY COST: LOVE, LIFE & DEATH AT SEA (Hardcover)
By Peter Tangvald; thrilling autobiography of a cruising sailor.

❑ $13.50   AT ANY COST: LOVE, LIFE & DEATH AT SEA (Paperback).

❑ $14.95   THE NATURE OF THE ISLANDS: PLANTS & ANIMALS OF THE
EASTERN CARIBBEAN by Chris Doyle and Virginia Barlow.

NEW ❑ $12.50   SOAP OPERAS OF THE SKY by Jeannie Kuich. A whimsical view of
stargazing tales for Caribbean latitudes.

NEW ❑ $10.00   A YEAR IN A YAWL by Russell Doubleday. A true-life 1800's adventure.

❑ $39.95   CARIBBEAN by Margaret Zellers with breathtaking photos by Bob Krist;
oversized coffee-table book—perfect tropical souvenir or gift.

❑ $25.00   CARIBBEAN: THE OUTDOOR TRAVELER'S GUIDE by Kay Showker;
lots of color photos illustrate flora, fauna & island geology.

❑ $18.95   DECK WITH A VIEW: VACATION SAILING IN THE CARIBBEAN by
Dale Ward & Dustine Davidson — adventure sailing for the novice.

❑ $13.95   UNDERSTANDING THE EASTERN CARIBBEAN AND THE
ANTILLES by Prof. Nelson Marshall (oceanography/marine affairs).

❑ $11.95   DIVING AND SNORKELING GUIDE TO THE BRITISH VIRGIN
ISLANDS by Linda Sorensen.

❑ $ 7.95 THE CONCH BOOK: ALL YOU EVER WANTED TO KNOW ABOUT THE QUEEN CONCH by Dee Carstarphen.

❑ $14.95 THE LEEWARD & VIRGIN ISLANDS RESTAURANT GUIDE & (Each) RECIPE BOOKS (Two separate books filled with color photos.)

❑ $14.95 SHIP TO SHORE I (A collection of 680 recipes & cooking tips from Caribbean charter yacht chefs) compiled by Capt. Jan Robinson.

❑ $14.95 SHIP TO SHORE II (440 more recipes from Capt. Jan Robinson).

❑ $14.95 SEA TO SHORE (280 recipes by Capt. Jan Robinson.)

❑ $14.95 SWEET TO SHORE (Robinson's ultimate dessert collection).

❑ $10.95 SIP TO SHORE (Robinson's cocktails and hors d'oeuvres collection).

❑ $ 7.95 MAVERICK SEA FARE: A CARIBBEAN COOK BOOK by Dee Carstarphen (Simple shipboard recipes you can prepare at home).

❑ $12.00 **CALENDAR:** THE BRITISH VIRGIN ISLANDS. Photography by Dougal Thornton (New year available in October of preceding year).

❑ $29.95 **VIDEO** VHS (or PAL *add $10*): SAILING THE WINDWARD ISLANDS by Chris Doyle & Jeff Fisher

❑ $29.95 **VIDEO** (VHS): ISLAND PORTRAITS: ST. VINCENT & THE GRENADINES by Chris Doyle & Jeff Fisher.

❑ $ 4.50 CLEAR, WATERPROOF CRUISING GUIDE COVERS

WATERPROOF CHARTS

❑ $16.95 U.S. & BRITISH VIRGIN ISLANDS

❑ $16.95 BRITISH VIRGIN ISLANDS

❑ $16.95 UPPER FLORIDA KEYS

❑ $16.95 LOWER FLORIDA KEYS

❑ $ 8.50 CLEAR, WATERPROOF, REUSABLE PLASTIC STORAGE TUBE

ORDER FORM ░DISCOVER░ ▨VISA▨ ⬤MasterCard *(For orders only, call 1-800-330-9542).*

To order, check the appropriate box(es), fill out coupon and send check or money order to: Cruising Guide Publications, P.O. Box 1017, Dunedin, FL 34697-1017. Florida residents add 7% sales tax. See schedule for shipping charges. All books are shipped via UPS within 10 days of receipt of order.

SHIPPING & HANDLING:

	U.S./Terr.	Canada	Other
Up to $15.00	$3.50	$5.50	$7.00
15.01-30.00	4.95	6.95	9.90
30.01-40.00	6.75	8.75	13.50
40.01-50.00	7.75	9.75	15.50
50.01-75.00	8.75	10.75	17.50
Over 75.00	9.75	11.75	19.50
Additional Address Add $3.25.			

$ _____ Total Merchandise

$ _____ Sales Tax 7% (Florida residents only)

$ _____ Shipping & Handling

$ _____ Total Enclosed

Name _____

Address _____

City _____ State _____ Zip _____

Daytime telephone (_____) _____

(Prices subject to change without notice)

INDEX

INDEX OF ADVERTISERS